P9-CMV-356

DEEP WATER CRUISING

DEEP WATER CRUISING

CRUISING

Gordon Stuermer
and
Nina Stuermer

David McKay Company, Inc.

NEW YORK

Copyright © 1980 by Gordon Stuermer and Nina Stuermer

All rights reserved, including the right to reproduce this book, or parts thereof, in any form, except for the inclusion of brief quotations in a review.

Book Design by Tere LoPrete

Library of Congress Cataloging in Publication Data

Stuermer, Gordon.
  Deep water cruising.
  1. Yachts and yachting. 2. Navigation.
I. Stuermer, Nina, joint author. II. Title.
GV813.S94   797.1   80-14902
ISBN 0-679-50976-3

10 9 8 7 6 5 4 3 2 1

MANUFACTURED IN THE UNITED STATES OF AMERICA

This book is dedicated to those who dream of cruising deep-water . . . and has the aim of helping them realize their dreams.

With grateful acknowledgement to:
Marty Luray, our editor, a master of constructive criticism, who showed us how to add by subtracting.
Jay and Robin Benford of Jay R. Benford and Associates, Inc., who contributed many photos and layouts of their most excellent cruising designs.
Jerry Kirschenbaum, who allowed us to use excerpts from his excellent series of articles on electrolysis and corrosion.
The Technical Committee of the Cruising Club of America, who allowed us to use excerpts from their valuable booklet: *Desirable Characteristics of Off-Shore Cruising/Racing Yachts.*
George Prentice, naval architect, who shared with us his knowledge of anchors and anchoring and the appurtenances thereto.
Don and Keren Dement, who opened their extensive "cruising files" to us.
Jim Louttit, our publisher, who suggested that we write this book and had faith in our ability to do so.
And to dozens of other friends who gave freely of their knowledge and advice.

Deep Water Cruising: A Preface

As our country's Bicentennial celebration approached its zenith, our big ketch *Starbound* eased her 35 tons back up against the dock tee in the colonial town of Annapolis from which she had departed almost three years before. From October 1973 to July 1976 we had sailed her 31,000 nautical miles around the world.

We returned to our jobs with a definite sense of unreality that has since been tempered by the swiftly passing days. The Navy Department in Washington, D.C. again employs Gordon's service as a naval architect. Nina again works at the U.S. Naval Academy and our son Ernie is studying marine biology at a local college. When weather and time permit, we take *Starbound* for a sail on the Chesapeake Bay. We still live aboard, as we have for many years; we would live no other way.

During these past months we've seen our book *Starbound* published and well received by the public. We are content—for the time being.

The human mind is unlimited in its capacity for remembrance and conjecture, and so much of the talk aboard *Starbound* concerns ships, voyages and voyaging. There have been moments when we've considered ourselves the resident experts on these subjects; usually short-lived moments, because we constantly meet people with more expertise on almost any subject than we possess. And so we ask questions to add to our store of knowledge, and we remember, and conjecture; when we go voyaging again, what will we do differently? Down what new avenues of investigation will our cruise planning take us? How much better will the preparation of our ship and ourselves stand the heavy-handed and unforgiving inspection of the deep ocean? During our sea passages and while in foreign lands, what are the not-so-obvious problems that we with our stores of knowledge gained from years of living aboard and cruising, should now be able to avoid, or solve?

Friends, acquaintances, and strangers have asked and discussed with us the same questions over and over again. So we have decided to write down everything we know as well as everything we have learned from others.

We hope that the information on these pages, the "getting it all together" of deep-water cruising, will help others fulfill the dream that we are realizing. And we hope to joggle that man who is perhaps sitting in front of his television set into at least one small, positive action toward the realization of his own dream-adventure. If we can influence him just enough—perhaps to order a sailing chart of the South Pacific or to sign up for a course in piloting and navigation—we will have succeeded.

Gordon Stuermer
Nina Stuermer

Annapolis, Md.
Summer, 1979

Contents

ONE

PLANNING

—leave all meaner things
To low ambition, and the pride of kings.
Let us, since life can little more supply
Than just to look about us and die,
Expatiate free o'er all this scene of man;
A mighty maze! but not without a plan.

An Essay on Man
Alexander Pope (1688–1744)

1
Cruising and Cruising Boats

A question we are always asked: How big should a cruising boat be?

The answer: 40 feet of length on deck is a very nice size boat in which to go cruising. Why 40 feet? Why not 30 feet, or 50 feet? Because it just seems to work out that a 40-foot boat is large enough to carry the comfort required, to allow a certain amount of privacy, and is still small enough to be sailed and maintained by a relatively small crew—even two people.

Then come more questions. How much comfort should a cruising boat have? The answer has to be: all she can hold. Look at it this way: a deep-water cruising yacht must carry food and water for many days and various pieces of ground tackle, including at least two anchors and a lot of chain. It should be able to carry a tender or dinghy capable of transporting the entire crew ashore, of bringing bulky stores aboard, and of putting a second anchor out in a blow. The yacht should have an engine, hopefully a diesel, and should have large enough fuel tanks to give her a good range. Refrigeration is not mandatory but is highly desirable for cruising deep water. Fresh stores can really be extended. And who can overlook the delights of a cold beer or an iced drink on a hot, tropical afternoon? A 40-foot boat can generally carry all of these things. A 30-foot boat generally cannot. A 50-foot boat certainly can, but the gear is commensurately heavier and the boat is much more expensive to maintain.

Privacy aboard is very important. Even if a husband and wife are the total crew, there are times when they need privacy from each other—some sort of physical separation. A semblance of privacy is possible to achieve on a 40-foot boat.

We've seen "successful" cruises made by boats of all sizes and rigs, if successful means that the boat eventually arrived at its ultimate destination still in one piece. There are certainly many definitions of that term, but experienced cruising people have only one definition for a successful cruise: *It is a cruise on which everyone aboard has a good time for the entire duration of the voyage.* Think of the implications.

There are an infinite variety of cruising boats plying the oceans of the world. There are multihulls as well as monohulls. There are pure sailers and there are motorsailers. There are the trawler yachts and the big converted working boats such as Brixham trawlers, Baltic traders, and North Sea pilot boats.

A very few deep-water cruising boats are powered by engine alone. These are limited in range by the amount of fuel they can carry. A slightly greater number are powered by sail alone; they have no engines on board. These purists play the winds and tides for their pleasure and their lives.

The vast majority of cruising boats have both sails and engines, and nearly all of these are true sailboats with a relatively small auxiliary engine that is used to get in and out of port and sometimes to power through a calm.

Motorsailers were originally defined as a motorboat that carries auxiliary sails. But the definition has seemingly evolved to mean any sailboat with an engine powerful enough to drive the boat at full speed and fuel tanks large enough to give her a meaningful range at sea under power alone. Motorsailers are ever popular and are often seen in various ports around the world, but they are definitely outnumbered by auxiliary sailboats.

Multihulls, that is, catamarans and trimarans, are relatively popular, at least with their owners, as cruising boats. They are roomy, fast, and have a very shallow draft. But they lack the ability to carry a lot of weight unless they are very large. And if they are very large, they are very expensive and difficult to find a berthing space for because of their extreme beam.

It is a fact that most deep-water cruising vessels are auxiliary sailboats between, say, 35 and 45 feet overall with long keels. And their rigs are myriad.

It is difficult for me to get down to cases when comparing various types of yacht construction. This is not because of a lack of knowledge but rather a bit too much of it. Being a naval architect for the government puts me in a position to know quite a lot about steel and aluminum. Living aboard a large, carvel-planked ketch for many years has given me a great deal of experience with traditional wooden yacht construction. Working on yachts belonging to friends has given me a good working knowledge of the attributes of fiberglass. I am not a stranger to ferro-cement yachts, having investigated several in some detail during our circumnavigation and having helped, in a minor way, in the construction of one.

MATERIALS

From the engineer's standpoint, I believe that any of the materials mentioned above, assembled in the proper manner, can result in a very satisfactory seagoing yacht. But despite the strength of steel, the lightness of aluminum, the noncorrosive sleekness of fiberglass, and the advertised inexpensiveness and availability of ferro-cement, my craftman's soul still prefers wood.

Wood has one of the highest strength-to-weight ratios of any material known. It can be cut, shaped, or bent to almost any form. It can be glued and fastened in a hundred ways. It is available almost

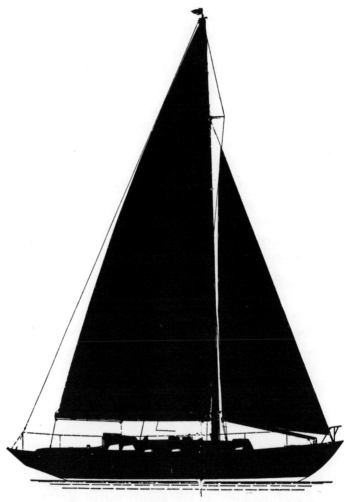

Sloop

anywhere in the world. It is pleasurable to work with and beautiful to look at.

The sole disadvantage of wood is its susceptibility to organic deterioration, otherwise known as rot. Rot can be minimized, even eliminated, by using properly seasoned wood of good quality, by designing the yacht with adequate ventilation, and by treating the wood chemically before and during construction, and periodically thereafter.

If I were to build a large yacht today—say 50 feet or bigger, I think I would build her of steel. Fine quality wood is expensive and very hard to find. Fine quality workmanship is even more expensive. Both can be found, with difficulty, but the cost is truly prohibitive. Steel is another story. While not exactly dirt-cheap, it is plentiful. There exists much design history regarding steel and there are many competent welders in all parts of the world.

A steel boat has two major problems: corrosion and electrolysis. Or maybe they should be called rust and galvanic action since there are many forms of corrosion. Careful construction and even more careful maintenance can reduce these problems to a bare minimum, although I've never seen them completely eliminated.

Aluminum is marvelous stuff. It is lightweight, strong, and weldable with the proper equipment. The alloys used for marine application are relatively free of oxidation-type corrosion. But electrolysis problems can be gross in aluminum hulls—much more so than in a steel boat—because aluminum is a relatively base metal. And the specialized welding equipment required for aluminum construction or repair is not nearly as available as is the standard welding equipment used for steel. Another big drawback to aluminum is its cost.

Ferro-cement is a controversial yacht construction material. Despite that fact, there are some very beautiful ferro-cement yachts taking their owners on long voyages today. During our circumnavigation we saw some exemplary ferro-cement yachts from 45 feet up to 70 feet, particularly in New Zealand and South Africa. Australian sailors were building a few ferro-cement boats on the northeast coast, but that wood-starved country seems to spawn more steel hulls than hulls from ferro-cement. Perhaps this is because of the expertise with steel that exists in that country.

I guess the most important point to make about ferro-cement yachts is that the use-factor is still too small for anyone to make valid judgments on just how well the material will stand up to the rigorous inspection of deep-water sailing. Of course, owners of ferro-cement yachts swear by them. But that's human nature; I've never heard of a deep-water sailor bad-mouth his own ship.

We have seen the topside and bottom paint of ferro-cement hulls peel off in sheets. We have watched agonized crews patching spalled hull surfaces that had the corroded reinforcing mesh showing through and bleeding rust down the hull. We have observed seeping leakage coming right through the hull in areas where, presumably, voids were left in the grout when the hull was plastered. We have noticed ferro-cement yachts burdened with excessive topside weight because the decks and cabin sides were made of that same material and then we have seen that error compounded by an interior overhead lined with wood sheathing to get away from the effect of living in a basement. On the other hand we have been guests on very beautiful yachts for as long as a half day before learning that their hulls were made of ferro-cement. We had thought they were fiberglass, so well-finished were they, with wood deck beams and decks and teak-lined interiors. Admittedly they were very new yachts.

Fiberglass is an admirable material. From a guy who has had a constant love affair with wooden boats, it might seem inconsistent to admit that I like fiberglass, but I do. It doesn't rust, rot, or corrode. It is not subject to electrolysis and there are no seams to caulk. The two major disadvantages of fiberglass are the high initial cost and the difficulty of repair.

Table 1 summarizes the assets and liabilities of the five construction materials just discussed. The points made are meant to be generally informative, not a treatise on yacht construction. Remember that Table 1 refers to the *hull material*, not to the total yacht.

The cost of the hull material, and maintainability of that mate-

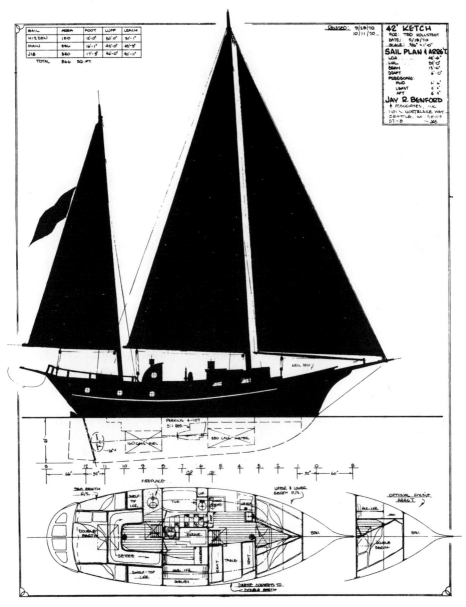

SAIL	AREA	FOOT	LUFF	LEACH
MIZZEN	180	15'-0"	50'-0"	51'-1"
MAIN	366	16'-1"	44'-0"	45'-8"
JIB	360	17'-8"	46'-0"	40'-11"
TOTAL	866	SQ.FT.		

REVISED: 9/28/70
10/11/70

42' KETCH
FOR: TED VOLLSTEDT
DATE: 5/18/70
SCALE: 3/16" = 1'-0"

SAIL PLAN & ARRGT

LOA	44'-6"
LWL	34'-0"
BEAM	13'-0"
DRAFT	6'-0"
FREEBOARD:	
FWD	6'-6"
LEAST	6'-4"
AFT	6'-4"

JAY R. BENFORD
& ASSOCIATES, INC.
1101 N. NORTHLAKE WAY
SEATTLE, WA 98103
57-B   -JRB

Ketch

TABLE 1

Hull Material	Assets	Liabilities
Wood	Beauty Relatively available Excellent workability Excellent strength-to-weight ratio Easy to repair No corrosion Good insulator	Subject to organic deterioration (rot) and marine borers Requires hull fastenings Flammable
Steel	Availability Workability Relative ease of repair Good strength-to-weight ratio Immune to marine borers Fireproof	Subject to oxidation corrosion Subject to galvanic corrosion Requires welding equipment and power tools for repairs Poor insulator
Aluminum	Relatively available Relatively workable Oxidation-corrosion resistance is good Good strength-to-weight ratio Immune to marine borers Fireproof	Expensive Requires special welding equipment and power tools for repairs Very subject to galvanic corrosion Poor insulator
Ferro-cement	Available Relatively inexpensive Relatively easy to repair Relatively immune to corrosion (the reinforcing is *not*)	Low flexibility Difficult to retain painted coatings Very difficult to add fittings Relatively poor insulator

TABLE 1

Hull Material	Assets	Liabilities
Ferro-cement (cont'd)	Relatively immune to marine borers (there are types that will attack concrete) Fireproof	Too heavy for deck and cabin construction
Fiberglass	Relatively available Relatively workable Good strength-to-weight ratio Immune to all corrosion and borers	Expensive Requires power tools to repair Difficult to add fittings (backing plates must be used) Subject to ultraviolet degradation Flammable Poor insulator

Notes: 1. *All* hull materials require maintenance.

2. Mars to the exterior of a fiberglass hull (the gel coat) may require an expert to repair if damage is extensive enough. The gel coat will eventually deteriorate and will require paint like all other hulls.

3. Remember that assets, particularly "immune to corrosion" refer to the hull material only; not to the hull fittings, shafts, propellers, stuffing boxes, etc.

4. The liability "poor insulator" means that condensation will form easily on the interior suface of the hull. This is usually combatted by the attachment of an insulating material such as one of the plastic foams.

5. When considering the asset "fireproof," remember that virtually all fires on yachts (or ships) start *below* decks where flammable material exists aplenty regardless of the hull material.

6. *It should be recognized that wood is the only hull material that can be effectively repaired at sea with hand tools—particularly if the hull is holed by collision.*

rial, are relatively unimportant factors. The basic material costs for a sea-going yacht outfitted for deep water used to be broken down as follows: one third for the hull, one third for outfitting the interior of the hull, and one third for outfitting the exterior of the hull. Nowadays, however, the hull itself is the most inexpensive part of the boat—approximately 25 percent of the total cost. Therefore, anyone who thinks he will "save lots of money" by constructing a yacht of the cheapest material is fooling himself in the long run. A yacht should be constructed of the best materials available, regardless of the cost of those materials.

HULL CONSTRUCTION

Construction costs follow the same tenet. The finest construction methods should be applied to whatever material is chosen. There will never be an adequate blue-water yacht that has been designed and/or built by an "amateur." A dictionary definition of an amateur is: "one lacking in experience and competence in an art or science." Any person who can design or build a sound seagoing yacht out of *any* material is no amateur; he is a competent expert, albeit he may have achieved that competency and expertise on his own.

About the term *maintainability.* It is foolish to try to apply it to a material. It has meaning only when applied to the total package: the completely outfitted seagoing yacht. If five relatively identical and complete cruising yachts were expertly built, one of each of the five different materials discussed, the maintenance, both cost-wise and time-wise would be almost identical for them all—with one proviso: The fiberglass yacht would perhaps require less top-side maintenance on the hull and decks for the first few years following construction.

To conclude these initial remarks on hull construction and hull materials, we have received permission to include excerpts from a very informative compendium published in 1977 by the Cruising Club of America, entitled *Desirable Characteristics of Offshore Cruising-Racing Yachts;* prepared and edited by the Technical

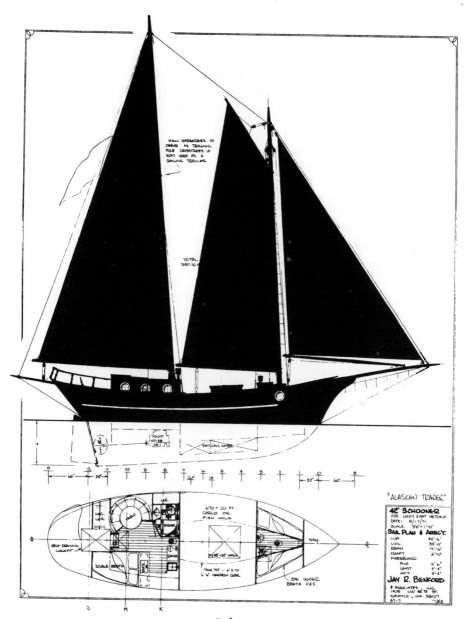

Schooner

Committee, 1975–1977. The section from which the following material is taken is called "Hull Construction" and its principal author is James A. McCurdy. For brevity's sake I have included only the primary points, interspersed with my own remarks and clarifications. Any italicizations are mine. I think the section admirably answers the most-asked question: How can I tell if the yacht hull I own/want to buy/want to build is (or will be) constructed well enough for deep-water cruising, and what do I need to know? I recommend this small spiral-bound book to everyone interested in boats which go to sea.

> The proper goal in hull construction is to produce the required strength with the least weight of material. Unnecessary weight makes a boat more difficult to manage and less enjoyable to sail. It also makes for greater material cost.

The questions immediately generated are: What is the "required strength" and "least weight"? The next sub paragraphs provide the clues.

Strength Required to Meet Sea Conditions

> The structural arrangements and scantlings of a hull must combine to produce sufficient strength to survive the stresses of intended service.

So, a cruising boat must be strong enough for whatever you intend to do with it—and more:

> For an offshore racing-cruising yacht the stresses of intended service are not limited to those which result from weather and sea conditions that the boat may *reasonably* be expected to encounter during her useful life. Rather, they are stresses caused by conditions rare enough to be met by the one boat in a thousand that is in the wrong place at the wrong time.

Stated another way, there are combinations of circumstances that a boat could statistically be expected to encounter once during a service life of say, one thousand years. Whether this will occur during the first year or the thousandth year cannot be predicted, but *if* its occurrence is not allowed for in hull construction the element of risk should not be acceptable to an owner who is not a gambler.

An interesting paragraph, and one, I am sure, that could receive its share of arguments. Frankly, my own criterion for hull strength is simply this: If the ship is pitchpoled while running before great seas or is rolled completely over after broaching, she must survive with her basic structure intact and without serious hull damage, even if the masts have carried away.

More excerpts relating to strength:

The entire hull structure is *not* uniformly stressed by the forces of the sea. . . .

Under bending loads the deck is heavily stressed before it functions as the top flange of the hull girder. For this reason the deck must possess strength of the same order of magnitude as the topsides of the hull along the deck edge. Deck strength should not be compromised by hatch or cockpit openings that are excessive in number or in size. This is particularly important amidships (or) near the deck edge. . . .

The sea also produces severe local loads when a yacht is being driven to windward. These result from slamming and are concentrated on the lee side of the forepart of the vessel. Typically this effect reaches a maximum halfway between stemhead and (fore) mast.

Structural Systems

The forces of the sea that work on the hull of a sailing yacht are not subject to calculation with a useful degree of precision. Fortunately this lack is made up for by a long history of trial and error, experience that can be used to design hull structures in additional, new, or yet to be developed materials. . . .

Time is required for proof of the efficacy of any new system, but if its calculated strength approximates that of time-tested systems it can be accepted initially with some degree of confidence.

The structural arrangements used by the manufacturers of production fiberglass boats are often dictated by considerations of material and labor economy. *Very few production boats are used as true offshore cruising-racing yachts and it is perhaps unrealistic to expect all of them to be built to the exacting standards required by that service.*

The last statement is a true one, but it is unintentionally misleading. Perhaps a more accurate version is: Relative to the very large number of companies building production boats, only a small percentage of those companies build to the standards desired for deep-water cruising.

Construction Details

The hull/deck joint is a notoriously weak point in some fiberglass hulls. Mechanical fastening alone is often not adequate to keep these two essential parts of the hull from parting company. Fiberglass bonding across the inside of this joint can be used to bring it up to the same strength as the adjoining hull and deck surfaces. A fiberglass hull laid up in a single rather than a split mold, avoids potential weaknesses along its centerline because there is no suggestion of a centerline joint.

We saw a hull several years ago that had broken in half lengthwise along this centerline joint.

Topsail Schooner

Centerboards

Centerboards can produce highly concentrated stresses on the hull and centerboard trunk in rough weather or grounding. These loads increase in proportion to the length of centerboard outside the boat as compared to the amount that remains inside the trunk. This is a simple leverage situation and as a rough rule the centerboard should extend up into the trunk at least half as far as it extends down below the keel when fully lowered. The centerboard trunk itself must be quite robust to withstand the centerboard forces and to give the crew confidence when the board is thumping.

The rudder on a centerboard boat should not extend below the maximum draft of the rest of the boat with the centerboard raised.

An extremely heavy centerboard or drop keel is not suitable for an offshore cruiser-racer because of the large forces that are required to handle it and that it imposes on the hull.

In general, a centerboard is not a desirable feature unless a boat is to be used in an area that requires shoal draft.

We can't think of such a cruising area unless the boat is very large. In general, deep-water sailors prefer more draft in lieu of less. The very few sailors of boats with centerboards that we chanced to meet swore *at* them, not by them.

Quality

In the case of custom-built boats the experience and reputation of designer *and* builder provide the best basis for judging the quality of hull construction. *For production boats the experience and reputation of the builder should be given more weight because the designer often has only weak control over the actions of the builder.*

We totally agree with this statement. Well-built production boats do exist but, without exception, cost more than the common run. Good buys can sometimes be found, but they always require being in the right place at the right time with a stack of cash in hand.

Merits of Construction Materials

Aluminum alloy is the material of choice for one-off custom designs. It offers a relatively rigid structure with the highest strength/weight ratio. This is as one might expect from its use in aircraft construction. It is not suited to production boats because very little of the labor required can be eliminated by investment in tooling.

The marine aluminum alloys currently in use are resistant to chemical corrosion to the extent that paint is not required to protect them from attack by sea water. It is, however, required for appearance' sake as is the application of surfacing compounds to smooth out plating distortion caused by welding heat. *On the other hand aluminum is quite vulnerable to electrolytic corrosion caused by contact with dissimilar metals or imposed by improperly designed and installed electrical systems.* With proper design, construction, and maintenance, all based on a thorough understanding of this vulnerability, it is not a problem. Unless something wrong is done, electrolytic corrosion will not occur.

Aluminum alloy construction requires insulation under the deck to reduce heat transfer and minimize noise. Insulation of the inside of the hull is required for the same reasons and to eliminate sweating. Sprayed-on flame-retardant urethane insulation can be applied quickly, easily, and permanently. Bilges below the level of the cabin sole should be left free of insulation.

Note the italicizations. Even though contact of dissimilar metals is held to an absolute minimum, the various electrical systems generally desired by a cruising sailor are almost sure to eventually result in some *stray-current corrosion* on an aluminum boat. Aluminum is a particularly unforgiving material in this sense; one small mistake or flaw in wiring can result in hull material deteriorating at a most alarming rate. Electrical systems installations and maintenance must be flawless.

And another big point to remember (see Table 1) is the expense of aluminum construction.

Fiberglass-reinforced plastic is the material of choice for production boats. The amount of skilled labor required can be drastically reduced by substantial tooling investment, the cost of which can be spread over a large number of hulls. A fiberglass hull should be designed for stiffness. If it is stiff enough it will be more than strong enough, *barring poor detail design and construction. . . .*

Quality control of fiberglass layups is not easy to maintain and flaws or lack of uniformity are difficult to detect in the finished product. The reputation of the builder is perhaps the surest, if not the only, guide in this connection.

Once again I will reiterate that I much admire well-designed and well-built fiberglass boats for deep-water cruising—and much decry the increasingly popular notion of the uninformed that just any production fiberglass hull popped out of a mold is suitable to stand the stresses imposed by heavy seas.

Cold molded-wood construction is a term that covers wood held together by glues and resins rather than a complete reliance on individual fastenings as in conventional wood construction. The word "cold" means that high temperatures requiring the special application of heat are not required for glue curing. Modern glues permit the construction of a wood hull, the parts of which are permanently bonded together and essentially one piece, with grain direction determined by

An example of a cutter is the 39-foot Prometheus, *designed by Jay Benford.*

lamination rather than steam bending or selection of natural curvature. The result is a hull with a strength/weight ratio second only to aluminum alloy and a rigidity exceeding that of fiberglass construction.

I've included the preceding paragraph only because I've not previously addressed cold molded-wood construction. This method of construction can produce a fine boat but is quite expensive. The excellent strength-to-weight ratio is of course more important to the racing sailor, although it is not to be scorned by the cruising devotee. It should be noted that hull repairs will be difficult, and any delamination of the skin provides an ideal environment for wood rot. Some construction of this type is now going on, employing wood that has been pressure treated with water-borne inorganic salts. This technique appears to be giving new life to wooden boat construction, even using conventional methods. The more inexpensive woods, including the sapwood portions of timber, normally not resistant to rot, can be made so by pressure treatment. I speculate that the wildly surging costs of fiberglass may precipitate a new era of wooden boats and wooden boat artisans.

I regret that the concluding portion of the HULL CONSTRUCTION section of CCA's fine little book gives short shrift to conventional wood, steel, and ferro-cement yachts. For wood, they claim the materials and skills are too scarce. The preceding paragraph gives a clue to a possible solution to this problem.

Steel is shrugged off as not suitable for offshore cruising yachts of less than 75 to 100 feet in length—and ferro-cement is dismissed as "not satisfactory for yacht construction."

We cannot agree with the concluding remarks regarding both steel and ferro-cement cruising yachts. We have seen too many good boats built of these materials. Conscientious hull maintenance will preclude the incidence of chemical corrosion on steel hulls; and, while we are not personally enamoured of ferro-cement yachts, as we remarked earlier, there are some beauties now making long, safe passages.

HULL SHAPES

The "best" hull shape for a cruising yacht will remain in contention as long as there are at least two cruising sailors to talk about it. Look at the sailing characteristics desired in a cruising yacht: *directional stability* (the ability of a boat to *track* in a straight line), *windward ability, liveliness* (maneuverability), *minimal wetted surface* (for speed in light airs), and *stability* (minimal pitching and rolling motion).

Many deep-water sailors think an extremely long-keel design is the only answer to directional stability. This is not true. While it is one element for such stability, a long waterline is the most important factor. Straight hull sides (in lieu of a rounded or vee-shaped form) also allow a yacht to track better. A shallow forefoot in conjunction with a deep run aft reduces yawing when running downward and will let the boat come about a lot easier.

Since directional stability is so important to a cruising yacht, here are some design factors to avoid: overly buoyant ends, high freeboard at the ends, long overhangs, a deep forefoot, a shallow run (aft), and pinched ends with a wide midship section. Generally, yachts with these factors designed into their hulls end up with the *center of gravity* (CG) located aft of the *center of lateral resistance* (CLR) and they will steer erratically. They might result in a good racing hull, but they'll make for a poor cruiser.

I have not yet said anything specifically derogatory about fin-keel/spade-rudder type hulls. If the hull has a spade rudder with a skeg in front of it, and the fin keel is carried relatively far aft, she just might make a fine cruising boat, other factors not excluded. (See hull sketches.)

During our circumnavigation we became acquainted with several multihulls, mostly trimarans, and their crews. We liked the crews more than the boats. Here is why, in what I feel is the correct order of importance:

•Multihulls are not self-righting and a lot of sailors have disappeared at sea to prove it.

HULL SHAPES LESS SUITABLE FOR CRUISING

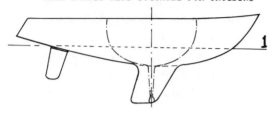

<u>NOTES</u>:

A poor hull for cruising but fast to windward. Factors detrimental to directional stability are the high freeboard fore & aft, the short waterline and the deep garboards. Downwind yawing is a common characteristic.

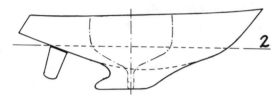

A better design than the #1 hull, but not by much. The hard bilge with deep, full garboards and relatively deep forefoot will cause erratic steering. Her CLR is forward of her CG which makes her hard to handle when running.

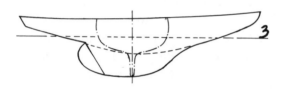

Basically a 'long-keel' boat, but with a quick motion and hard to steer in any seaway; a wet boat not suitable for cruising. She's very reminiscent of the old racing designs.

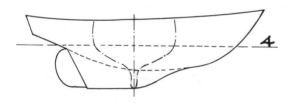

A better cruising hull design than #1, #2, or #3 but still with the undesirable characteristics of the overhanging, pinched ends, deep forefoot, deep garboards, hard bilge and shallow, flat run. She'll 'wander around' downwind.

TYPICAL PLAN OF THE ABOVE HULLS:

Note the short waterline, round hull sides and wide beam concentrated amidships; none of these are desirable cruising hull characteristics.

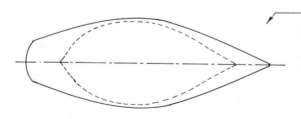

HULL SHAPES MORE SUITABLE FOR CRUISING

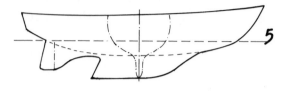

NOTES:

A good cruising hull despite the
'fin' keel. Observe the shallow
forefoot and garboards, the moderate beam and soft bilges, the
long deep after run; all are conducive to directional stability.
Her CLR is aft of her CG which
is highly desirable for downwind
work - and she'll still go well
to windward.

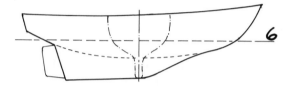

This is our personal favorite
cruising hull design, 'tho we
like more beam than she shows.
She'll have all the attributes of
#5 but will be slower to windward
offset by working easier when off
the wind.

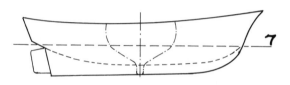

Now the hull design is moving
toward the opposite extreme.
This is sometimes called the
'pickle' shape. A great offwind
boat, slow and comfortable, with
lots of living space - but a poor
performer to windward. Our ship
Starbound has lines much like
this, but with a more shallow
forefoot.

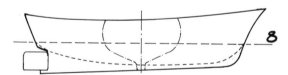

Here's a good cargo carrier hull
reminiscent of the Baltic traders
and their ilk. They are terrible
to drive to windward without the
help of their engines, but they're
a great tradewind boat when rigged
with some squaresail.

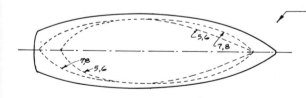

TYPICAL PLAN OF THE ABOVE HULLS:

Note the long waterline and long,
straight hull sides which contri-
bute so much to directional stability.

•Their light displacement precludes carrying the weight of sufficient stores, water, fuel, spares, ground tackle, and other gear required for comfortable, safe, deep-water cruising.

•Despite their speed in smooth water, they are much slower in rough seas. And if loaded down past their design waterline, they are slower yet.

•The connections of the transverse braces to the floats and hulls have a distressing habit of coming apart at sea. These connection points are put under immense stress in a seaway.

•The motion of a multihull at sea is uncomfortably quick. In a rough anchorage with no sail up, the motion can be really obnoxious.

•Multihulls don't tack very well.

•There are problems in maneuvering in tight places and in finding berths in marinas because of their extreme beam.

The preceding comments are not made with the intention of infuriating devotees of multihulls; they are simple facts. I love sailing a fast multihull in smooth water. A Hobie 16 has given me some real thrills. But for deep-water cruising I'll stick to a monohull with its heavy keel and its weight-carrying ability.

WHAT RIG?

Papeete, during the Bastille Day fete in July, is a gathering place for deep-water cruisers. Their crews stroll the quai and exchange compliments, and there is always discussion about rigs. Within a few hundred yards one may see sloops and cutters, ketches and yawls, schooners and brigantines—a few with square rigs, more with twin genoa arrangements. An interesting point becomes obvious during these quai-side gatherings: There is no single cruising rig that evidences a clear superiority over any of the others on *all* points of sail. In other words any rig a sailor happens to prefer can be an adequate rig for deep-water cruising if one learns to use it properly. Another conspicuous item: a downward rig of some sort

DEEP-WATER CRUISING RIGS: KETCH vs CUTTER

40 ft. KETCH

ASSETS:
1. More total sail area
2. Smaller main is more easily managed
3. Less reefing - it's easier to drop it
4. Better balance with staysail and mizzen than with staysail and reefed main
5. Loss of one mast still leaves one, assuming masts are independently stayed
6. Easier to heave to with mizzen
7. More places for annemometers, antennas, radar reflector, flag halyards, lights, awnings
8. Mizzen useful for weather cocking during anchoring and in anchorage

LIABILITIES:
1. Initial cost and ultimate maintenance is one-third more
2. Main tends to backwind mizzen when close hauled
3. Mizzen boom end must be designed inboard to avoid interference with wind vane

40 ft. CUTTER

ASSETS:
1. Will point higher and foot faster to windward
2. Cutter rig is one third less the cost of the ketch rig.
3. Less windage and deck obstruction
4. No interference with self-steering wind vane

LIABILITIES:
1. Greater chance of tripping boom
2. Higher center of effort because of taller mast
3. Reefing mainsail necessary to achieve balanced rig in heavy going
4. Harder to heave to - must reef or change to trysail

Another Benford design is Harambee, *a 60-foot ferro-cement ketch.*

is almost mandatory for deep-water cruising. This is because most cruises are planned to take advantage of favorable winds—fair winds—where the boat will be running with the sea and the prevailing winds are abeam or aft of the beam.

Any discussion of cruising rigs generally degenerates into a simple squabble over the merits of one mast versus two masts. Most blue-water sailors prefer one mast (usually a cutter rig) on cruising boats up to 40 or perhaps 45 feet overall (LOA). And they prefer two masts (nearly always a ketch rig) on cruising boats larger than this, say up to 60 feet LOA (perhaps the maximum size manageable with a small crew).

I've used 40 to 45 feet as a nebulous dividing line, primarily because of hull types. A 40-foot, traditionally designed and built, relatively heavy displacement hull will generally have a bowsprit and a ketch rig, primarily because this rig can be split and spread, essentially lowered for easier handling. Also, in my opinion, the more traditional hulls look better with bowsprit and low-aspect ratio sails than they would with a high, single-masted rig. Conversely, a 45-foot, relatively light displacement hull of a more modern design will have a minimal bowsprit or none and be cutter- or sloop-rigged with high-aspect ratio sails. The 40- to 45-foot LOA range is a very popular size of cruising boat and I've seen them rigged all ways, even as a three-masted brigantine.

With hull-size increase or decrease, the arguments (rather perversely) seem to die down to a low rumble: "Well, if you're talking about big/small yachts, I'll agree that a ketch/cutter rig is the only way to fly! Let's have another beer!"

So let's do a comparison study. We'll take two identical hulls of a salubrious cruising design, rig one as a cutter and one as a ketch, then list their assets and liabilities—sailing and otherwise. Assume the masts, sails, and rigging for both boats are made expertly by the same manufacturers and are of the best, most modern design. Assume furthermore that both boats are provided with downwind gear, since deep-water sailors try to plan their passages for maximum reaching and running. Also, we must define a cutter as having the mast stepped about 40 percent of the LOA aft of the bow

This stern view of Starbound shows her massive rudder, broad transom, and high cockpit coamings, altogether suitable for cruising.

and having a double headsail rig with jumper struts or running backstays to offset the pull of the inner forestay. Likewise, we must define a ketch as having a mizzen large enough to be a true working sail, at least three-eighths the area of the main, and also having an inner forestay. The mizzen boom will extend no further than the transom to allow the self-steering gear vane enough clearance in which to work.

Table 1, as simple as it looks, is the result of considerable research, conducted with all emotions cast aside. Please note that only assets and liabilities that are meaningful to deep-water cruising are listed.

Our personal preference leans toward the ketch rig. We like the way it looks, we like the way it handles and, most of all, we like its versatility. To illustrate our point we'd like to say that during our circumnavigation never did we have to reef the main of our big ketch, *Starbound*. When the wind came on to blow a gale, we'd drop it completely. Sure, we could have kept more speed on her by taking in a reef, or even two, but a cruising sailor doesn't want speed in a gale, either on or off the wind. He wants to noodle along easily and slowly, with the weather or across it, perhaps flying staysail and mizzen.

To conclude these general comments on cruising rigs, a few statements are in order regarding sloops, yawls, and schooners.

A *sloop* rig generally has the mast placed about 30 percent of the LOA aft of the bow and has a single headstay. The sloop is an adequate cruising rig, but it lacks the cutter's advantage of having an additional headsail and a generally shorter main boom, hence a more manageable mainsail. An additional stay is often added forward, but then jumper stays or running backstays must be added and the fore triangle is relatively small to accommodate two headsails.

A *schooner* is a pretty boat, particularly with a fore topmast, which almost never seems to be carried anymore. A schooner will outreach any other rig. But downwind they suffer a real degradation in performance. Swinging the long main boom out allows a

TABLE 2

GENERAL SOURCES FOR THE
NORTH ATLANTIC & NORTH PACIFIC

Source	Frequency	Area & Coverage
1. Commercial Radio	0.45 to 1.6 MHz	Local waters
2. Weather Bureaus	VHF-FM, Wx1 & Wx2 162.40 & 162.55 MHz	Coastal to immediate waters up to 200 miles offshore
3. Coast Guard	2182, 2670 & VHF Channel 22	Storm and small craft warnings, local weather conditions
4. Coast Guard	High frequency single sideband 4,6,8,13 & 17 MHz	Offshore oceanic weather conditions and forecasts
5. High Seas Telephone Service	High frequency single sideband 4 to 22 MHz	Offshore oceanic weather conditions and forecasts
6. WWV & WWVH	2.5,5,10,15,20 MHz	Major storms and other extreme weather conditions on a general oceanic scale

NOTE

Weather—an all-important subject no matter which boat you choose—is discussed in detail in Chapter 5.

TABLE 2

GENERAL SOURCES FOR THE
NORTH ATLANTIC & NORTH PACIFIC

Source	Frequency	Area & Coverage
7. British, Canadian & other national broadcasts	Various frequencies	Weather and navigational information
8. U.S. Naval Radio	Various frequencies	Emergency and extreme weather information

SOURCES FOR THE CENTRAL PACIFIC
(NORTH: from equator to 50°N Lat. & between 140°W to 160°E Long.)
(SOUTH: from equator to 25°S Lat. & between 110°W to 160°E Long.)

Station	Frequency	Time (GMT)
KQM High Seas Marine Operator Honolulu	17,272.5 KHz 8,751.2 KHz	2025 0525 (except Sundays)
NMO U.S. Coast Guard Honolulu	6,523.2 KHz 8,762.2 KHz	0545 (except Sundays)
	8,762.2 KHz 13,145.4 KHz	1745 (except Sundays)
WWVH Kekaha-Kanai (Female Voice)	2.5, 5, 10, 15, 20 MHz	48, 49, 50th minutes of each hour

TABLE 2

SOURCES FOR EASTERN NORTH PACIFIC
(AREA A: equator to 30°N & from
shore to 140°W Long.)
(AREA B: 30°N to 60°N Lat. & from
shore to 140°W Long.)

Station	Frequency	Time (GMT)
KMI High Seas Marine Operator Point Reyes, California	4,371.0 KHz 8,735.2, 8,738.4 KHz 13,151.0, 13,161.5 KHz 17,307.5 KHz	0000, 0600, and 1500
NMC U.S. Coast Guard San Francisco	4,393.4 KHz 8,760.8 KHz 13,144.0 KHz 13,144.0 KHz 8,760.8 Khz	0430, 1030, 1230
BC Telephone Company Vancouver, B.C., Canada	4,422.2 KHz	0230, 1530, 2115
WWV Fort Collins, Colorado (Male Voice)	2.5, 5, 10, 20, 25 MHz	Tenth minute of every hour

SOURCES FOR SOUTH PACIFIC

Mahina Radio, Tahiti	8,764.0	2100 08°S –28°S, 134°W –155°W (IN FRENCH)

TABLE 2

SOURCES FOR WESTERN NORTH ATLANTIC

Station	Frequency	Time (GMT)
WOO High Seas Marine Operator Ocean Gate, New Jersey	4,390.2, 4,403.0 KHz 8,757.6, 8,754.4 KHz 13,175.5, 13,172.0 KHz 17,321.5, 17,318.0 KHz 22,657.0, 22,653.5 KHz	0100, 1300, and 1900
WOM High Seas Marine	4,428.6, 8,792.8 KHz 13,137.0, 17,325.0 KHz 22,699.5 KHz	0430 and 1230
Operator Fort Lauderdale, Florida	4,422.2, 8,796.0 KHz 13,140.5, 17,286.5 KHz 22,692.0 KHz	0530 and 1130
NMF US Coast Guard Boston, Massachusetts	8,765.4 KHz	0130, 0730, 1330, 1930
WWV Fort Collins, Colorado (Male Voice)	2.5, 5, 10, 20, 25 MHz	8th and 9th minute of every hour
NMN Portsmouth, Virginia	4,393.4 KHz 6,521.8 KHz 8,760.8 KHz 13,144.0 KHz 17,290.0 KHz	0530 1130, 2330, 1730

TABLE 2

SOURCES FOR THE INDIAN OCEAN

Station	Frequency	Time (GMT)
VIE Esperance, Australia	4,136.3 KHz	0103, 0833 30°S –45°S 100°E –125°E
5YE Nairobi, Kenya	9,086 KHz	1240 12°N –11°S, Indian Coast to 60°E
3BB Port Louis Harbour, Mauritius	4,403 KHz	0435, 1635 10°S –30°S, 50°E –85°E
ZSD Durban, South Africa	8,744.8 4,377.4	0918 1703 S of 15°S to Agulhas

Sources for areas not shown above can be obtained from the pamphlet: *Worldwide Marine Weather Broadcasts* and from:

 H.O. 117A—RADIO NAVIGATIONAL AIDS, ATLANTIC &
    MEDITERRANEAN AREA

 H.O. 117B—RADIO NAVIGATIONAL AIDS, PACIFIC &
    INDIAN OCEANS AREA

Starbound's *deck from aloft shows general arrangement and stow-age.*

real chance of tripping it on waves when rolling. The headsails rigged on stays from a baldheaded foremast just don't have enough area to pull well, even when winged out. Of course, with a fore topmast added and a small yard crossed, we have a topsail schooner, a much better downwind proposition. Schooners are also mediocre performers to windward—again unless that fore topmast exists, which enables the crew to set headsails with a meaningful length of luff. So at the expense of extra rigging, they'll get to windward about as well as a ketch—but not as well as a sloop or a cutter.

The mizzen or jigger on a *yawl* is quite small. It was invented, I believe, to beat the racing rules. It's possible to achieve a minor balance with it, but the small area just isn't worth the extra rigging. Also, it always overhangs the stern and interferes with the wind vane. Still, people cruise long distances with yawls.

To summarize, successful cruises have been made with every type of rig. What is really important is to learn to refine and use whatever rig is being employed to its best advantages, and to remember its disadvantages and plan the cruise accordingly.

"*Seakindliness* is a term relating to the ease of motion or behavior of a vessel in heavy weather, particularly in regard to rolling and pitching and shipping water on deck. The term should not be confused with *seaworthiness*, which implies that the vessel is able to sustain, without structural damage, heavy rolling and pitching. Seakindliness is a desirable but not essential adjunct to seaworthiness." So states the International Maritime Dictionary by DeKerchove (2nd Edition, 1961, D. Van Nostrand Co., Inc.).

Those are very meaningful words, but I'll make one proviso: A cruising yacht *must* be seakindly. A happy voyage depends on it!

The big question for a person contemplating buying or building a cruising yacht is: How do I know if this boat will have that mandatory quality called seakindliness?

It is a difficult question. If the vessel is in the water, it would be wise to take her for a sail in relatively heavy weather and see how she goes. An experienced deep-water sailing friend can help make the judgment. Similarity of design to a proven seakindly yacht might give an indication. A word of caution: Don't believe all the

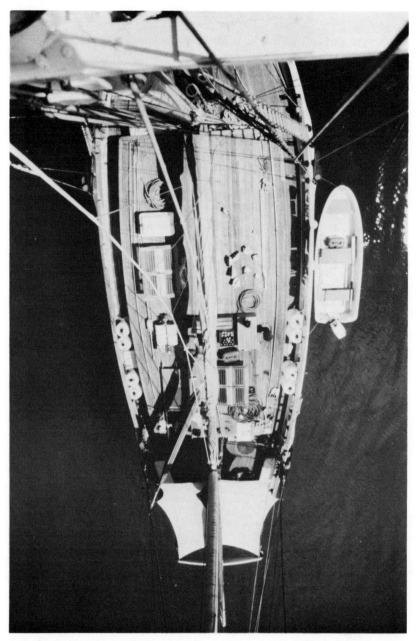

Another view from aloft at anchor. Note extra fuel and water containers and launch.

literature put out by yacht brokers and manufacturers. They claim the virtue of seakindliness for everything that floats.

The term *carrying ability* is one I have coined to discuss the various attributes of a cruising yacht. What I mean by the term is the ability of a yacht to carry everything that must be put in her and on her for a long deep-water cruise and still allow her to float on her design-load waterline and sail as she should.

Consider these items: two anchors (minimum), 100 feet of chain (minimum), 300 feet of anchor rode, an anchor windlass, a dinghy and raft, an outboard motor (hopefully), a full load of fuel and water (with possibly extra cans on deck), all the food that can possibly be stowed, paint, oil, spare rigging, machinery spares and tools of every description, three kinds of radios (VHF-FM, SSB, and a good multiband receiver), a radio direction finder (RDF), navigational tables, volumes of sailing directions and pilot books, a big load of charts (as many as 300), plus all the sails! And the crew!

I do not believe that many of the so-called production boats can handle the required cruising load without seriously handicapping their basic sailing qualities. The ability to carry weight must be inherent in the basic design.

There is no single, perfect combination of characteristics that make up the deep-water cruising boat. If there were, all cruising boats would have evolved from the same set of lines. A design must account for the way the hull responds to sea conditions, the desired rig, the appearance and layout requirements, possible draft restrictions, and displacement.

So how does a sailor make the optimum choice of a cruising boat that will meet his requirements for beauty, safety, comfort, directional stability, seakindliness, and performance both on and off the wind? *The best choice will be found only in a design that avoids extremes.* Choosing any single design factor without consideration of all the others will surely result in an unsatisfactory deep-water cruising boat.

2

The Crew and the Cruising Accommodations

It seems practical to assume that having determined to cruise a yacht deep water and having chosen the boat with which one intends to enter this fascinating realm, the problem of the ship's company must be considered. We call it a problem because as crew size increases arithmetically (1–2–3) the entity of cruising complexity increases geometrically (2–4–8).

After sailing *Starbound* around the world and meeting the crews of more than 100 boats, we will say that the most successful long deep-water cruises were made, in descending order of their success, with the following kinds of crew (remember our definition of a successful cruise):

First (most successful): a family consisting of a couple and their children.

Second: a married couple with no children.

Third: an unmarried couple who have been living together for at least a year (two years are better).

Fourth: the singlehander, man or woman.

Fifth: two men whose friendship has stood all tests (save that of a cruise).

Sixth: all others.

Of course, there are always exceptions, but they are not the rule. Let us mention two exceptions of which we have personal knowledge:

First: A man, his wife, and their two children, generally the optimum crew for a successful cruise, sailed a beautiful cutter from California to Tahiti and planned to continue around the world. Because of the incredible "Bligh syndrome" with which the skipper was infected, by the time they reached Tahiti his wife was distraught and exhausted, and the two kids—nice kids, a boy and a girl—were psychological wrecks who hated the boat, the cruise, and the skipper. We do not choose to set down the conclusion of this sad story; it is too depressing.

Second: The yacht *Topaz*, a 37-year-old, 86-foot schooner owned and crewed by eleven people in their twenties and thirties, made a very happy (that is, successful) cruise around the world. The factors of that cruise—the multiple ownership, the diversity of personalities, the age and size of the schooner—would seemingly spell eventual disaster to such an undertaking. But the cruise was a success because of the care with which the crew formed their partnership and planned their great adventure. Their story is told in a series of articles written for *Motor Boat and Sailing* magazine, starting with the April 1974 issue. It makes fascinating reading and is a good study of human relations at their best.

In general the less crew, the more successful the cruise. Sure, it is great fun to take a bunch of friends on a short coasting hop, where antagonistic relationships either don't have time to form or can be brushed off because of their limited duration. But take that same group aboard for a serious ocean cruise encompassing weeks, and all hell can break loose—especially when both sexes are involved. The sex drive of the human animal has destroyed more friendships than anyone can count, regardless of age, marital status, or seemingly liberal ideas about sex.

We would decry the possibility of success for two couples on a really long deep-water cruise. We personally know of very few who have accomplished it successfully. We do know of at least two cases in which the cruise ended in divorce court. With that particular crew makeup it does seem that the reverse of the general rule is true: Three couples on a boat, or four, have a better chance of maintaining stable personal relationships than two couples. And naturally, with three or four couples aboard, the size of the boat must be adequate to afford the absolute privacy required, as well as the additional stores and water.

These preceding paragraphs are intended to start the reader really thinking about his crew: Who, actually, is going to go with him on his boat and help sail her across the deep ocean.

Most people will say, "Why, my wife/husband will be my crew, naturally. And maybe (assuming there are no children) if I'm going to need other people, we will ask the Smiths—a wonderful couple who have done some sailing on the bay and with whom we get along so well."

We have mentioned above the problems of two couples on a long cruise, but there are other problems too, not necessarily insurmountable. If two couples do decide to go deep-water cruising together, they should be as close as family or *be* family—perhaps a brother and his wife. Remember, that charming idiosyncrasy a person might have while living in the suburbs can be transformed into a royal pain-in-the-neck at sea. In fact it probably will be.

It is very wise to have done a lot of coastal and bay sailing with any crew before going off on a really extended, deep-water passage with them. That statement also relates to one's spouse. The most common problem a man has who wants to cruise is that his wife doesn't. A wife generally can't be talked into deep-water cruising because she's had such a miserable time on that little production "Tupperware" sloop every damn summer weekend for the last five years. She's done all the supplying, cooking, and cleaning—in addition to cranking up the main and jib while the noble skipper handles the tiller and sheets.

The head isn't big enough for comfort, the bunk is too small for making love (she's too tired anyway), and she's got to lean over the smelly alcohol stove to get into the icebox for the skipper's cold beer, which she is expected to locate, open, and deliver to him while he relaxes in the cockpit.

If a man wants his wife to enjoy cruising, he had better take a hard look at her as a human being. We have seen men sailing with their wives on a weekend and treating them (admittedly unconsciously) in a fashion that would get them a punch in the nose from another man. Or at least earn them a blast of profanity. Deepwater sailing is the most partnership there is. Everyone on a small boat is equal, notwithstanding the fact that there is only one captain. That means that he is the boss when it comes to running the ship, but it doesn't mean that everyone else aboard is his slave, including his wife and kids.

Here are some general rules to think about. We have found them mandatory for happy cruising and they should be kept in mind while planning the crew.

Each crew member must have a standing berth: a private bunk, which is always available and in which they can sleep at any time, other duties aside. They must also have some small amount of drawer space and part of a hanging locker, as well as a clothes hammock next to their bunk. This is important; the human animal needs a nest of his own.

Couples need adjacent bunks, or a single large bunk, and some way to maintain privacy. It is pure hell when the only time one can make love is in the middle of the night watch after waking up one's partner (who usually just got off watch) and saying, "Look, it's Jack's watch next. I've got an hour left on mine—why don't you come out on the afterdeck with me and admire the stars for a while?"

Cooking is a full-time job for one person on a deep-water cruise and must be shared by all, including the captain. Aboard *Starbound* my wife, Nina, is the storekeeper and more or less determines the menus (subject to discussion and votes). She has final say on what we eat in order to achieve balanced meals as well as balanced stores. But she cooks *only* when it is her turn. When it is someone else's turn to play "Peggy-for-the-day," she will give all the preparation instruction needed, but she doesn't cook or clean up afterward. "Peggy" does that. If Nina, or any other person (with the exception of a paid cook), had to do all the cooking and cleaning, there'd be a mutiny on board—and well there should be.

Meals can be a social event and ought to be, to some extent anyway. Breakfast usually gets eaten in ones and twos, because someone is usually navigating or sleeping. Lunch is usually a simple, light meal served topside. We find it is a good thing to keep the evening meal relatively formal—the table is set; everyone sits down together; "Peggy" serves, then sits down, too. People "dress" *before* dinner and the art of gentle conversation is employed by all. It is a time of gathering. This is another technique conducive to a happy ship.

All hands stand night watches. Kids too, with an adult if they are too young or too inexperienced. Children should not be deprived of sharing the responsibility of watch-standing. It is a rare and particularly valuable experience for everyone, especially at night.

More than one person should know how to navigate. If the skipper gets really ill, God forbid, someone else will have to get the ship into port. A pecking order should be avoided. This is not a normal occurrence with cruising people who are all, usually, an outgoing, gregarious bunch of extroverts, but we have seen it happen on rare occasions, with a crew of three or more. For instance, with two or three men and one woman making up the crew, the tendency is for the men to pick on the woman. Not because she's deficient in any way—just because she's different from the rest. Any difference in one member of the crew may lead to this all too human trait of establishing a pecking order. It even occurs within families. The problem can usually be avoided through careful crew selection. But if not, it is the captain's duty to nip in the bud any flowering tendencies of this sort, using brains, tact, and diplomacy to do so. It may be too late by the time the downtrodden individual decides he has had enough and makes it clear to one and all.

THE SKIPPER

A few words about the captain: This paragon is responsible for everything and everyone—the ship, the crew, the cruise, the navigation—virtually the success of the entire venture. If he is frightened, not only can he not show it, but he must make the right decisions as well as display outward confidence to the crew in order to bolster theirs. It is easy to appear competent and confident under good sailing conditions, but a storm at sea can turn anyone's knees into noodles.

There are occasions in a person's life when he finds out a lot about himself in a very short time. The skipper of a deep-water sailing boat gets more than his normal share of these times on a cruise. The ability to think rationally and transmit that thought into competent action and confident orders when one is frightened oneself is a definite requirement for a good captain. Sometimes making decisions when under stress calls for employing the old *triage method* that medics still use during times of chaos, such as on a battlefront or during some great disaster when casualties far outnumber available care. The cases requiring attention are divided into three groups; those who will recover regardless of care, those who will die regardless of care, and finally those who need immediate care to save them. The first two groups are ignored and all attention is given the third.

When a boat is in trouble at sea, the captain had better have a cool head, frightened or not. It would be very nice if the captain were one of those people usually referred to as "a born leader." Unfortunately, such people are relatively rare, even though, among deep-water cruising folk, hidden leadership abilities tend to emerge simply through necessity—and often from unsuspected sources.

The thought we want to provide is simply this: While considering a crew for the cruise, don't forget a stringent self-examination. And to reuse an old cliché: If you don't think you can cut it, remember, there are ways to nick it and break it.

Double berth in Starbound's *master stateroom.*

LAYOUT PLANS

Layouts are a compromise. There is no such thing as a perfect layout. And in deep-water cruising boats this problem of compromise becomes even more acute because of the large amount of required stowage that must be accommodated in the small, oddly shaped interior space that is also one's home. It is important to remember that the deep-water cruising yacht will most likely be in port for at least two-thirds of the total duration of a cruise and that comfortable living space is a necessity for a happy ship, and thus a happy cruise.

"How many does she sleep?" How many times have we on *Starbound* heard that question! We're usually very polite, though. We answer that she sleeps four for deep-water work, five or six for a weekend on the bay, and forty or so if we stack them like cordwood, topside.

Starbound has standing berths for just four people when at sea (see layout). There are two lower bunks in the forecastle stateroom and a double in the master's stateroom. The portside upper bunk in the forecastle has 24 inches of vertical clearance and is converted to sail-bag stowage for long cruises. The small forward head generally has the sea cocks closed and is used as a rigging locker. The quarterberth aft has hardly ever been used, save as a receptacle for a current job's odds and ends and is now being converted into a small radio cubby/workspace. We can sleep two more on the transom seats in the main saloon, but that is not a good arrangement for deep-water work, simply because there is always a body or two in the way of comfortable living.

We like to go to sea with just four aboard, but when a couple joins us for a relatively short-term cruise, in the nature of two or three weeks, our son Ernie sleeps in the main saloon. But he generally slings a hammock topside when the weather is clement—which, if we planned well, is almost always. We can rig two hammocks, one on either side, and they are lovely on a hot night in the tropics. People prone to *mal de mer* like them, too. When rolling downwind, the ship's motion is considerably dampened.

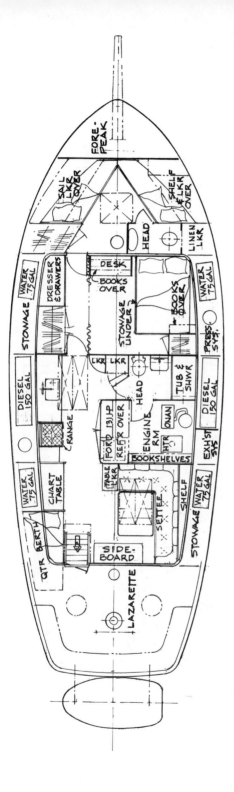

STARBOUND ~ ACCOMODATION

0   5   10   15   20 FT

Fig. 2-2 Starbound: accomodation plan.

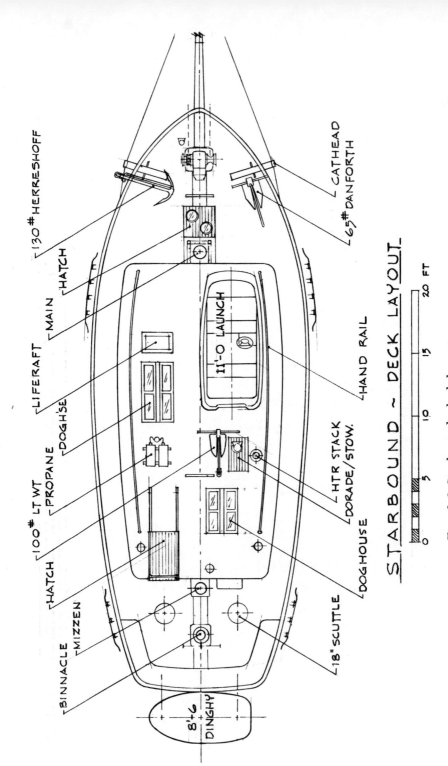

STARBOUND ~ DECK LAYOUT

130# HERRESHOFF
HATCH
MAIN
LIFERAFT
PROPANE
DOGH'SE
100# LT WT
HATCH
MIZZEN
BINNACLE
8'-6
DINGHY
18" SCUTTLE
DOGHOUSE
HTR STACK
DORADE/STOW.
HAND RAIL
11'-0 LAUNCH
CATHEAD
65# DANFORTH

0   5   10   15   20 FT

Fig. 2-3 Starbound: deck layout.

I've included four additional cruising layouts of a 45-footer for the reader's consideration. They differ only in two key factors: location of cockpit and location of galley. This size boat and these four general arrangements characterize so many cruising yachts today that we feel they are worthy of study, although the assets of one arrangement become the liabilities of another, and vice versa. Compromise again.

A center cockpit allows living quarters aft, albeit not large in a 45-footer. It is generally protected from a pooping wave. The running gear can be easily led to it. A wide engine room can be tucked under it (even though there is no headroom), and tankage, battery lockers, work space, and stowage can be built into the engine compartment on both sides of the engine. A wide, livable center cockpit is a nice place to while away a hot afternoon; it is essentially an additional living space. It is hard to fall out of a center cockpit during rough weather and motion is felt less than in an after cockpit. An awning can easily be rigged over it.

The liabilities: Living space aft is about as large as a doghouse unless the after deck is raised considerably, which makes the after deck a hazardous place on which to work while at sea. An option on the raised deck aft is to give the ship very full buttock lines to increase beam and headroom in that after cabin. This results in hull lines that tend to make the ship pull a hole in back of her, slowing her down. And opening the transom portlights (if any) for badly needed ventilation is an invitation to a following wave. The center cockpit is placed just about at the extreme beam of the boat, where the best use of it could be made below for the main saloon, galley, and navigation space. Ventilation to the engine space is a problem, as is the length of shaft required to reach aft. The lazaret has disappeared and the multitude of gear normally stowed there must have other space found for it. The steering gear will almost certainly have to be hydraulic, else a mess of wire, chain, and sheaves will be strung about the after quarters. (Not that hydraulic steering is a liability. It is a good system if one knows how to care for it.)

Now look at the aft cockpit arrangements and, while doing so, reverse the assets and liabilities just discussed. We will not recom-

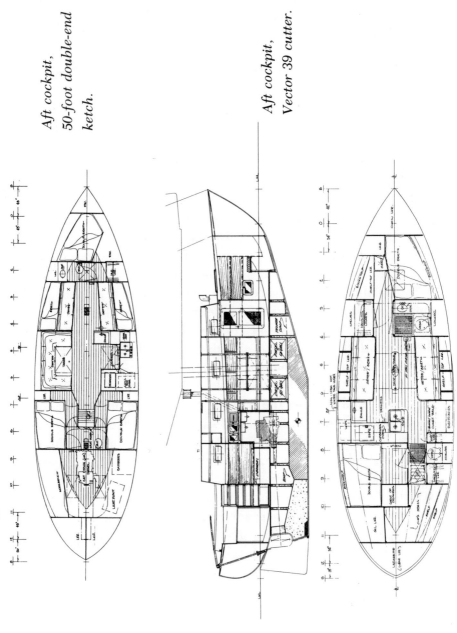

Fig. 2-1 SOME TYPICAL CRUISING LAYOUTS

Aft cockpit,
50-foot double-end
ketch.

Aft cockpit,
Vector 39 cutter.

*Center cockpit,
43-foot ketch motorsailer.*

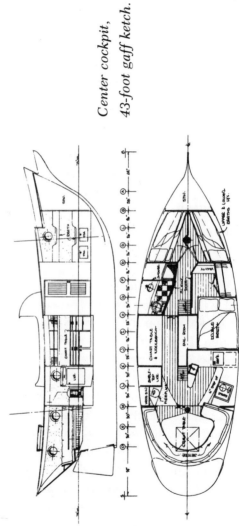

*Center cockpit,
43-foot gaff ketch.*

(COURTESY JAY R. BENFORD & ASSOC.)

mend, per se, one over any other for deep-water cruising; the decision is too much one of personal preference. Our personal preference, however, is the after cockpit arrangement, primarily because of the after stowage it affords and the flexibility of arrangements amidships it allows. Too often living space on cruising boats is made subsidiary to all other factors. On a 30-footer this might be its proper status, simply because of the small total existing cubic space. But a deep-water cruising boat, don't forget, will spend at least two-thirds of her time in port and that comfortable living space is a very necessary luxury—a contradiction in terms, we know.

Location of the galley is the second key factor. While cruising, one person is almost always in the galley and the remainder of the crew rummage around in it for goodies several times each day (and night). It is a center of activity.

Ideally the galley should be out of the way of traffic. Realistically that's almost impossible on a 45-foot boat. On a 60-footer the galley can be made totally separate, but on smaller boats the traffic must be lived with.

An *after galley* must endure the companionway traffic, including that with dripping-wet foul-weather gear. It is also subject to an occasional dollop from a wave top, when the companionway hatch is open. However, air and ventilation are good (a definite asset for those who tend toward seasickness) and the after location is handy for passing goodies to those on deck.

An amidships galley, because of the greater beam in that location, can more easily be arranged in the desirable U-shaped configuration that allows the cook to brace on either tack or when rolling downwind. Traffic is still a problem, but generally only when someone goes forward, and is less than the companionway traffic. An amidships galley also acts as a buffer zone between main saloon and forward sleeping quarters, allowing a bit more privacy to those sleeping. Of course at night, someone clanking about looking for the cookies can disturb everyone, unless the galley has a goodie locker with easy access. A primary attribute for the amidships location is that the motion is easier there, and anyone who has cooked at sea knows that the cook needs all the help he can get.

A few basics should apply to all galleys. Sinks should be located as close to the centerline of the boat as possible, if they gravity-drain via through-hull openings. They should be constructed deep enough to prevent water from slopping out and should be a set of double narrow sinks rather than a single wide one. Stoves should be gimbaled against heeling and rolling. Iceboxes, refrigerators, and deep freezes should be top opening. If they are big enough to require side doors, the doors should open forward or aft. Useable (reachable) storage should be installed in every location not taken up by basic galley equipment.

This general discussion regarding accommodation has so far touched on only the prime requirements of berthing, cockpits, and galleys. Of course, there are many other items and factors of lesser importance that must be considered when contemplating accommodation niceties. They might seem obvious, which is why they are often overlooked or ignored. Here are some of them.

The head should contain at least a w.c. and a wash basin. The w.c. should face either fore or aft. A shower, piped for both fresh and salt water, is desirable, as is linen storage.

The navigational space should be separate, with a built-in chart table, hopefully a seat, enough chart "ready" stowage to accommodate at least 20 charts, and racks and stowage for all navigational equipment and texts. All electronic instruments should be located within easy reach. The space should be totally protected from salt spray, wavetops, rain, and wet people. Generally ideal navigating space cannot be had on yachts less than 45 feet. But on any deep-water cruiser, some sort of dedicated space is a must, even if it is a simple drop-leaf plywood board hinged to the cabin trunk and hooked to the overhead when not in use.

Cabin tables must be sailor-proof, which means brutally strong. Tables that fold up against the bulkhead are ingenious, but they tend to collapse when a 200-pound man is thrown against one. A permanent table, mounted on solid stanchions, with a drop leaf on the passage side, is highly desirable.

Sail stowage cannot be overlooked. Wet sails must often go below—and not in someone's bunk. Suitable storage either forward or aft must be provided, and that stowage must be reached without trundling said wet sail down the main companionway and through the living spaces. And remember, whatever stowage is being used, it must have a hatchway large enough to accommodate the unfolded, but bagged, mainsail. The stowage area must drain and be ventilated.

The library is a necessity. Everyone reads at sea. Besides which, space must be available for navigation books. We would estimate six linear feet of shelves to be an absolute minimum. *Starbound* contains 30 feet of shelves throughout the ship. Our sailing directions, light lists, and radio aids alone take up six feet.

Grab-rails and handholds should be located throughout the vessel and where they can be reached. It is a fact that everything that can be grabbed, stepped on, leaned against, or struck by a hurled human body, will be. These items—grab-rails, fiddles, tables, settees, or whatever—must be strong enough to stand the strain. Sharp edges must be rounded or fendered (cushioned) to avoid injury.

Companionways should face aft and, if possible, be protected by a dodger. The companionway opening should be sized so that a person can stand on an intermediate step, head and shoulders extending above the coamings, and brace himself, facing in any direction, while using a sextant.

3
The Planning Book

About 18 months before we left on our world cruise, we were questioning a good friend of ours, George Prentice, about the availability of nautical charts and other hydrographic data. An experienced deep-water sailor, George looked at the lists we had prepared and asked us a question. "Haven't you started a planning book?" Which led to the initiation of a very valuable planning tool for us—a way of insinuating a necessary degree of discipline into the cruise-planning process.

I told him we had many lists and our little green notebooks.

He said, "Those are all just fine, but you should have a real planning book with everything in it. Get yourselves a big, fat, three-ring binder, a bunch of separators with index tabs and some lined paper. Assign categories to the index tabs: charts, weather, books, tools, spares, bosun's stores, food, medicine—every damn thing there is on the boat and everything you'll have to get. Keep all your information in that one book. When you jot down notes to yourself at work, transfer them into the book when you get home.

It'll become the most valuable book you have; an instant ready reference."

George was right. So the main purpose of this chapter is to tell our readers how to develop a planning book as well as to provide guidance on obtaining much of the required information.

First, collect a "big, fat, three-ring binder, a bunch of separators with index tabs, and some lined paper." Second, consider the following categories to apply to the index tabs:

Charts
Sailing Directions
Navigation Tools/Texts
Weather Notes
Provisioning
Bosun's Stores
Spare Parts
Tools
Emergency Equipment
Emergency Repairs
Medical Stores
Documents: Ship's and Crew's
Cable and Mail Addresses
Personal Gear
Stowage Plan (ship layout)
Layouts (misc.)
 Sails
 Awnings, Covers, Boots
Rigging
 Standing
 Running
 Fittings
Docking Plans/Photos
Book List
Address List
Conversion Tables

The foregoing is a somewhat abbreviated reference list and the categories are in no particular order—only as we added them to *Starbound's* planning book.

An additional binder is necessary to accommodate all of the various equipment manuals. If a repair manual, parts list, wiring diagram, etc., is missing for any piece of mechanical or electrical equipment aboard, it should be obtained from the manufacturer. The same rule applies when buying a new piece of gear; make sure the "software" comes with it.

CHARTS AND NAVIGATIONAL REFERENCES

Charts always seem to be the initial thought in anyone's mind when planning a cruise. But which charts? There has to be a starting point for planning the course of a deep-water cruise and a way of calculating which charts are needed. We think the best way to start is to obtain the following four publications: The *American Practical Navigator* by N. Bowditch, *Ocean Passages of the World* (a hefty British Admiralty publication), *Pilot Charts* for the planned cruise area, and *The Catalog of Nautical Charts and Publications*.

The American Practical Navigator, more commonly and fondly known as Bowditch, should be the first book in any sailor's library. It is and has been the epitome of navigation since its initial publication in 1802.

Ocean Passages is valuable to the sailor because it contains over 100 pages of sailing-ship routes, including many charts that suggest the best ways to cross oceans under sail at various times of the year. We know of no other publications that contain such information.

Pilot Charts are general ocean charts that present, in graphic form, more facts and conclusions relative to navigation, oceanography, and meteorology than any other single source. Pilot Charts are available for each month of the year, a separate set for (1) the North Atlantic, (2) the North Pacific, (3) the Northern North Atlantic, (4) the South Atlantic and Central American Waters, and (5) the South Pacific and Indian Oceans.

Nina at ease in large double bunk in master cabin. Note the storage space under the bunk.

The Catalog of Nautical Charts and Publications (pub. no. 1-N series) is a series of catalogs that lists all the various U.S. Oceanographic charts and publications available. Just what area each chart covers is shown graphically.

Bowditch, *Pilot Charts,* and the *Catalog* can be obtained through authorized sales agents for the U.S. Naval Oceanographic Office, and also through the Superintendent of Documents, U.S. Government Printing Office, Washington, D.C. 20402. *Ocean Passages* is a bit more difficult to find. Try the American sales agents first. Two suggested sources are:

Weems and Plath, Inc.
222 Severn Avenue
Annapolis, Maryland 21403
(301) 263-6700

New York Nautical Instruments and Repair Co.
140 West Broadway
New York, N.Y. 10013
(212) 944-9191

Or, one might write directly to the source of British Admiralty publications:

Hydrographer of the Navy
Ministry of Defense
Paunton, Somerset, London, England

CRUISE PLANNING

Once having the above described publications in hand, the second and more enjoyable step toward the actual course planning of the cruise can begin. The absolute primary concerns in planning the course of a deep-water cruise are: *Avoid severe storms* and *employ fair winds.* With these two concerns firmly in mind, the problem becomes one of juggling dates to minimize the ship's exposure to the first and maximize exposure to the second.

The way Nina and I did the initial planning for our world cruise was this: We sat down amongst a welter of books and pilot charts and began to clarify on paper the sailing route we had talked and thought about for many months. We found the pilot charts to be the best cruise-planning guide of all. As we actually started putting dates down in writing, some of our problems began solving themselves.

We had a total of three years in which to sail the world—a decision based primarily on future career considerations and available funds. Second, there are places in the world that a cruising yacht generally finds untenable at certain times of the year. These places, along our loosely defined route, are the North Atlantic in winter, the Caribbean in summer, the southwest Pacific in "down under" summer (November to April), the Tasman Sea in "down under" winter, Indonesian waters from October to April, and the Cape of Good Hope anytime. (However, January is considered the best time of year to sail around the "Cape of Storms.")

So we drew pencil lines on the charts and discussed it. "We'll leave the Chesapeake before November, spend the winter in the West Indies, get to the Panama Canal by mid-February, and play around in the South Pacific until October, by which time we should leave Suva, Fiji, for New Zealand.

"Then we'll work in New Zealand during their summer and by the following April, five or six months later, we'll be on our way across the Tasman Sea to Sydney or Brisbane, and then go north up the Australian Coast inside the Great Barrier Reef.

"And then on to Thursday Island and around the top of Australia to Darwin; from there to Bali and as much more of Indonesia as we can see; out of Indonesia by the first of October and down to South Africa before Christmas, probably at Durban; then around the Cape in January, hang it up in Capetown awhile, leave in March and sail a long slant across the South Atlantic back to the West Indies, with a stop at Saint Helena along the way."

We made up our sailing schedule and based it on departure dates from each port. Arrival dates depend on how fast we might sail and are too nebulous to contemplate.

That is a very general idea of how we went about our cruise planning. But let us make some additional suggestions. Buy two or three inexpensive world maps from the local stationery store. Refer to Chapter XXXIX in Bowditch. This chapter defines the areas of *tropical cyclones* of the world and their seasons. Using a soft lead pencil, encircle these hazardous general areas on one of the inexpensive maps and crosshatch the area lightly. Write in the dates of the hazardous seasons.

Now break out the pilot charts and *Ocean Passages* and using their more detailed information, refine the areas and dates. Once satisfied that the information on the "working" map is complete, it will probably be a mess. Tape it on a suitable sunny window and tape a clean map over it. Trace the final crosshatched amorphous blobs of the hazardous areas onto the new working map with a felt-tip pen. Put the dates back on in large figures, using a different color.

It is time to lay out the actual course of the cruise. So lay it out roughly—again with soft pencil. Then, figuring an average speed at sea of 100 nautical miles per day, estimate the dates of departure and arrival at all the places to be visited. When the courses and ports lie within the hazardous areas, make sure that the dates of the cruise do not coincide with the dates of the defined storm seasons. And since these seasons are only averages, allow some leeway. Try not to cut the bad seasons too close on either end. An early or late typhoon or hurricane can upset the best laid plans.

When the dates have all been printed on the working map, it is time to break out the Pilot Charts again. Lightly transpose the course and dates onto the appropriate charts for the months that reflect the cruise dates. Perhaps the course will have to stop in the middle of an ocean on a chart for one month and take up again on the next month's chart.

Once the entire planned course has been transposed, study the pilot charts very closely. Look at the limits of the trade winds. Does the course take maximum advantage of these incredibly steady winds? How about ocean currents? They are all shown on the pilot charts. Is the course laid against an equatorial countercurrent in the area of *doldrums*? Study the wind roses defined for each of the five-degree square areas along the planned route. Do they indicate favorable winds?

Now the heavy thinking begins. Cruise planning is an iterative process, and you must change the course and the cruise timing wherever necessary to ensure that the ship will be in the right part of the ocean at the right time of year.

Finally, when completely satisfied with the planned course, check it once more against *Ocean Passages* and transcribe the changes back to the working map, which is now probably cluttered with notes. So, once again trace all the final data onto a new working map. Pin this final map up on a wall someplace, where it can be referred to. It will be, frequently.

If a truly beautiful cruise chart is desired, buy a large world chart from National Geographic Magazine, 1145 17th Street, N.W., Washington, D.C. 20036 and transpose the cruise route onto it with 1/16-inch wide mapping tape. Write in the arrival and departure dates with white ink or colored pencils and define the storm areas and seasons in the same fashion. Make sure when ordering the chart that it is the one that contains hydrographic data (winds and currents) for the ocean areas, shown as superimposed small arrows on the depth-defining graduated blue.

The decision as to which charts to order has now been very much simplified. Spread the chart catalogs out and once again transpose the planned course; this time, directly onto the catalog, which is itself a type of chart. All that is left to do is to list all the charts through which the course is laid.

Some might ask why all the preliminary work is necessary. Why not start with the chart catalog, draw the course on it, and order the desired charts? A few extras won't hurt, and since the small-scale ocean charts are not so date dependent, why not get them first?

That is one way to do it, but the preliminary work just discussed needs to be done anyway. And once completed, a much greater understanding of the entire planned route will have been achieved. It is a mind-settler to really know the course of the cruise

Navigation area aboard Starbound *has stowage for Aids to Naviga-tion,* Sailing Directions, *and radio. A portion of ship's library is begind Nina.*

route, the arrival and departure times, and the reasoning behind them. Also, charts are expensive, and in quantity take up much more space and weight than one would think. Enough charts should be ordered to completely cover the planned route, plus a reasonable number of alternate routes and ports, but no more than that. However, if one is in doubt about a certain chart, buy it.

It is really best to buy Pilot Charts for the entire calendar year so that the average seasonal changes can be tracked. Also, since the *charts* are a compendium of averages over a great number of years, they are never out-of-date.

Small-scale charts, covering entire oceans, are needed for detail planning and navigational use. Medium-scale charts, covering certain ocean areas, are positively required for the approaches to coastlines and islands. Large-scale charts are the ones containing detailed information on ports and harbors and how to get into them safely. The harbor charts should always be up-to-date with the latest information on them.

We mentioned the high cost of charts. It is not unusual to spend $1000 on charts for a world cruise. Hal Roth mentions in his fine book, *After 50,000 Miles,* that he carries about 200 charts on *Whisper* just for the Pacific Basin. Since the average cost is about $2.50 per chart, his investment might be $500 or more—probably more.

To save money, old charts can be updated through the *Notice to Mariners,* issued periodically by the Defense Mapping Agency, Hydrographic and Topographic Office, Washington, D.C.

There is another way to bring old charts up to date: Make contact with an owner of new charts and pen in the necessary changes on your old ones. This evolution takes time but is generally well worth it. Other cruising yachtsmen are always willing to help out, as are, perhaps surprisingly, the officers of big ships—freighters and the like. We know one cruising family, Al and Helen Gehrman, now on their fourth trip around the world on their ketch, *Myonie,* who operate mostly with very old charts that they have kept updated for many years. They pay particular attention to harbor and area charts, making sure the lights and radio-beam signatures are correct and that harbor construction and anchorage information is current.

When cruising waters of foreign countries we found it wise, in many cases, to use the harbor and area charts issued by that country. The Great Barrier Reef along the northeast coast of Australia is an area that illustrates the case in point. Our American charts for the Reef, although new, contained several errors. At each port we would find a friendly trawler and spread out our charts for the captain's perusal. Too often he would say, "Bloody hell, mate! That's all wrong there. There's no passage between those islands; it's up here, between these. That other pass is filled with a lot of bloody coral. Take the bottom right out of 'er." Then he would spread his charts and have us "put right."

We bought some select British charts for the British West Indies and French charts for certain areas of French Polynesia, notably the Tuamotu Archipelago. And we wish we had obtained some Dutch charts for Indonesian waters, but we couldn't get them when we needed them. Also, Indonesia has been independent for some time now and we are not certain how recently surveys of those waters have been made.

Regardless of which charts are being used though, the proper technique is to maintain extreme caution off any foreign coast or when entering any foreign harbor. When we on *Starbound* face tricky piloting in strange waters and are beset by sudden doubt, we perform a "*Starbound* maneuver," which is a fast 180-degree turn, always making sure we have room to do so, and proceed back on a reciprocal of our entrance course. Then we think it over and make sure that everything looks right before trying it again.

Before ordering a stack of navigational charts, the reader should be aware of the other navigational publications that are available through various government offices. Chapter IV and Appendix N in Bowditch lists in detail what these publications are and where they can be obtianed. Instructions for their use are also given in various sections through Bowditch.

For planning's sake, as well as to ease the strain on one's bank account, it would be wise to exercise some restraint on one's first order of navigational data. Once the procedure for ordering has been established, follow-up orders are simple. Desired publications can be listed in the planning book, then checked off as they are obtained, or stricken if it is decided they are not required.

We would suggest that at least one volume of *Sailing Directions* should be included in the first order. Contained in a pocket at the back of each volume of *Sailing Directions* is a catalog in chart form that shows the numbers of all the available volumes and the areas they cover. Subsequent orders can be made using this catalog as a guide. We put the catalog in our planning book as a fold-out page and simply circled the desired volume numbers with red pencil. As we obtained them, we shaded in the circle. We've included a reproduction of one of these chart/catalogs to give the reader an idea of what he should first order. For instance, if the cruise is going to include French Polynesia, Hydrographic Office Publication (H.O. Pub.) No. 80 should be obtained with the first chart order.

A clarification is in order: *Sailing Directions* are often called *Pilots*, especially in other countries. But *Sailing Directions* do not cover the coasts of the United States and its possessions, including the Intercoastal Waterways. These are covered by *Coast Pilots*, published by NOAA (National Oceanic and Atmospheric Administration) and are not to be confused with *Sailing Directions*, which cover the rest of the world and are published in looseleaf form by the U.S. Naval Oceanographic Office.

A cautionary note: Supplements to coast pilots are published annually, and change pages to *Sailing Directions* are published periodically. It takes real dedication to stay up with the changes, so order only what is needed and not too soon before the planned cruise date. The more important changes are listed in *Notice to Mariners*, which is published weekly and distributed to "qualified users." It can be consulted at offices of sales agents for products of the U.S. Naval Oceanographic Office, NOAA, and the U.S. Coast Guard. It can also be found in their branch and district offices. When abroad, United States consulates should have it.

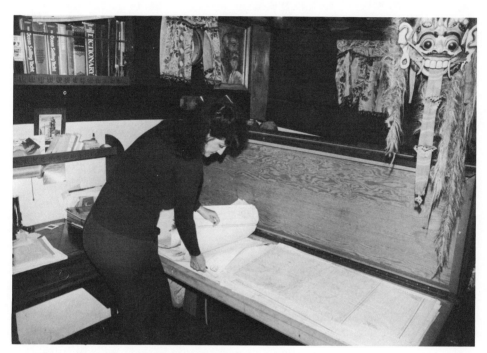

Chart stowage under berth has room for large charts.

Other publications that we find of value and have on board are: *Radio Navigational Aids, Light Lists, Table of Distances Between Ports,* and of course, the *Sight Reduction Tables.* There are dozens of others available but we again caution the reader to think carefully before ordering: Charts and *Sailing Directions* themselves take up a lot of weight and space.

We have mentioned the ship's library. As far as we're concerned, there is no such thing as too many books—until one tries to fit them all on a boat. We try to reserve our shelf space, in descending order of priority, for navigational texts, informational and reference books such as cruising guides, and books of passage accounts, of which there are very many. These alone will overfill the shelves on most boats.

Hardback novels are a waste of shelf space. Buy paperbacks instead and keep them in a big plastic bag, doubled, and stuffed into an out-of-the-way locker. At each port have book trading sessions with other yachts to maintain a fresh supply. *Starbound* started her cruise with over 100 paperbacks and we traded at every port. It is a deep-water cruising institution.

At the start of this chapter, we indicated a number of categories that should be included in the planning book and thus far, we have written a somewhat detailed exposition on the first two of these: charts and *Sailing Directions.* Subsequent chapters deal with the remaining subjects in detail, so as a reference, here we will simply comment on them and give some guidance on how to obtain more information.

Navigation: The tools and texts for this not-very-difficult art are covered in Chapter 4, along with a comparison study of the various methods that may be employed. We have included our recommendation of the simplest means to find one's position when at sea.

Weather is another subject to which we have devoted a section of this book. Chapter 5 contains general thoughts about weather, climate, and seasons as they relate to the deep-water cruiser and how to get up-to-date information both before and during a cruise.

Provisioning is not a topic of heavy importance while in the plan-

Nina works on the Planning Book.

ning stage of a cruise, but information-gathering should begin. Nina is the principal expert in this field and she writes on the subject in Chapter 15.

Bosun's stores refers to all those supplies and spares, excluding tools, needed to care for the hull and rig of the ship. (See Chapter 12.)

Spare parts refers to all mechanical and electrical supplies and spares, again excluding tools. (See Chapter 12.)

Tools, a very self-explanatory term, are discussed in detail in Chapter 12.

Emergency equipment and repairs is a section that should list all the material and equipment needed to effect at-sea repairs to the hull and/or rig in case of a real emergency, such as a holed hull, a lost rudder, a broken mast, or similar occurrences. Chapter 13 gets into the subject.

Medical stores are covered in Chapter 16.

Documents, those precious pieces of paper required by all countries for both ship and crew, are covered in Chapter 7.

Addresses are easy to misplace—particularly cable addresses for banks, embassies, and machinery manufacturers. Start listing them—now!

Personal gear, including clothes, is included in Chapter 14.

The stowage plan can be very simple and very handy. Draw a rough full-page (8½ x 11 inches) diagram of the ship's interior layout. Measure the spacing between bulkheads, both fore and aft and athwartship. Using an architect's or engineer's scale (ruler), redraw the layout to an appropriate scale (a 40-foot boat drawn to ¼ inch = 1 foot scale will be 10 inches long on paper). Accentuate with heavy lines all the storage areas. Now list everything to be carried aboard and see if it will all fit. Pay attention to what is stowed where. Heavy tools and spare parts must be kept dry and handy, but they must be stowed so as not to foul up the ship's trim. Medical stores must be kept cool, dry and handy—where? Food stores are generally kept near the galley if possible, but for long passages the bilge volumes are often full of tinned food. How much can they hold?

Miscellaneous layouts should include scale drawings, or pat-

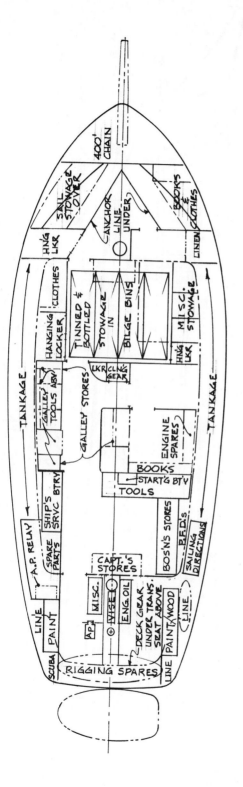

STARBOUND ~ STOWAGE PLAN

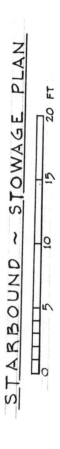

0   5   10   15   20 FT

Fig. 3-1 Starbound's stowage plan.

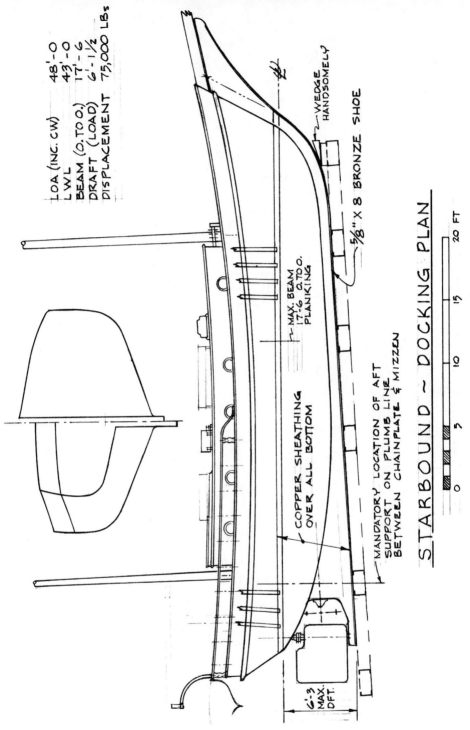

LOA (INC. CW) ——— 48'-0
LWL ——— 43'-0
BEAM (O.TO.O.) ——— 17'-6
DRAFT (LOAD) ——— 6'-1½
DISPLACEMENT 75,000 LBs

WEDGE HANDSOMELY

⅝" X 8 BRONZE SHOE

MAX. BEAM
17-6 O.TO.O.
PLANKING

COPPER SHEATHING
OVER ALL BOTTOM

MANDATORY LOCATION OF AFT
SUPPORT ON PLUMB LINE
BETWEEN CHAINPLATE ¢ MIZZEN

6'-3
MAX.
DFT.

0   5   10   15   20 FT

STARBOUND ~ DOCKING PLAN

Fig. 3-2 *Starbound's docking plan.*

terns, of sails, sail covers, awnings, dodgers, doghouse covers, mast boots and other items which will have to periodically be remade.

The planning book section on *rigging* should list every piece of standing and running rigging aboard, with its dimension, length, and material. All spare line and wire should also be listed. If a 600-foot reel of ½-inch nylon is aboard and 140 feet of it is used for a new sheet, the 600 should be changed to 460. It sounds like a simple procedure, but very few people do it and so have no idea how much spare line is left in the lazaret—or even how much is required for a new sheet or halyard without remeasuring each time it needs changing.

Docking plans are very necessary if the planned cruise is long enough to require intermediate haulouts. We are constantly surprised by the number of skippers who don't have a docking plan for their ship, and some who have never even seen her hauled. It is wise to have a very good idea of where she is likely to be hauled during the cruise and what facilities are available. We saw boats that had always been hauled by a Travel-lift in the states get put into a small drydock or onto a huge marine railway, or even get propped against pilings on the "hard" while a 15-foot tide went out. We personally supervise every facet of our haulouts, even when there is a language barrier. A poorly engineered facility for hauling can induce more structural damage to a ship, regardless of her construction, than any storm at sea.

Reflecting on the hectic months of our own cruise planning, my father's words, spoken when regarding a somewhat difficult project, come to mind: "It's like building a barn, son. By the time you've got it done, you know how!"

4

Piloting and Navigation: You Must Take Notes!

Several years ago I was sitting in a classroom in a large Eastern university, listening to the introductory lecture of a class in analytical geometry by a learned professor of mathematics. The professor must have impressed me, because I still remember some of what he said.

"You must take notes!" he cried in his penetrating nasal-toned voice. "There is little hope for you—no, I say that it is *impossible*—to pass this course unless you take notes, *all* the notes!"

His gaze swept the front row of students, halting at a large, red-faced young man, whose size 14 feet projected far into the front cross-aisle. The professor pointed a nicotine-stained index finger at that unfortunate individual and cried again in his high, grating voice, "Observe Landuski there! Year after year he sits in the front row—*looking* at me! You must take notes!"

I tell this story to show that formal classes of one kind or another are a very good way to learn what needs to be learned about piloting and navigation. Once enrolled in a class, there exists the personal obligation to attend that class and to perform the assigned homework (for which class notes must be taken). And, of course, the psychological aid of group learning gives added impetus to the necessary discipline required for the learning process. The classes are not difficult. It is simply a fact that the human animal tends to be lazy unless some form of discipline is imposed. Paying for and attending a class seems to do the trick better than independent learning at home.

Many people confuse these two nautical terms; simply stated, *piloting* is for coastal work and *navigation* is for offshore. *Navigation* is the art of fixing the position of the boat at sea by observation of the sun, stars, planets, and moon. Good navigation depends to a certain extent upon good piloting. That is to say, one must *pilot* one's boat away from the harbor and the coastline before celestial navigation becomes necessary. And even then the position of the vessel must be roughly known by *deduced (ded or dead) reckoning*, again a form of piloting. Celestial navigation is not difficult and enough can be learned relatively quickly to do an adequate job of finding the boat's position when out of sight of land.

Piloting is the much more difficult art and requires a good deal of study and practice. Piloting is involved with every facet of directing the course of the boat, from the time the mooring is dropped until it is picked up again, perhaps on the other side of an ocean.

Most owners of pleasure boats today cruise only their home waters and depend on their local knowledge to get from place to place during good weather. If low visibility conditions catch them while away from their dock, they—most of them—find themselves seriously handicapped.

We believe that every boat owner/operator should be schooled in at least the basics of piloting. If extensive coasting work is to be engaged in, instruction in piloting is very necessary. We are constantly bemused by the ever-increasing number of inexperienced people who buy a nice little production fiberglass sailboat and charge out of the harbor with her, knowing not one thing about even the basic rules of the road.

While coming back through the Caribbean, we chanced to meet not one but three different boats—beautiful, well-found boats—

whose owners knew little of piloting and nothing of celestial navigation. They had made their way to where they were by courtesy of electronics, luck, and the grace of God. Then something happened to their electronic navigation systems—and they were stuck without the expertise to repair them. No one knew how to work a simple sun line, despite the fact that each boat had a beautiful sextant aboard and the proper tables. Our son, Ernie, twenty at the time, fixed the electronics equipment on two of the boats. He taught the owner of the third, whose Loran needed some unavailable parts, how to use his showpiece sextant to obtain a sun shot and to work out a line of position. What surprised us then was the lack of interest displayed by the two owners whose electronics had been repaired in learning how to use their sextants.

I put in a good deal of thought on how much technical information about piloting to include in this chapter. My conclusion has to be that there is no way that I can improve on that marvelous book, *Piloting, Seamanship and Small Boat Handling* by Charles F. Chapman. This should be one of the first books purchased for any sailor's library.

I've already noted that formal classwork is the best method to learn piloting, which can be done via the United States Coast Guard Auxiliary and the United States Power Squadron. Here are two nonprofit organizations that offer free instruction in basic boating to the general public.

After passing the U.S.P.S. Boating Course, which is open to everyone, male graduates of the course are invited to join the organization.* The membership is very active and offers advanced courses of several kinds, including seamanship, advanced piloting and navigation. Additional courses are given in sailing, meteorology, electronics, and engine maintenance.

Our strong recommendation to anyone whose future plans include deep-water cruising, is to join the U.S. Power Squadron as soon as possible and take advantage of these really valuable

---

*It is, perhaps, unfortunate that only males can become members of the U.S.P.S., a matter which is being tested in the courts. Please make note that women are allowed to take all the offered courses. As far as I'm concerned, that is the important thing.

courses. The cost is minimal: just the yearly dues and the price of the course materials. The rewards are incalculable.

If you choose to take the U.S. Coast Guard Auxiliary's basic course, be advised that the organization also offers advanced courses. These are made available to their members on a more informal basis and schedule than are the U.S.P.S. courses and include subjects such as Communications, Search and Rescue, Weather, and Seamanship. However, be aware that the U.S.C.G.A. courses are primarily geared to boating on coastal and inland waters. While their value is obvious, their content is, for the deep-water cruising sailor, somewhat limited.

CELESTIAL NAVIGATION BY COOKBOOK

I believe that the advertised difficulty of learning celestial navigation is exaggerated. This opinion is shared by all of our cruising friends. While recognizing that volumes have been written on the subject, the amount of knowledge needed to fix one's position at sea is actually not at all large or difficult. However, a full understanding of all the involved theories can be confusing and quite time-consuming. So our recommendation to those who want to learn how to use a sextant and thereby find their position at sea, is to forget the theory for the time being and learn by rote, that is, by following an established recipe. All that has to be learned before going to sea is how to obtain a *line of position* (LOP) as it is designated, and how to put it on a chart. The theory can be learned later—at sea during the night watches is a perfect time to engage one's mind in advanced studies.

"Cookbook navigation" is what we call this method. I've taught my wife and son and several friends to navigate by employing this technique. When I say "celestial navigation" I mean locating oneself at sea, using a sextant, an almanac, and the appropriate tables. That's all we have on *Starbound,* except for a radio direction finder, which is handy when there are reliable radio beacons around.

With a sextant, the navigator can shoot the sun, the moon, certain navigational stars, and four of the planets. The sun is easiest because there's no mistaking it, the horizon is obvious, and the calculation is simple. Stars are almost as easy, but the timing has to be right. In either the morning or evening it has to be dark enough to see the primary stars and light enough to have a clearly discernible horizon. The same applies to planets, except for Venus, which is so bright that it can often be seen in broad daylight. The moon is, in my opinion, the most difficult heavenly body to use for navigation. Being closest to the earth, it moves fast. Also, the calculations involve some corrections that are confusing to the beginner.

The best procedure for the beginner is to learn to shoot the sun, calculate a line of position, and place it on the chart. When you reach the point of asking yourself, "Is this all there is to it?" then it's time to start shooting stars and planets.

A question I am often asked is: How do you know which star to shoot out of all that glittering stuff up there? I have to say it's easier at sea. There's a horizon all around and the atmosphere is generally free of dust and smoke. The answer is, use a *Starfinder* and study the constellations—a perfect way to while away the night watches. I'll simplify it further: The *Nautical Almanac* lists fifty-seven stars. There are only twenty that I consider to be bright enough to shoot at any time and on a given evening, or morning, only four to six of those twenty will be available to shoot. The others will be too low, too high, or below the horizon. So it isn't that difficult. During the day there is the sun and sometimes the moon. In the evening there are four to six stars and a planet or two. In the morning the same.

A single shot of a single body, be it sun, moon, star, or planet, will give the navigator one line of position and the navigator will know he is on that line. If it's daylight, only a sun LOP is possible. Most commonly the sun will be shot again a few hours after the first shot; then the first sun LOP will be advanced however many miles the ship has sailed to the point when the second sun shot was taken, and a *running fix* (R. Fix) is thus obtained—accurate enough when the ship is far from land.

When approaching islands or a coastline, position accuracy is

mandatory. We've been in places where the wind has been blowing fresh, with the ship on a beam reach, and we were approaching
a harbor on a long, inhospitable coastline. We knew that if we
raised the coast downwind of our harbor, we would play veritable
hell motoring back against sea and wind. We shot evening stars and
got an accurate fix. Then we adjusted the ship's speed so we would
raise the coastline about 0900 next morning. At first light we shot
more stars, plus a planet, and adjusted our course accordingly. We
hit the harbor buoys perfectly and ran in safely with much relief.
Two other yachts were not so careful and spent a rotten day and
lots of fuel trying to get back up the coast.

Most books on navigation list all the tables available and then try
to show how each is used. Cutting through all that confusion, there
are two sets worth considering: the *Nautical Almanac*, used with
Sight Reduction Tables for Marine Navigation, H.O. 229, and the
Air Almanac, used with Sight Reduction Tables for Air Navigation,
H.O. 249. Taking it one step further, most deep-water yachtsmen
engaged in lengthy voyages prefer H.O. 229, the marine tables,
because the almanac is good for the entire year and the tables are
good forever. The *Air Almanac* allows a method of calculation that
is slightly faster, but it comes out every four months and if the
yacht is on a long cruise, the navigator is liable to find himself with
the latest almanac unobtainable. Also, the shortcut method used
with the air tables gives results not quite as accurate as those calculated with the marine tables. (Because of an aircraft's speed during
the time between two sights, it is not necessary for the *Air Almanac* to be as accurate. But the resulting shortcut in the air method
may cause a ship's navigator to be appreciably off, relatively speaking, from his true location—not an important factor when well
clear of land but much more so when approaching a tricky landfall,
such as the Tuamotu Archipelago or Bermuda's northern reef.)

We use the current *Nautical Almanac* and H.O. 229. H.O. 229
comes in six volumes, each one covering 15 degrees of latitude, up
to 90 degrees. If the navigator doesn't plan on sailing north or
south of 60 degrees of latitude, he can get by with four volumes of
the set: 0–15 degrees, 15–30 degrees, 30–45 degrees, and 45–60

degrees. The current year's *Nautical Almanac* can be obtained in most seaboard cities in the world. The American version has an orange cardboard cover. The British version has a blue cloth cover. The contents are identical in every respect.

The only other equipment necessary is a set of parallel rules (a draftsman's triangle is handy), charting or drafting dividers, a sharp pencil for plotting, another pencil or pen for calculations, some means of identifying stars (we have Star Identifier No. 2101-D put out by Weems and Plath, and Bowditch's diagrams), a chronometer, a shortwave radio receiver, and a sextant.

About *sextants:* We use an old Mark 2 Navy sextant with a micrometer-type readout on it and it works fine. We also have an ancient instrument of World War I vintage with a vernier readout, which is also quite accurate. We have met several yachtsmen who navigate with a cheapie plastic sextant—not as accurate as ours, but they found the same islands as we did.

When a beginning navigator obtains a sextant, he should carefully study the instructions before taking the instrument from its case (which should also not be dropped, thumped, banged, or in any way treated roughly). If it's a used sextant, he should study Bowditch's chapter on the subject before manipulating the instrument. We allow no one to handle our sextants—unless we know that they know what they're doing. One careless rap and the least you've got is a lengthy readjustment job (Bowditch tells how to do that too). If a used sextant is obtained from an instrument firm, make sure it has been checked out. If it is obtained from a private individual, take it to a reputable precision instrument shop and have it checked out before purchase—it could be beyond adjustment, in which case it'll make an interesting conversation piece for the den or bar.

The *chronometer* and the *shortwave radio receiver* are used to obtain accurate time—to the second. Four seconds of time equal one nautical mile of distance—that's how fast the earth turns. A stopwatch is handy also so that one doesn't have to gallop from topside to below to read the time. Many navigators employ a very good chronometer-rated wristwatch, such as a Bulova Accuquartz or a Rolex Seamaster. Bulkhead-mounted quartz crystal, battery-driven chronometers are now quite common and reasonable in price. The shortwave receiver is used to get a time tick so the rate of the chronometer can be checked from time to time. We check ours every day and keep track of the rate in the *Nautical Almanac*. We just write in how fast or slow it is opposite the (Greenwich) day and hour.

To expand the explanation on time, it is this simple: All navigational time is based on the *Greenwich Mean Time* (GMT), which is now called *Coordinated Universal Time* (CUT). It is the time at the zero-degree meridian, the meridian that passes north and south through Greenwich, England. We have never failed to get a time tick on our shortwave receiver anywhere we've gone. So why a chronometer? Easy answer: When somebody drops the radio, the chronometer becomes important. For a time tick around the world, we usually use WWV, Colorado, and WWVH, Hawaii, on 2.5, 5, 10, 15, and 20 mHz. At night 2.5 and 5 mHz are good; during the day 15 and 20 mHz are good; and 10 mHz works almost all the time. Also, BBC stations give a time tick on the hour every hour.

Now that all the tools are present, the navigator can take his sun shot. A nice time for a morning sun line is 0930 (local time)—or any time when the sun's altitude is between 30 and 60 degrees above the horizon. So he takes his shot and punches his stopwatch. I'm not going to explain the shot-taking procedure—it's all in Bowditch anyway and taking accurate shots from the rolling deck of a yacht is a matter of practice. Someone has said that after two thousand shots, a navigator becomes proficient. I think it depends on the person. Ernie became capable in one day and expert in two weeks by working diligently.

The navigator goes below, looks at his chronometer, and punches the stopwatch again when the second hand passes a handy mark. Then he writes down the chronometer time, the stopwatch time, and the sextant reading—all this without letting go of the sextant, which he is holding carefully. He never lays the sextant on a bunk or a chart table. He puts the sextant away in its box and the box away in its safe and permanent storage spot. (Even a slightly damaged sextant can wreck your ship.) Now he can calculate his sun line and plot the line of position on the sailing chart.

The answer the navigator is looking for is similar to the following: "*x*" number of miles toward (or away from) the sun at a true azimuth of "*y*" degrees. Actually he'll scribble something like: 6 miles T @ 106°. How the navigator gets to this point is the process that beginners seem to dread. My suggestion is: Forget the theory! "Cookbook" the problem and learn the theory after the sun line is on the chart. Ernie learned this way. He knew how to find his position at sea long before he fully understood the theory behind it. He studied the theory during his night watches purely out of interest and learned it quickly because he was *employing* it.

An experienced navigator can shoot the sight, make the calculation, and plot the LOP on a chart in less than five minutes. The first time I did it, it took me over an hour. The second time, half an hour. The third time, twenty minutes. Now, both Ernie and I can work a sight in five minutes. It takes practice.

Printed forms can be purchased that may help the beginner with the calculation for each shot. Most deep-water sailors don't bother with them. If we shoot five stars in the morning, a 1000 sun line, a noon latitude shot, a 1500 sun line, and five evening stars, we would use 13 forms each day. Instead, we employ an inexpensive, thick, bound notebook with lined paper and work all our shots in it. We can calculate three shots on a page.

I've mentioned that we shoot five stars (one or two might be planets) in the morning or evening when we want an accurate fix. Actually, a fix can be obtained by just shooting two bodies if they're at near right angles (90-degree angles) to each other. But if a mistake is made on one of them, the fix could be off a good distance. If we shoot three bodies and the final plot gives us a small triangle, which it usually does, we know we're somewhere in the triangle. But if we screw up one shot, say because of a bad horizon or a misreading of the sextant, we might end up with a very large triangle—then we're in the quandary of not knowing which shot was faulty, so we shoot five bodies (in quick succession). One of them might be off, but the others will give us a good fix. A five-body fix can be worked in about thirty minutes.

Let's see what happens when you make a sextant shot and plot the results on a chart. Just a bit of basic theory to begin. Our yacht is in the North Atlantic (see Figure 4-1). We're east of the Caribbean and our destination is Martinique. We break out our sextant and shoot an evening star. The angle we read from the sextant is called the *sextant altitude* and is abbreviated H_s. I've shown that angle on Figure 4-1 as well as that line called the *circle of equal altitude*. Each star (or other heavenly body) we shoot will have, at that instant, its own circle of equal altitude, and the important thing to remember is that our ship is *on that circle*. Also, please note that if our ship is located *anywhere* on that circle, we would get the same sextant altitude, or H_s. We would simply be looking at the star from a different direction; that is, the *azimuth* of the star would change.

Consider a flagpole in the middle of a large, flat field. A line is tied from the top of the flagpole to your neck. If you walked around the flagpole while keeping the line tight, you'd walk in a perfect circle—and the angle formed by the top of the flagpole to your eye to the base of the pole would not change. But the direction in which you are looking would. So when we shoot a star at sea, we know that we are somewhere on a circle of equal altitude for that star. We also know the approximate azimuth of the star by looking at our compass. We will want to know the *exact* azimuth, but we'll get that from our calculations.

Azimuth is the horizontal direction of a celestial point from a geographic point—an angle, as we'll use it, clockwise from true north to the star's *geographical position* (GP) in degrees. If a line were drawn between the star and the earth's center, where that line pierces the surface of the earth is called that star's GP. It is analogous to the base of the flagpole that we were talking about earlier.

Now for the trick. If we could plot a very short section of that circle of equal altitude on a chart—say, just the section that is under our ship—we'd have a *line of position*, an LOP. And that's just

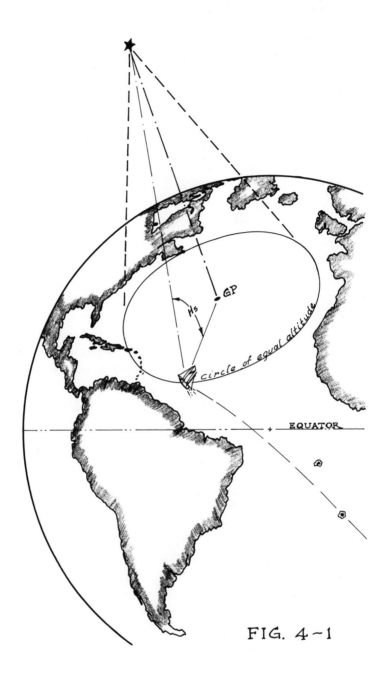

FIG. 4-1

what we'll do, and we'll know that we're on that line. But we won't plot a curved line because the circle of equal altitude has such an immense diameter that the very tiny segment of line on which our boat is sitting looks straight, and for the purposes of navigation, it is.

But we still haven't *fixed* our position. All that we know so far is that we're on that one LOP. So, it is rather obvious that if we take a sight of a different star, preferably one located about 90 degrees of azimuth away from the first star, we'll get a second circle of equal altitude, and that small section of the second circle that passes under our ship will give us a second LOP, and where it crosses the first LOP is where we are! Our position is now fixed.

But cast a glance at Figure 4-2. Note that two circles of equal altitude that intersect each other have to do so at two places. Obviously our ship can't be in two locations at once. And that's where the piloting comes in; we will always have a general idea of our position from our *deduced reckoning* (DR). Besides, the two intersections are so far apart, it is not realistic to assume that we'd make a mistake in DR of so many miles. So generally speaking, we can ignore that second intersection as if it were not there. All the navigator has to have is a very general idea of his DR in order to navigate.

I've already mentioned why we on *Starbound* use the marine tables for navigation, H.O. 229, and the *Nautical Almanac*. In essence we believe it is wise to sacrifice a little time to gain more accuracy. Also, the *Nautical Almanac* is good for the entire year. Therefore, the reader should remember that the following explanation of how to reduce a sextant shot to a line of position on a chart is given using H.O. 229.

The navigational tables perform all the really complicated math for the navigator. To "cookbook" a shot, he has only to do a few simple additions or subtractions to arm himself with the three *arguments* (a mathematical term) with which to enter the navigational tables. These three arguments are: the *local hour angle* of the heavenly body (LHA), the *assumed latitude* of the ship (L_a), and the *declination* of the heavenly body (dec).

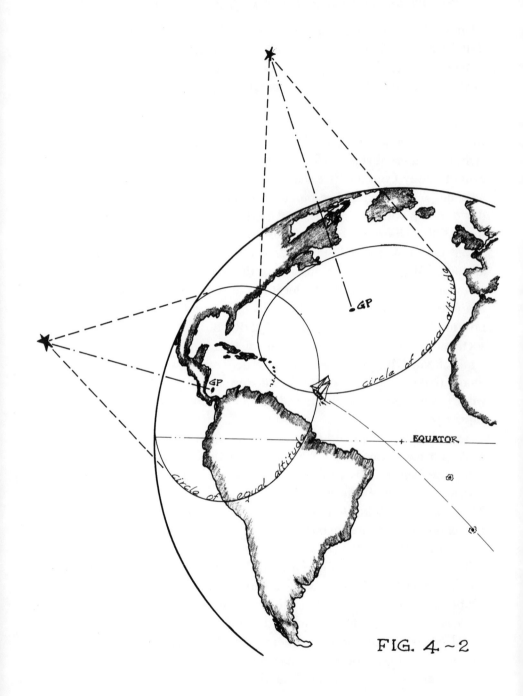

FIG. 4~2

Since the assumed latitude, L_a, is already known from the ship's DR, the navigator needs only to find the LHA and dec. of the heavenly body. He obtains these values via the *Nautical Almanac*, then enters the navigational tables armed with his three arguments, and within a minute he will have the information needed to plot his LOP, that short segment of the circle of equal altitude on which his ship is navigating.

Now let's go through a *sun shot*, since most people consider the sun the easiest body to shoot. We'll do it in three parts. The first two parts start together—taking the shot with the sextant and marking the line at which the shot was taken to the nearest second. Then we'll finish the first part by making some simple arithmetical corrections: the *sextant altitude* (H_s) is corrected for height of eye above the water, the refraction caused by the earth's atmosphere, and since we're shooting a large body (the sun), its semidiameter. We'll finish with the *observed altitude* (H_o), which we'll set aside until we get to the third part of the problem.

We'll complete part two by converting the exact time at which we took the shot into the local hour angle (LHA) of the sun at that time. Then we'll compute its declination (dec.) and conclude the second part of the problem by setting down the assumed latitude of the ship (L_a).

Finally, for part three, we'll enter H.O. 229 with the LHA, L_a, and dec. and come up with the *computed altitude* (H_c) and the azimuth. Comparing the computed altitude (H_c) with the observed altitude (H_o) from part one will tell us how far our actual position is from our assumed position, and the calculated azimuth will tell us in which direction we should apply the correction.

Before we look at an actual problem, here is a list of abbreviations and symbols in the order in which we'll use them, with a brief explanation of where their value is found:

H_s *sextant altitude:* read directly from the sextant.

IE ($\pm$)   *index correction:* peculiar to each sextant and usually marked inside the sextant box.

Dip (−)   *height of eye correction:* measured from eye to water level at the location from where shots are taken.

H_a *apparent altitude:* the altitude corrected for IE and Dip.

AC (±)   *altitude correction:* given explicitly for the stars and planets and incorporated into the correction tables for the sun and moon. The correction tables for the sun include the effects of semidiameter and parallax, as well as the mean refraction.

H_o *observed altitude:* the final corrected sextant altitude. This value is set aside until time to compare it with the computed altitude H_c, derived from H.O. 229.

CT   *chronometer time:* taken from the ship's chronometer which is usually set to GMT.

SW (−)   *stopwatch time:* if used, the interval between the instant of the shot and the instant of reading the chronometer.

CE (±)   *clock error:* how fast or slow the chronometer is at the time of the shot.

GMT   *Greenwich (mean) time:* the time at the prime meridian at Greenwich, England, on which the tables contained in the *Nautical Almanac* are based. If the ship's chronometer is set to GMT, then the GMT of the shot may be obtained by correcting CT by SW and CE.

GHA   *Greenwich hour angle:* the angular distance of the celestial body west from the Greenwich meridian. GHA is tabulated in the almanac for the Sun, Moon, planets, and Aries.

λ_a (±)   *assumed longitude:* the closest longitude to the ship's DR position which, when added or subtracted from the GHA, will result in an LHA expressed in a round number of degrees.

LHA   *local hour angle:* the angular distance of the celestial body west from the meridian of the observer (navigator). LHA can be obtained by the formula LHA = GHA $^{+\ \text{east}}_{-\ \text{west}}$ λ_a.

L$_a$ *assumed latitude:* the closest latitude, suffixed north (N) or south (S), to the ship's DR latitude that can be expressed in a round number of degrees.

dec.   *declination:* the celestial equivalent of the earth's latitude, suffixed north (N) or south (S), as applied to the celestial body and measured in the same way, through 90 degrees (in degrees and tenths of degrees) north or south of the celestial equator.

Two additional terms that apply only to stars are:

γ   *Aries:* an arbitrary reference point in the sky, defined as the point at which the Sun on its annual swing northward crosses the celestial equator. This takes place about March 21st each year. The navigator thinks of Aries as a true but unseen celestial body and uses it to find the GHA of navigational stars (see SHA below).

SHA   *sidereal hour angle:* the angular distance of a star west from the hour circle of Aries. The SHA of the navigational stars is listed in the almanac, as is the GHA of Aries. So we can find the GHA of a star by adding the SHA of that star to the GHA of Aries. (Note: The reason the almanac doesn't list the actual GHAs of stars as they do for the Sun, Moon and planets is because there are 57 navigational stars, which would make for a very fat almanac. Since the SHA of a star changes very slowly, the almanac needs only to show the SHAs once per page [every three days] for these 57 stars. Then, by using the GHA of Aries and an easy addition, we come up with the star's GHA. Actually, it's a handy shortcut.)

FIG. 4-3 ~ SUNSHOT CALCULATION
DATE 8 MAY 1978 - LOCAL TIME 0838 - LOG 3145

PART I

H_s 33° 27.4	SEXTANT	
IE 0	SEXTANT BOX	
DIP(-) 2.8	ALMANAC INSIDE COVER (FIG. 4-3)	
H_a 33° 24.6		
A.C. (+) 14.6	ALMANAC INSIDE COVER (FIG. 4-3)	
H_o 33° 39.2	FINAL RESULT OF PART I; TO BE COMPARED WITH H_c BELOW	

PART III

FROM H.O. 229 (FIG 4-6)

	H_c	d	Z
DEC.(17°)	33° 21.3	+ 0.7	76.2

NOW WE ADJUST THE VALUE OF H_c TO ACCOUNT FOR THE DECLINATION INCREMENT OF 03.6' BY USING THE INTERPOLATION TABLE PRINTED ON THE INSIDE COVER OF H.O. 229. WE ENTER THE TABLE WITH d=+0.7 (FROM ABOVE) & OUR DEC. INC. = 03.6' SEE FIG. 4-7 & NOTICE THAT IN THIS CASE OUR ADJUSTMENT IS NIL (0.0).

FROM THE AZIMUTH RULES PRINTED AT THE TOP & BOTTOM OF EACH PAGE OF H.O. 229, NOTICE THAT SINCE WE ARE IN N. LATITUDE & LHA IS GREATER THAN 180°, THEN $Z = Z_N$ (THE _TRUE_ AZIMUTH; i.e., 76.2° CLOCKWISE FROM TRUE N.)

PART II

CT 11h 36m 10s	CHRONOMETER	
SW (-) 14s	STOPWATCH	
11:35:56		
CE (+) 2:36	TIME TICK	
GMT 11:38:32	WHICH WE CONVERT TO:	
GHA (11h): 345° 53.3	ALMANAC FOR 8 MAY (FIG. 4-4)	
(38m 32s): 9° 38.0	ALMANAC YELLOW PGS. (FIG. 4-5)	
GHA ☉ (TOTAL) 355° 31.3		
λ_a (WEST) 53° 31.3	ASSUMED LONGITUDE CLOSEST TO OR ALLOW'S RESULT TO BE ROUNDED TO NEAREST WHOLE DEGREE	
LHA 302°	
L_a 10° (N)	ASSUMED LATITUDE CLOSEST TO OR ROUNDED TO NEAREST WHOLE DEGREE
DEC. (GMT/11h) N 17° 03.2	ALMANAC FOR 8 MAY (FIG. 4-4)
(38m, d=.7) (GMT) (+) 0.4	ALMANAC YELLOW PGS. (FIG. 4-5)
DEC. (TOTAL) (N) 17° 03.6	

NOTE BOTH N, i.e. SAME NAME

THIS ENDS PART II & GIVES US THE THREE ARGUMENTS WE NEED TO ENTER THE SIGHT REDUCTION TABLES: THE LHA, L_a & DEC.. NOW WE PROGRESS TO PART III

SO NOW WE COMPARE H_c WITH H_o FROM PART I & USE THE DIFFERENCE IN MINUTES AS NAUTICAL MILES:

H_o 33° 39.2'
H_c 33° 21.3'
17.9'

THE RULE IS "CGA"; i.e. COMPUTED GREATER = AWAY, & SINCE IN OUR CASE THE _OBSERVED_ ALTITUDE (H_o) IS GREATER, WE WILL MEASURE _TOWARD_ THE OBSERVED BODY (SUN) FROM OUR ASSUMED POSITION (L_a, λ_a).

THEREFORE, OUR "ANSWER" IS: 17.9 N.M. TOWARD THE SUN AT A TRUE AZIMUTH OF 76.2°

WHICH IS USUALLY WRITTEN: 17.9 T @ 76.2°

ALTITUDE CORRECTION TABLES 10°-90° — SUN, STARS, PLANETS

OCT.—MAR. SUN APR.—SEPT.

App. Alt.	Lower Limb	Upper Limb	App. Alt.	Lower Limb	Upper Limb
9 34	+10.8	−21.5	9 39	+10.6	−21.2
9 45	+10.9	−21.4	9 51	+10.7	−21.1
9 56	+11.0	−21.3	10 03	+10.8	−21.0
10 08	+11.1	−21.2	10 15	+10.9	−20.9
10 21	+11.2	−21.1	10 27	+11.0	−20.8
10 34	+11.3	−21.0	10 40	+11.1	−20.7
10 47	+11.4	−20.9	10 54	+11.2	−20.6
11 01	+11.5	−20.8	11 08	+11.3	−20.5
11 15	+11.6	−20.7	11 23	+11.4	−20.4
11 30	+11.7	−20.6	11 38	+11.5	−20.3
11 46	+11.8	−20.5	11 54	+11.6	−20.2
12 02	+11.9	−20.4	12 10	+11.7	−20.1
12 19	+12.0	−20.3	12 28	+11.8	−20.0
12 37	+12.1	−20.2	12 46	+11.9	−19.9
12 55	+12.2	−20.1	13 05	+12.0	−19.8
13 14	+12.3	−20.0	13 24	+12.1	−19.7
13 35	+12.4	−19.9	13 45	+12.2	−19.6
13 56	+12.5	−19.8	14 07	+12.3	−19.5
14 18	+12.6	−19.7	14 30	+12.4	−19.4
14 42	+12.7	−19.6	14 54	+12.5	−19.3
15 06	+12.8	−19.5	15 19	+12.6	−19.2
15 32	+12.9	−19.4	15 46	+12.7	−19.1
15 59	+13.0	−19.3	16 14	+12.8	−19.0
16 28	+13.1	−19.2	16 44	+12.9	−18.9
16 59	+13.2	−19.1	17 15	+13.0	−18.8
17 32	+13.3	−19.0	17 48	+13.1	−18.7
18 06	+13.4	−18.9	18 24	+13.2	−18.6
18 42	+13.5	−18.8	19 01	+13.3	−18.5
19 21	+13.6	−18.7	19 42	+13.4	−18.4
20 03	+13.7	−18.6	20 25	+13.5	−18.3
20 48	+13.8	−18.5	21 11	+13.6	−18.2
21 35	+13.9	−18.4	22 00	+13.7	−18.1
22 26	+14.0	−18.3	22 54	+13.8	−18.0
23 22	+14.1	−18.2	23 51	+13.9	−17.9
24 21	+14.2	−18.1	24 53	+14.0	−17.8
25 26	+14.3	−18.0	26 00	+14.1	−17.7
26 36	+14.4	−17.9	27 13	+14.2	−17.6
27 52	+14.5	−17.8	28 33	+14.3	−17.5
29 15	+14.6	−17.7	30 00	+14.4	−17.4
30 46	+14.7	−17.6	31 35	+14.5	−17.3
32 26	+14.8	−17.5	33 20	+14.6	−17.2
34 17	+14.9	−17.4	35 17	+14.7	−17.1
36 20	+15.0	−17.3	37 26	+14.8	−17.0
38 36	+15.1	−17.2	39 50	+14.9	−16.9
41 08	+15.2	−17.1	42 31	+15.0	−16.8
43 59	+15.3	−17.0	45 31	+15.1	−16.7
47 10	+15.4	−16.9	48 55	+15.2	−16.6
50 46	+15.5	−16.8	52 44	+15.3	−16.5
54 49	+15.6	−16.7	57 02	+15.4	−16.4
59 23	+15.7	−16.6	61 51	+15.5	−16.3
64 30	+15.8	−16.5	67 17	+15.6	−16.2
70 12	+15.9	−16.4	73 16	+15.7	−16.1
76 26	+16.0	−16.3	79 43	+15.8	−16.0
83 05	+16.1	−16.2	86 32	+15.9	−15.9
90 00			90 00		

STARS AND PLANETS

App. Alt.	Corrn	App. Alt. Additional Corrn
9 56	−5.3	**1978**
10 08	−5.2	**VENUS**
10 20	−5.1	Jan. 1-July 20
10 33	−5.0	42 + 0.1
10 46	−4.9	
11 00	−4.8	July 21-Sept. 2
11 14	−4.7	47 + 0.2
11 29	−4.6	
11 45	−4.5	Sept. 3-Sept. 29
12 01	−4.4	46 + 0.3
12 18	−4.3	
12 35	−4.2	Sept. 30-Oct. 14
12 54	−4.1	11 + 0.4
13 13	−4.0	41 + 0.5
13 33	−3.9	
13 54	−3.8	Oct. 15-Oct. 22
14 16	−3.7	6 + 0.5
14 40	−3.6	20 + 0.6
15 04	−3.5	31 + 0.7
15 30	−3.4	
15 57	−3.3	Oct. 23-Nov. 25
16 26	−3.2	4 + 0.6
16 56	−3.1	12 + 0.7
17 28	−3.0	22 + 0.8
18 02	−2.9	
18 38	−2.8	Nov. 26-Dec. 3
19 17	−2.7	6 + 0.5
19 58	−2.6	20 + 0.6
20 42	−2.5	31 + 0.7
21 28	−2.4	
22 19	−2.3	Dec. 4-Dec. 19
23 13	−2.2	11 + 0.4
24 11	−2.1	41 + 0.5
25 14	−2.0	
26 22	−1.9	Dec. 20-Dec 31
27 36	−1.8	46 + 0.3
28 56	−1.7	
30 24	−1.6	
32 00	−1.5	**MARS**
33 45	−1.4	Jan. 1-Mar. 22
35 40	−1.3	41 + 0.2
37 48	−1.2	75 + 0.1
40 08	−1.1	
42 44	−1.0	Mar. 23-Dec. 31
45 36	−0.9	60 + 0.1
48 47	−0.8	
52 18	−0.7	
56 11	−0.6	
60 28	−0.5	
65 08	−0.4	
70 11	−0.3	
75 34	−0.2	
81 13	−0.1	
87 03	0.0	
90 00		

DIP

Ht. of Eye (m)	Corrn	Ht. of Eye (ft)	Ht. of Eye (m)	Corrn
2.4	−2.8	8.0	1.0	−1.8
2.6	−2.9	8.6	1.5	−2.2
2.8	−3.0	9.2	2.0	−2.5
3.0	−3.1	9.8	2.5	−2.8
3.2	−3.2	10.5	3.0	−3.0
3.4	−3.3	11.2	See table	
3.6	−3.4	11.9	←	
3.8	−3.5	12.6		
4.0	−3.6	13.3	m	
4.3	−3.7	14.1	20	−7.9
4.5	−3.8	14.9	22	−8.3
4.7	−3.9	15.7	24	−8.6
5.0	−4.0	16.5	26	−9.0
5.2	−4.1	17.4	28	−9.3
5.5	−4.2	18.3		
5.8	−4.3	19.1	30	−9.6
6.1	−4.4	20.1	32	−10.0
6.3	−4.5	21.0	34	−10.3
6.6	−4.6	22.0	36	−10.6
6.9	−4.7	22.9	38	−10.8
7.2	−4.8	23.9		
7.5	−4.9	24.9	40	−11.1
7.9	−5.0	26.0	42	−11.4
8.2	−5.1	27.1	44	−11.7
8.5	−5.2	28.1	46	−11.9
8.8	−5.3	29.2	48	−12.2
9.2	−5.4	30.4	ft.	
9.5	−5.5	31.5	2	−1.4
9.9	−5.6	32.7	4	−1.9
10.3	−5.7	33.9	6	−2.4
10.6	−5.8	35.1	8	−2.7
11.0	−5.9	36.3	10	−3.1
11.4	−6.0	37.6	See table	
11.8	−6.1	38.9	←	
12.2	−6.2	40.1	ft.	
12.6	−6.3	41.5	70	−8.1
13.0	−6.4	42.8	75	−8.4
13.4	−6.5	44.2	80	−8.7
13.8	−6.6	45.5	85	−8.9
14.2	−6.7	46.9	90	−9.2
14.7	−6.8	48.4	95	−9.5
15.1	−6.9	49.8		
15.5	−7.0	51.3	100	−9.7
16.0	−7.1	52.8	105	−9.9
16.5	−7.2	54.3	110	−10.2
16.9	−7.3	55.8	115	−10.4
17.4	−7.4	57.4	120	−10.6
17.9	−7.5	58.9	125	−10.8
18.4	−7.6	60.5		
18.8	−7.7	62.1	130	−11.1
19.3	−7.8	63.8	135	−11.3
19.8	−7.9	65.4	140	−11.5
20.4	−8.0	67.1	145	−11.7
20.9	−8.1	68.8	150	−11.9
21.4		70.5	155	−12.1

App. Alt. = Apparent altitude = Sextant altitude corrected for index error and dip.
For daylight observations of Venus, see page 260.

1978 MAY 7, 8, 9 (SUN., MON., TUES.)

G.M.T.	SUN G.H.A.	Dec.	MOON G.H.A.	v	Dec.	d	H.P.	Lat.	Twilight Naut.	Civil	Sunrise	Moonrise 7	8	9	10
d h	° '	° '	° '	'	° '	'	'	°	h m	h m	h m	h m	h m	h m	h m
7 00	180 51.9	N16 39.1	182 10.6	12.0	N12 54.7	7.1	55.6	N 72	////	////	00 34	02 53	02 47	02 39	▭
01	195 52.0	39.8	196 41.6	12.1	13 01.8	7.0	55.6	N 70	////	////	01 49	03 17	03 24	03 36	04 02
02	210 52.0	40.5	211 12.7	12.1	13 08.8	7.0	55.6	68	////	////	02 26	03 36	03 50	04 11	04 43
03	225 52.1 ··	41.2	225 43.8	12.0	13 15.8	6.8	55.5	66	////	01 07	02 51	03 51	04 10	04 35	05 11
04	240 52.1	41.8	240 14.8	12.0	13 22.6	6.8	55.5	64	////	01 53	03 11	04 03	04 26	04 55	05 33
05	255 52.2	42.5	254 45.8	12.1	13 29.4	6.8	55.5	62	////	02 22	03 27	04 14	04 39	05 10	05 50
06	270 52.2	N16 43.2	269 16.9	12.0	N13 36.2	6.7	55.5	60	01 00	02 43	03 41	04 23	04 50	05 24	06 04
07	285 52.3	43.9	283 47.9	12.0	13 42.9	6.6	55.5	N 58	01 41	03 01	03 52	04 31	05 00	05 35	06 17
08	300 52.3	44.6	298 18.9	12.0	13 49.5	6.5	55.4	56	02 08	03 15	04 02	04 38	05 09	05 45	06 27
S 09	315 52.3 ··	45.3	312 49.9	12.0	13 56.0	6.5	55.4	54	02 28	03 27	04 11	04 44	05 17	05 54	06 36
U 10	330 52.4	46.0	327 20.9	12.0	14 02.5	6.3	55.4	52	02 44	03 38	04 18	04 50	05 23	06 02	06 45
N 11	345 52.4	46.7	341 51.9	12.0	14 08.8	6.4	55.4	50	02 58	03 47	04 25	04 55	05 30	06 09	06 52
D 12	0 52.5	N16 47.4	356 22.9	12.0	N14 15.2	6.2	55.4	45	03 25	04 07	04 40	05 06	05 43	06 24	07 08
A 13	15 52.5	48.1	10 53.9	11.9	14 21.4	6.2	55.3	N 40	03 46	04 22	04 52	05 15	05 54	06 36	07 21
Y 14	30 52.5	48.8	25 24.8	12.0	14 27.6	6.1	55.3	35	04 02	04 35	05 03	05 23	06 04	06 47	07 33
15	45 52.6 ··	49.5	39 55.8	11.9	14 33.7	6.0	55.3	30	04 15	04 46	05 12	05 30	06 12	06 56	07 42
16	60 52.6	50.2	54 26.7	12.0	14 39.7	5.9	55.3	20	04 36	05 04	05 27	05 43	06 27	07 12	07 59
17	75 52.7	50.8	68 57.7	11.9	14 45.6	5.9	55.3	N 10	04 53	05 19	05 41	05 53	06 39	07 26	08 14
18	90 52.7	N16 51.5	83 28.6	12.0	N14 51.5	5.8	55.3	0	05 06	05 31	05 53	06 03	06 51	07 40	08 28
19	105 52.7	52.2	97 59.6	11.9	14 57.3	5.7	55.2	S 10	05 18	05 43	06 05	06 14	07 03	07 53	08 42
20	120 52.8	52.9	112 30.5	11.9	15 03.0	5.7	55.2	20	05 29	05 55	06 18	06 24	07 16	08 07	08 56
21	135 52.8 ··	53.6	127 01.4	11.9	15 08.7	5.5	55.2	30	05 39	06 08	06 33	06 37	07 31	08 23	09 13
22	150 52.9	54.3	141 32.3	11.9	15 14.2	5.5	55.2	35	05 45	06 15	06 42	06 44	07 40	08 33	09 23
23	165 52.9	55.0	156 03.2	11.9	15 19.7	5.4	55.2	40	05 50	06 23	06 51	06 52	07 49	08 44	09 35
8 00	180 52.9	N16 55.7	170 34.1	11.9	N15 25.1	5.4	55.1	45	05 56	06 31	07 03	07 02	08 01	08 57	09 48
01	195 53.0	56.3	185 05.0	11.9	15 30.5	5.2	55.1	S 50	06 02	06 41	07 16	07 14	08 15	09 12	10 04
02	210 53.0	57.0	199 35.9	11.9	15 35.7	5.2	55.1	52	06 05	06 46	07 23	07 19	08 22	09 19	10 12
03	225 53.1 ··	57.7	214 06.8	11.9	15 40.9	5.1	55.1	54	06 08	06 51	07 30	07 25	08 29	09 27	10 20
04	240 53.1	58.4	228 37.7	11.8	15 46.0	5.0	55.1	56	06 11	06 56	07 37	07 32	08 37	09 37	10 30
05	255 53.1	59.1	243 08.5	11.9	15 51.0	5.0	55.1	58	06 15	07 02	07 46	07 39	08 46	09 47	10 40
06	270 53.2	N16 59.8	257 39.4	11.9	N15 56.0	4.8	55.0	S 60	06 18	07 09	07 56	07 48	08 57	09 59	10 53
07	285 53.2	17 00.4	272 10.3	11.8	16 00.8	4.8	55.0								
08	300 53.2	01.1	286 41.1	11.9	16 05.6	4.7	55.0	Lat.	Sunset	Twilight Civil	Naut.	Moonset 7	8	9	10
M 09	315 53.3 ··	01.8	301 12.0	11.8	16 10.3	4.5	55.0								
O 10	330 53.3	02.5	315 42.8	11.9	16 15.0	4.5	55.0	°	h m	h m	h m	h m	h m	h m	h m
N 11	345 53.3	03.2	330 13.7	11.8	16 19.5	4.5	55.0	N 72	▭	////	////	22 21	24 09	00 09	▭
D 12	0 53.4	N17 03.8	344 44.5	11.8	N16 24.0	4.3	54.9	N 70	22 10	////	////	21 45	23 12	24 26	00 26
A 13	15 53.4	04.5	359 15.3	11.9	16 28.3	4.3	54.9	68	21 31	////	////	21 20	22 39	23 46	24 36
Y 14	30 53.4	05.2	13 46.2	11.8	16 32.6	4.2	54.9	66	21 04	22 54	////	21 00	22 14	23 18	24 08
15	45 53.5 ··	05.9	28 17.0	11.8	16 36.8	4.2	54.9	64	20 44	22 05	////	20 45	21 55	22 56	23 46
16	60 53.5	06.6	42 47.8	11.9	16 41.0	4.0	54.9	62	20 28	21 34	////	20 32	21 40	22 39	23 29
17	75 53.6	07.2	57 18.7	11.8	16 45.0	4.0	54.9	60	20 14	21 12	23 01	20 21	21 27	22 25	23 15
18	90 53.6	N17 07.9	71 49.5	11.8	N16 49.0	3.9	54.8	N 58	20 02	20 54	22 16	20 12	21 16	22 13	23 02
19	105 53.6	08.6	86 20.3	11.8	16 52.9	3.8	54.8	56	19 52	20 40	21 48	20 03	21 06	22 02	22 52
20	120 53.7	09.3	100 51.1	11.9	16 56.7	3.7	54.8	54	19 44	20 27	21 27	19 56	20 57	21 53	22 42
21	135 53.7 ··	09.9	115 22.0	11.8	17 00.4	3.7	54.8	52	19 36	20 16	21 10	19 49	20 50	21 45	22 34
22	150 53.7	10.6	129 52.8	11.8	17 04.1	3.5	54.8	50	19 29	20 07	20 56	19 43	20 43	21 37	22 27
23	165 53.8	11.3	144 23.6	11.8	17 07.6	3.5	54.8	45	19 14	19 47	20 29	19 31	20 28	21 22	22 11
9 00	180 53.8	N17 12.0	158 54.4	11.8	N17 11.1	3.4	54.8	N 40	19 01	19 31	20 08	19 20	20 16	21 09	21 57
01	195 53.8	12.6	173 25.2	11.8	17 14.5	3.3	54.7	35	18 51	19 18	19 52	19 11	20 06	20 57	21 46
02	210 53.9	13.3	187 56.0	11.9	17 17.8	3.2	54.7	30	18 42	19 07	19 38	19 03	19 57	20 48	21 36
03	225 53.9 ··	14.0	202 26.9	11.8	17 21.0	3.1	54.7	20	18 26	18 49	19 17	18 50	19 41	20 31	21 20
04	240 53.9	14.6	216 57.7	11.8	17 24.1	3.1	54.7	N 10	18 12	18 35	19 00	18 38	19 27	20 17	21 05
05	255 53.9	15.3	231 28.5	11.9	17 27.2	2.9	54.7	0	18 00	18 22	18 47	18 27	19 15	20 03	20 51
06	270 54.0	N17 16.0	245 59.3	11.8	N17 30.1	2.9	54.7	S 10	17 48	18 09	18 35	18 15	19 02	19 49	20 37
07	285 54.0	16.7	260 30.1	11.9	17 33.0	2.8	54.6	20	17 34	17 57	18 24	18 04	18 48	19 35	20 22
08	300 54.0	17.3	275 01.0	11.8	17 35.8	2.7	54.6	30	17 20	17 45	18 13	17 50	18 33	19 18	20 05
T 09	315 54.1 ··	18.0	289 31.8	11.8	17 38.5	2.6	54.6	35	17 11	17 38	18 08	17 42	18 24	19 08	19 55
U 10	330 54.1	18.7	304 02.6	11.8	17 41.1	2.6	54.6	40	17 01	17 30	18 02	17 33	18 14	18 57	19 44
E 11	345 54.1	19.3	318 33.4	11.9	17 43.7	2.4	54.6	45	16 50	17 21	17 56	17 23	18 02	18 44	19 31
S 12	0 54.2	N17 20.0	333 04.3	11.8	N17 46.1	2.4	54.6	S 50	16 36	17 11	17 50	17 10	17 47	18 29	19 15
D 13	15 54.2	20.7	347 35.1	11.8	17 48.5	2.2	54.6	52	16 30	17 06	17 47	17 05	17 40	18 21	19 07
A 14	30 54.2	21.3	2 05.9	11.9	17 50.7	2.2	54.6	54	16 23	17 01	17 44	16 58	17 33	18 13	18 59
Y 15	45 54.2 ··	22.0	16 36.8	11.8	17 52.9	2.2	54.5	56	16 15	16 56	17 41	16 51	17 25	18 04	18 49
16	60 54.3	22.7	31 07.6	11.9	17 55.1	2.0	54.5	58	16 06	16 50	17 37	16 43	17 15	17 53	18 38
17	75 54.3	23.3	45 38.5	11.8	17 57.1	1.9	54.5	S 60	15 56	16 43	17 34	16 34	17 04	17 41	18 26
18	90 54.3	N17 24.0	60 09.3	11.9	N17 59.0	1.9	54.5								
19	105 54.4	24.7	74 40.2	11.9	18 00.9	1.7	54.5	Day	SUN Eqn. of Time 00ʰ	12ʰ	Mer. Pass.	MOON Mer. Pass. Upper	Lower	Age	Phase
20	120 54.4	25.3	89 11.1	11.9	18 02.6	1.7	54.5								
21	135 54.4 ··	26.0	103 42.0	11.8	18 04.3	1.6	54.5		m s	m s	h m	h m	h m	d	
22	150 54.4	26.6	118 12.8	11.9	18 05.9	1.5	54.5	7	03 28	03 30	11 57	12 15	24 39	00	
23	165 54.5	27.3	132 43.7	11.9	18 07.4	1.4	54.4	8	03 32	03 33	11 56	13 03	00 39	01	
	S.D. 15.9	d 0.7	S.D. 15.1		15.0		14.9	9	03 35	03 37	11 56	13 51	01 27	02	🌑

└ THE FACTOR FOR INCREMENTS & CORRECTIONS IN THE "YELLOW PAGES"!

└ USEFUL FOR A NOON LATITUDE SHOT!

SOURCE: the Nautical Almanac for 1978

(38ᵐ) INCREMENTS AND CORRECTIONS **39ᵐ**

38	SUN PLANETS	ARIES	MOON	v or Corr d	v or Corr d	v or Corr d
00	9 30·0	9 31·6	9 04·0	0·0 0·0	6·0 3·9	12·0 7·7
01	9 30·3	9 31·8	9 04·3	0·1 0·1	6·1 3·9	12·1 7·8
02	9 30·5	9 32·1	9 04·5	0·2 0·1	6·2 4·0	12·2 7·8
03	9 30·8	9 32·3	9 04·7	0·3 0·2	6·3 4·0	12·3 7·9
04	9 31·0	9 32·6	9 05·0	0·4 0·3	6·4 4·1	12·4 8·0
05	9 31·3	9 32·8	9 05·2	0·5 0·3	6·5 4·2	12·5 8·0
06	9 31·5	9 33·1	9 05·5	0·6 0·4	6·6 4·2	12·6 8·1
07	9 31·8	9 33·3	9 05·7	0·7 0·4	6·7 4·3	12·7 8·1
08	9 32·0	9 33·6	9 05·9	0·8 0·5	6·8 4·4	12·8 8·2
09	9 32·3	9 33·8	9 06·2	0·9 0·6	6·9 4·4	12·9 8·3
10	9 32·5	9 34·1	9 06·4	1·0 0·6	7·0 4·5	13·0 8·3
11	9 32·8	9 34·3	9 06·7	1·1 0·7	7·1 4·6	13·1 8·4
12	9 33·0	9 34·6	9 06·9	1·2 0·8	7·2 4·6	13·2 8·5
13	9 33·3	9 34·8	9 07·1	1·3 0·8	7·3 4·7	13·3 8·5
14	9 33·5	9 35·1	9 07·4	1·4 0·9	7·4 4·7	13·4 8·6
15	9 33·8	9 35·3	9 07·6	1·5 1·0	7·5 4·8	13·5 8·7
16	9 34·0	9 35·6	9 07·9	1·6 1·0	7·6 4·9	13·6 8·7
17	9 34·3	9 35·8	9 08·1	1·7 1·1	7·7 4·9	13·7 8·8
18	9 34·5	9 36·1	9 08·3	1·8 1·2	7·8 5·0	13·8 8·9
19	9 34·8	9 36·3	9 08·6	1·9 1·2	7·9 5·1	13·9 8·9
20	9 35·0	9 36·6	9 08·8	2·0 1·3	8·0 5·1	14·0 9·0
21	9 35·3	9 36·8	9 09·0	2·1 1·3	8·1 5·2	14·1 9·0
22	9 35·5	9 37·1	9 09·3	2·2 1·4	8·2 5·3	14·2 9·1
23	9 35·8	9 37·3	9 09·5	2·3 1·5	8·3 5·3	14·3 9·2
24	9 36·0	9 37·6	9 09·8	2·4 1·5	8·4 5·4	14·4 9·2
25	9 36·3	9 37·8	9 10·0	2·5 1·6	8·5 5·5	14·5 9·3
26	9 36·5	9 38·1	9 10·2	2·6 1·7	8·6 5·5	14·6 9·4
27	9 36·8	9 38·3	9 10·5	2·7 1·7	8·7 5·6	14·7 9·4
28	9 37·0	9 38·6	9 10·7	2·8 1·8	8·8 5·6	14·8 9·5
29	9 37·3	9 38·8	9 11·0	2·9 1·9	8·9 5·7	14·9 9·6
30	9 37·5	9 39·1	9 11·2	3·0 1·9	9·0 5·8	15·0 9·6
31	9 37·8	9 39·3	9 11·4	3·1 2·0	9·1 5·8	15·1 9·7
32	9 38·0	9 39·6	9 11·7	3·2 2·0	9·2 5·9	15·2 9·8
33	9 38·3	9 39·8	9 11·9	3·3 2·1	9·3 6·0	15·3 9·8
34	9 38·5	9 40·1	9 12·1	3·4 2·2	9·4 6·0	15·4 9·9
35	9 38·8	9 40·3	9 12·4	3·5 2·2	9·5 6·1	15·5 9·9
36	9 39·0	9 40·6	9 12·6	3·6 2·3	9·6 6·2	15·6 10·0
37	9 39·3	9 40·8	9 12·9	3·7 2·4	9·7 6·2	15·7 10·1
38	9 39·5	9 41·1	9 13·1	3·8 2·4	9·8 6·3	15·8 10·1
39	9 39·8	9 41·3	9 13·3	3·9 2·5	9·9 6·4	15·9 10·2
40	9 40·0	9 41·6	9 13·6	4·0 2·6	10·0 6·4	16·0 10·3
41	9 40·3	9 41·8	9 13·8	4·1 2·6	10·1 6·5	16·1 10·3
42	9 40·5	9 42·1	9 14·1	4·2 2·7	10·2 6·5	16·2 10·4
43	9 40·8	9 42·3	9 14·3	4·3 2·8	10·3 6·6	16·3 10·5
44	9 41·0	9 42·6	9 14·5	4·4 2·8	10·4 6·7	16·4 10·5
45	9 41·3	9 42·8	9 14·8	4·5 2·9	10·5 6·7	16·5 10·6
46	9 41·5	9 43·1	9 15·0	4·6 3·0	10·6 6·8	16·6 10·7
47	9 41·8	9 43·3	9 15·2	4·7 3·0	10·7 6·9	16·7 10·7
48	9 42·0	9 43·6	9 15·5	4·8 3·1	10·8 6·9	16·8 10·8
49	9 42·3	9 43·8	9 15·7	4·9 3·2	10·9 7·0	16·9 10·8
50	9 42·5	9 44·1	9 16·0	5·0 3·2	11·0 7·1	17·0 10·9
51	9 42·8	9 44·3	9 16·2	5·1 3·3	11·1 7·1	17·1 11·0
52	9 43·0	9 44·6	9 16·4	5·2 3·3	11·2 7·2	17·2 11·0
53	9 43·3	9 44·8	9 16·7	5·3 3·4	11·3 7·3	17·3 11·1
54	9 43·5	9 45·1	9 16·9	5·4 3·5	11·4 7·3	17·4 11·2
55	9 43·8	9 45·3	9 17·2	5·5 3·5	11·5 7·4	17·5 11·2
56	9 44·0	9 45·6	9 17·4	5·6 3·6	11·6 7·4	17·6 11·3
57	9 44·3	9 45·8	9 17·6	5·7 3·7	11·7 7·5	17·7 11·4
58	9 44·5	9 46·1	9 17·9	5·8 3·7	11·8 7·6	17·8 11·4
59	9 44·8	9 46·4	9 18·1	5·9 3·8	11·9 7·6	17·9 11·5
60	9 45·0	9 46·6	9 18·4	6·0 3·9	12·0 7·7	18·0 11·6

39	SUN PLANETS	ARIES	MOON	v or Corr d	v or Corr d	v or Corr d
00	9 45·0	9 46·6	9 18·4	0·0 0·0	6·0 4·0	12·0 7·9
01	9 45·3	9 46·9	9 18·6	0·1 0·1	6·1 4·0	12·1 8·0
02	9 45·5	9 47·1	9 18·8	0·2 0·1	6·2 4·1	12·2 8·0
03	9 45·8	9 47·4	9 19·1	0·3 0·2	6·3 4·1	12·3 8·1
04	9 46·0	9 47·6	9 19·3	0·4 0·3	6·4 4·2	12·4 8·2
05	9 46·3	9 47·9	9 19·5	0·5 0·3	6·5 4·3	12·5 8·2
06	9 46·5	9 48·1	9 19·8	0·6 0·4	6·6 4·3	12·6 8·3
07	9 46·8	9 48·4	9 20·0	0·7 0·5	6·7 4·4	12·7 8·4
08	9 47·0	9 48·6	9 20·3	0·8 0·5	6·8 4·5	12·8 8·4
09	9 47·3	9 48·9	9 20·5	0·9 0·6	6·9 4·5	12·9 8·5
10	9 47·5	9 49·1	9 20·7	1·0 0·7	7·0 4·6	13·0 8·6
11	9 47·8	9 49·4	9 21·0	1·1 0·7	7·1 4·7	13·1 8·6
12	9 48·0	9 49·6	9 21·2	1·2 0·8	7·2 4·7	13·2 8·7
13	9 48·3	9 49·9	9 21·5	1·3 0·9	7·3 4·8	13·3 8·8
14	9 48·5	9 50·1	9 21·7	1·4 0·9	7·4 4·9	13·4 8·8
15	9 48·8	9 50·4	9 21·9	1·5 1·0	7·5 4·9	13·5 8·9
16	9 49·0	9 50·6	9 22·2	1·6 1·1	7·6 5·0	13·6 9·0
17	9 49·3	9 50·9	9 22·4	1·7 1·1	7·7 5·1	13·7 9·0
18	9 49·5	9 51·1	9 22·6	1·8 1·2	7·8 5·1	13·8 9·1
19	9 49·8	9 51·4	9 22·9	1·9 1·3	7·9 5·2	13·9 9·2
20	9 50·0	9 51·6	9 23·1	2·0 1·3	8·0 5·3	14·0 9·2
21	9 50·3	9 51·9	9 23·4	2·1 1·4	8·1 5·3	14·1 9·3
22	9 50·5	9 52·1	9 23·6	2·2 1·4	8·2 5·4	14·2 9·3
23	9 50·8	9 52·4	9 23·8	2·3 1·5	8·3 5·5	14·3 9·4
24	9 51·0	9 52·6	9 24·1	2·4 1·6	8·4 5·5	14·4 9·5
25	9 51·3	9 52·9	9 24·3	2·5 1·6	8·5 5·6	14·5 9·5
26	9 51·5	9 53·1	9 24·6	2·6 1·7	8·6 5·7	14·6 9·6
27	9 51·8	9 53·4	9 24·8	2·7 1·8	8·7 5·7	14·7 9·7
28	9 52·0	9 53·6	9 25·0	2·8 1·8	8·8 5·8	14·8 9·7
29	9 52·3	9 53·9	9 25·3	2·9 1·9	8·9 5·9	14·9 9·8
30	9 52·5	9 54·1	9 25·5	3·0 2·0	9·0 5·9	15·0 9·9
31	9 52·8	9 54·4	9 25·7	3·1 2·0	9·1 6·0	15·1 9·9
32	9 53·0	9 54·6	9 26·0	3·2 2·1	9·2 6·1	15·2 10·0
33	9 53·3	9 54·9	9 26·2	3·3 2·2	9·3 6·1	15·3 10·1
34	9 53·5	9 55·1	9 26·5	3·4 2·2	9·4 6·2	15·4 10·1
35	9 53·8	9 55·4	9 26·7	3·5 2·3	9·5 6·3	15·5 10·2
36	9 54·0	9 55·6	9 26·9	3·6 2·4	9·6 6·3	15·6 10·3
37	9 54·3	9 55·9	9 27·2	3·7 2·4	9·7 6·4	15·7 10·3
38	9 54·5	9 56·1	9 27·4	3·8 2·5	9·8 6·5	15·8 10·4
39	9 54·8	9 56·4	9 27·7	3·9 2·6	9·9 6·5	15·9 10·5
40	9 55·0	9 56·6	9 27·9	4·0 2·6	10·0 6·6	16·0 10·5
41	9 55·3	9 56·9	9 28·1	4·1 2·7	10·1 6·6	16·1 10·6
42	9 55·5	9 57·1	9 28·4	4·2 2·8	10·2 6·7	16·2 10·7
43	9 55·8	9 57·4	9 28·6	4·3 2·8	10·3 6·8	16·3 10·7
44	9 56·0	9 57·6	9 28·8	4·4 2·9	10·4 6·8	16·4 10·8
45	9 56·3	9 57·9	9 29·1	4·5 3·0	10·5 6·9	16·5 10·9
46	9 56·5	9 58·1	9 29·3	4·6 3·0	10·6 7·0	16·6 10·9
47	9 56·8	9 58·4	9 29·6	4·7 3·1	10·7 7·0	16·7 11·0
48	9 57·0	9 58·6	9 29·8	4·8 3·2	10·8 7·1	16·8 11·1
49	9 57·3	9 58·9	9 30·0	4·9 3·2	10·9 7·2	16·9 11·1
50	9 57·5	9 59·1	9 30·3	5·0 3·3	11·0 7·2	17·0 11·2
51	9 57·8	9 59·4	9 30·5	5·1 3·4	11·1 7·3	17·1 11·3
52	9 58·0	9 59·6	9 30·8	5·2 3·4	11·2 7·4	17·2 11·3
53	9 58·3	9 59·9	9 31·0	5·3 3·5	11·3 7·4	17·3 11·4
54	9 58·5	10 00·1	9 31·2	5·4 3·6	11·4 7·5	17·4 11·5
55	9 58·8	10 00·4	9 31·5	5·5 3·6	11·5 7·6	17·5 11·5
56	9 59·0	10 00·6	9 31·7	5·6 3·7	11·6 7·6	17·6 11·6
57	9 59·3	10 00·9	9 32·0	5·7 3·8	11·7 7·7	17·7 11·7
58	9 59·5	10 01·1	9 32·2	5·8 3·8	11·8 7·8	17·8 11·7
59	9 59·8	10 01·4	9 32·4	5·9 3·9	11·9 7·8	17·9 11·8
60	10 00·0	10 01·6	9 32·7	6·0 4·0	12·0 7·9	18·0 11·9

SOURCE: the "yellow pages" of the Nautical Almanac for 1978

58°, 302° L.H.A.   **LATITUDE SAME NAME AS DECLINATION**

	8°			9°			10°			11°			12°			13°		
Dec.	Hc	d	Z	Hc	d	Z	Hc	d	Z	Hc	d	Z	Hc	d	Z	Hc	d	Z	
°	° ′	′	°	° ′	′	°	° ′	′	°	° ′	′	°	° ′	′	°	° ′	′	°	
0	31 39.1 + 9.5	95.0		31 33.6 +10.7	95.6		31 27.5 +11.9	96.2		31 20.7 +13.1	96.8		31 13.3 +14.2	97.4		31 05.2 +15.5	98.0		5
1	31 48.6 8.9	93.8		31 44.3 10.1	94.4		31 39.4 11.3	95.0		31 33.8 12.5	95.7		31 27.5 13.7	96.3		31 20.7 14.8	96.9		3
2	31 57.5 8.2	92.6		31 54.4 9.4	93.3		31 50.7 10.6	93.9		31 46.3 11.8	94.5		31 41.2 13.1	95.1		31 35.5 14.3	95.7		3
3	32 05.7 7.6	91.5		32 03.8 8.8	92.1		32 01.3 10.0	92.7		31 58.1 11.3	93.4		31 54.3 12.4	94.0		31 49.8 13.7	94.6		31
4	32 13.3 6.9	90.3		32 12.6 8.2	90.9		32 11.3 9.4	91.6		32 09.4 10.6	92.2		32 06.7 11.8	92.8		32 03.5 13.0	93.4		31
5	32 20.2 + 6.3	89.1		32 20.8 + 7.5	89.8		32 20.7 + 8.7	90.4		32 20.0 - 9.9	91.0		32 18.5 −11.2	91.7		32 16.5 +12.4	92.3		32
6	32 26.5 5.6	88.0		32 28.3 6.8	88.6		32 29.4 8.1	89.2		32 29.9 9.3	89.9		32 29.7 10.6	90.5		32 28.9 11.7	91.1		32 :
7	32 32.1 4.9	86.8		32 35.1 6.2	87.4		32 37.5 7.4	88.0		32 39.2 8.7	88.7		32 40.3 9.8	89.3		32 40.6 11.1	90.0		32 4
8	32 37.0 4.3 −85.6			32 41.3 5.5	86.2		32 44.9 6.8	86.9		32 47.9 8.0	87.5		32 50.1 9.3	88.2		32 51.7 10.5	88.8		32 5.
9	32 41.3 3.6	84.4		32 46.8 4.9	85.0		32 51.7 6.1	85.7		32 55.9 7.3	86.3		32 59.4 8.5	87.0		33 02.2 9.8	87.6		33 0<
10	32 44.9 + 3.0	83.2		32 51.7 + 4.2	83.9		32 57.8 + 5.4	84.5		33 03.2 + 6.6	85.1		33 07.9 + 7.9	85.8		33 12.0 + 9.1	86.5		33 15.
11	32 47.9 2.2	82.0		32 55.9 3.5	82.7		33 03.2 4.7	83.3		33 09.8 6.0	84.0		33 15.8 7.2	84.6		33 21.1 8.4	85.3		33 25.
12	32 50.1 1.6	80.8		32 59.4 2.8	81.5		33 07.9 4.1	82.1		33 15.8 5.3	82.8		33 23.0 6.5	83.4		33 29.5 7.8	84.1		33 35.
13	32 51.7 0.9	79.7		33 02.2 2.1	80.3		33 12.0 3.3	80.9		33 21.1 4.6	81.6		33 29.5 5.9	82.2		33 37.3 7.1	82.9		33 44.
14	32 52.6 + 0.3	78.5		33 04.3 1.5	79.1		33 15.3 2.7	79.7		33 25.7 3.9	80.4		33 35.4 5.1	81.0		33 44.4 6.4	81.7		33 52.7
15	32 52.9 − 0.5	77.3		33 05.8 + 0.8	77.9		33 18.0 + 2.0	78.5		33 29.6 + 3.2	79.2		33 40.5 + 4.5	79.8		33 50.8 + 5.7	80.5		34 00.3
16	32 52.4 1.1	76.1		33 06.6 + 0.1	76.7		33 20.0 + 1.3	77.3		33 32.8 2.6	78.0		33 45.0 3.8	78.6		33 56.5 5.0	79.3		34 07.3
17	32 51.3 1.8	74.9		33 06.7 − 0.6	75.5		33 21.3 + 0.7	76.2		33 35.4 1.8	76.8		33 48.8 3.0	77.4		34 01.5 4.3	78.1		34 13.5
18	32 49.5 2.4	73.7		33 06.1 1.3	74.3		33 22.0 − 0.1	75.0		33 37.2 1.2	75.6		33 51.8 2.4	76.2		34 05.8 3.5	76.9		34 19.0
19	32 47.1 3.2	72.5		33 04.8 1.9	73.1		33 21.9 0.8	73.8		33 38.4 − 0.4	74.4		33 54.2 1.6	75.0		34 09.3 2.9	75.7		34
20	32 43.9 − 3.8	71.3		33 02.9 − 2.7	71.9		33 21.1 − 1.4	72.6		33 38.8 − 0.2	73.2		33 55.8 + 1.0	73.8		34 12.2 − 2.2	74.6		
21	32 40.1 4.4	70.1		33 00.2 3.3	70.7		33 19.7 2.1	71.4		33 38.6 1.0	72.0		33 56.8 + 0.2	72.6		34 14.4 1.4			
22	32 35.7 5.2	69.0		32 56.9 4.0	69.6		33 17.6 2.9	70.2		33 37.6 1.6	70.8		33 57.0 − 0.4	71.4		34 15.8 +			
23	32 30.5 5.8	67.8		32 52.9 4.6	68.4		33 14.7 3.5	69.0		33 36.0 2.4	69.6		33 56.6 1.2	70.2		34 16.4			
24	32 24.7 6.5	66.6		32 48.3 5.4	67.2		33 11.2 4.1	67.8		33 33.6 3.0	68.4		33 55.4 1.8	69.0		34			
25	32 18.2 − 7.1	65.4		32 42.9 − 6.0	66.0		33 07.1 − 4.9	66.6		33 30.6 − 3.7	67.2		33 53.6 − 2.6	67.8					
26	32 11.1 7.7	64.2		32 36.9 6.6	64.8		33 02.2 5.5	65.4		33 26.9 4.4	66.0		33 51.0 3.3						
27	32 03.4 8.4	63.1		32 30.3 7.3	63.6		32 56.7 6.3	64.2		33 22.5 5.1	64.8		33 47.7						
28	31 55.0 9.1	61.9		32 23.0 8.0	62.5		32 50.4 6.8	63.0		33 17.4 5.8	63.6		33 43.9						
29	31 45.9 9.7	60.7		32 15.0 8.6	61.3		32 43.6 7.6	61.8		33 11.6 6.4	62.4		33						
30	31 36.2 −10.3	59.6		32 06.4 − 9.3	60.1		32 36.0 − 8.2	60.7		33 05.2 − 7.2	61.2								
31	31 25.9 10.9	58.4		31 57.1 9.9	59.0		32 27.8 8.8	59.5		32 58.0 7.8									
32	31 15.0 11.5	57.3		31 47.2 10.5	57.8		32 19.0 9.5	58.3		32 50.2 8									
33	31 03.5 12.2	56.1		31 36.7 11.2	56.6		32 09.5 10.2	57.2		32 41.8									
34	30 51.3 12.7	55.0		31 25.5 11.7	55.5		31 59.3 10.8	56.0		32 3									
35	30 38.6 −13.4	53.8		31 13.8 −12.4	54.3		31 48.5 −11.4	54.8											
36	30 25.2 13.9	52.7		31 01.4 13.0	53.2		31 37.1 12.0	53.7											
37	30 11.3 14.5	51.6		30 48.4 13.6	52.0		31 25.1 12.6												
38	29 56.8 15.0	50.5		30 34.8 14.1	50.9		31 12.5												
39	29 41.8 15.6	49.3		30 20.7 14.8	49.8		30 5?												
40	29 26.2 −16.2	48.2		30 05.9 −15.3	48.7														
41	29 10.0 16.7	47.1		29 50.6 15.8	47														
42	28 53.3 17.3	46.0		29 34.8 16.4															
43	28 36.0 17.7	44.9		29 18.4															
44	28 18.3 18.3	43.9		29 01															
45	28 00.0 −18.8	42.8																	
46	27 41.2 19.2	41																	
47	27 22.0 19.8																		
48	27 02.2																		
49	26 42																		
50	2:																		
51																			

Note that this is the <u>only</u> page of
the Sight Reduction Tables which
coincides with our three entering
arguments:

    LHA 302°
    La   10°N
    Dec. N17°

and the latitude and declination
have the <u>same</u> names; i.e., both North.

SOURCE: the Sight Reduction Tables for Marine Navigation; H.O. Pub. 229, Vol. 1

≈ 3.6 *= 0.7*

INTERPOLATION TABLE

Dec Inc	10'	20'	30'	40'	50'	Dec.	0'	1'	2'	3'	4'	5'	6'	7'	8'	9'	Double Second Diff. and Corr.
0.0	0.0	0.0	0.0	0.0	0.0	.0	0.0	0.0	0.0	0.0	0.0	0.0	0.0	0.0	0.1	0.1	
0.1	0.0	0.0	0.0	0.0	0.1	.1	0.0	0.0	0.0	0.0	0.0	0.0	0.1	0.1	0.1	0.1	0.0 / 48.2 0.0
0.2	0.0	0.0	0.1	0.1	0.1	.2	0.0	0.0	0.0	0.0	0.0	0.0	0.1	0.1	0.1	0.1	
0.3	0.0	0.1	0.1	0.2	0.2	.3	0.0	0.0	0.0	0.0	0.0	0.0	0.1	0.1	0.1	0.1	
0.4	0.1	0.1	0.2	0.3	0.3	.4	0.0	0.0	0.0	0.0	0.0	0.0	0.1	0.1	0.1	0.1	
0.5	0.1	0.2	0.3	0.3	0.4	.5	0.0	0.0	0.0	0.0	0.0	0.1	0.1	0.1	0.1		
0.6	0.1	0.2	0.3	0.4	0.5	.6	0.0	0.0	0.0	0.0	0.0	0.1	0.1	0.1	0.1		16.2 / 48.6 0.1
0.7	0.1	0.3	0.4	0.5	0.6	.7	0.0	0.0	0.0	0.0	0.0	0.1	0.1	0.1	0.1		
0.8	0.2	0.3	0.4	0.6	0.7	.8	0.0	0.0	0.0	0.0	0.0	0.1	0.1	0.1	0.1		
0.9	0.2	0.3	0.5	0.6	0.8	.9	0.0	0.0	0.0	0.0	0.0	0.1	0.1	0.1	0.1		
1.0	0.1	0.3	0.5	0.6	0.8	.0	0.0	0.0	0.0	0.1	0.1	0.1	0.1	0.2	0.2	0.2	
1.1	0.2	0.3	0.5	0.7	0.9	.1	0.0	0.0	0.0	0.1	0.1	0.1	0.1	0.2	0.2	0.2	
1.2	0.2	0.4	0.6	0.8	1.0	.2	0.0	0.0	0.1	0.1	0.1	0.1	0.2	0.2	0.2	0.2	
1.3	0.2	0.4	0.6	0.9	1.1	.3	0.0	0.0	0.1	0.1	0.1	0.1	0.2	0.2	0.2	0.2	8.2 / 24.6 0.1
1.4	0.2	0.5	0.7	0.9	1.2	.4	0.0	0.0	0.1	0.1	0.1	0.1	0.2	0.2	0.2	0.2	41.0 0.2
1.5	0.3	0.5	0.8	1.0	1.3	.5	0.0	0.0	0.1	0.1	0.1	0.1	0.2	0.2	0.2	0.2	
1.6	0.3	0.5	0.8	1.1	1.3	.6	0.0	0.0	0.1	0.1	0.1	0.1	0.2	0.2	0.2	0.2	
1.7	0.3	0.6	0.9	1.2	1.4	.7	0.0	0.0	0.1	0.1	0.1	0.1	0.2	0.2	0.2	0.2	
1.8	0.3	0.6	0.9	1.2	1.5	.8	0.0	0.0	0.1	0.1	0.1	0.1	0.2	0.2	0.2	0.2	
1.9	0.4	0.7	1.0	1.3	1.6	.9	0.0	0.0	0.1	0.1	0.1	0.1	0.2	0.2	0.2	0.2	
2.0	0.3	0.6	1.0	1.3	1.6	.0	0.0	0.0	0.1	0.1	0.2	0.2	0.2	0.3	0.3	0.4	
2.1	0.3	0.7	1.0	1.4	1.7	.1	0.0	0.0	0.1	0.1	0.2	0.2	0.2	0.3	0.3	0.4	
2.2	0.3	0.7	1.1	1.4	1.8	.2	0.0	0.0	0.1	0.1	0.2	0.2	0.2	0.3	0.3	0.4	
2.3	0.4	0.8	1.1	1.5	1.9	.3	0.0	0.1	0.1	0.1	0.2	0.2	0.3	0.3	0.4	0.4	5.0 / 15.0 0.1
2.4	0.4	0.8	1.2	1.6	2.0	.4	0.0	0.1	0.1	0.1	0.2	0.2	0.3	0.3	0.4	0.4	25.0 0.2
2.5	0.4	0.8	1.3	1.7	2.1	.5	0.0	0.1	0.1	0.2	0.2	0.3	0.3	0.4	0.4		35.1 0.3
2.6	0.4	0.9	1.3	1.7	2.2	.6	0.0	0.1	0.1	0.2	0.2	0.3	0.3	0.4	0.4		
2.7	0.5	0.9	1.4	1.8	2.3	.7	0.0	0.1	0.1	0.2	0.2	0.3	0.3	0.4	0.4		
2.8	0.5	1.0	1.4	1.9	2.4	.8	0.0	0.1	0.1	0.2	0.2	0.3	0.3	0.4	0.4		
2.9	0.5	1.0	1.5	2.0	2.5	.9	0.0	0.1	0.1	0.2	0.2	0.3	0.3	0.4	0.4		
3.0	0.5	1.0	1.5	2.0	2.5	.0	0.0	0.1	0.2	0.2	0.3	0.3	0.4	0.5	0.5		
3.1	0.5	1.0	1.5	2.0	2.6	.1	0.0	0.1	0.2	0.2	0.3	0.3	0.4	0.5	0.5		
3.2	0.5	1.0	1.6	2.1	2.6	.2	0.0	0.1	0.2	0.2	0.3	0.4	0.4	0.5	0.5		3.6 / 10.9 0
3.3	0.5	1.1	1.6	2.2	2.7	.3	0.0	0.1	0.2	0.2	0.3	0.4	0.4	0.5	0.5		
3.4	0.6	1.1	1.7	2.3	2.8	.4	0.0	0.1	0.2	0.2	0.3	0.4	0.4	0.5	0.5		
3.5	0.6	1.2	1.8	2.3	2.9	.5	0.0	0.1	0.2	0.2	0.3	0.3	0.4	0.5			
3.6	0.6	1.2	1.8	2.4	3.0	.6	0.0	0.1	0.2	0.2	0.3	0.3	0.4	0.4			
3.7	0.6	1.3	1.9	2.5	3.1	.7	0.0	0.1	0.2	0.2	0.3	0.3	0.4				
3.8	0.7	1.3	1.9	2.6	3.2	.8	0.0	0.1	0.2	0.2	0.3	0.3					
3.9	0.7	1.3	2.0	2.6	3.3	.9	0.1	0.1	0.2	0.2	0.3	0.3					
4.0	0.6	1.3	2.0	2.6	3.3	.0	0.0	0.1	0.1								
4.1	0.7	1.3	2.0	2.7	3.4	.1	0.0	0.0	0.1								
4.2	0.7	1.4	2.1	2.8	3.5	.2	0.0	0.0	0								
4.3	0.7	1.4	2.1	2.9	3.6	.3	0										
4.4	0.7	1.5	2.2	2.9	3.7	.4											
4.5	0.8	1.5	2.3	3.0	3												
4.6	0.8	1.5	2.3	3.1													
4.7	0.8	1.6	2.4														
4.8	0.8	1.6	2														
4.9	0.9	1.7															
5.0	0																
5.																	

Dec. Inc.	10'	20'	30'	40'
8.0	1.3	2.6	4.0	5.3
8.1	1.3	2.7	4.0	5.4
8.2	1.3	2.7	4.1	5.4
8.3	1.4	2.8	4.1	5.5
8.4	1.4	2.8	4.2	5.6
8.5	1.4	2.8	4.3	5.7
8.6	1.4	2.9	4.3	5.7
8.7	1.5	2.9	4.4	5.8
8.8	1.5	3.0	4.4	5.9
8.9	1.5	3.0	4.5	6.0
9.0	1.5	3.0	4.5	6.0
9.1	1.5	3.0	4.5	6.0
9.2	1.5	3.0	4.6	6.1
9.3	1.5	3.1	4.6	6.2
9.4	1.6	3.1	4.7	6.3
9.5	1.6	3.2	4.8	6.3
9.6	1.6	3.2	4.8	6.4
9.7	1.6	3.3	4.9	6.5
9.8	1.7	3.3	4.9	6.6
9.9	1.7	3.3	5.0	6.6
10.0	1.7	3.3	5.0	6.6
10.1	1.7	3.3	5.0	6.7
10.2	1.7	3.4	5.1	6.8
10.3	1.7	3.4	5.1	6.9
10.4	1.7	3.5	5.2	6.9
10.5	1.8	3.5	5.3	
10.6	1.8	3.5	5.3	
10.7	1.8	3.6		
10.8	1.8	3.6		
10.9	1.9			
11.0				
11.				

Note that with our d=+0.7 and Dec. Inc. of 3.6' that our adjustment to H_C is 0.0

Just as an educational example, if our d=+43.2 with the same Dec. Inc. of 3.6', our adjustment to H_C would be:

tens: 40' = +1.8
units: 3' &
decimals : .2 = +0.2
+2.0 and so we would add 2.0' to our H_C.

SOURCE: Inside front cover of the Sight Reduction Tables; H.O. Pub. 229

MONDAY / 8 MAY / 0830 SL / LOG 3145

H_S 33° 27.4   CT   11 : 36 : 10

      − 2.8   SW   − 14

H_a 33° 24.6   11 : 35 : 56

      + 14.6   CE   + 2 : 36

H_o 33° 39.2   GMT   11 : 38 : 32

                   GHA (11ₕ)   345° 53.3

                   (38ₘ 32ₛ)   9° 38.0

                            355° 31.3

H_c d   Z λ_a 53° 31.3

33° 21.3   +0.7   76.2   LHA   302°

        0.0 L_a 10° N

   39.2   DEC   N 17° 03.2   +0.4

   21.3   = N 17° 03.6

   17.9 T @ 76.2

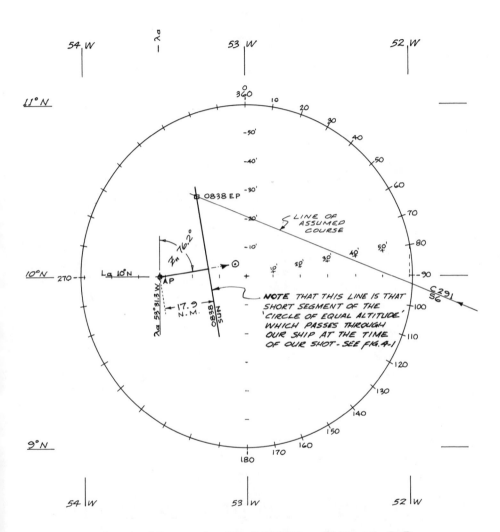

FIG. 4-10 ~ A PLOTTED SUN LOP

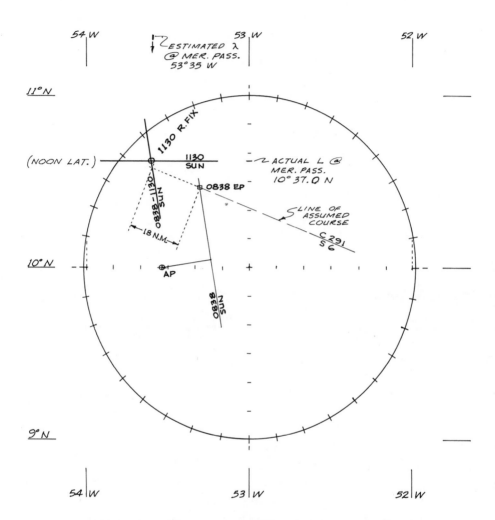

FIG. 4-12 ~ A PLOTTED RUNNING FIX

We're on our yacht at sea, heading for the West Indies from St. Helena Island. It's been a long trip. We've crossed the equator, slopped our way across the doldrums, and finally picked up the trades. It is a beautiful morning and, as is our normal habit, we want to get a *morning sun LOP* on our sailing chart. Later on, at high noon, we'll shoot a *noon latitude shot* and advance this LOP to obtain a running fix. This is our normal procedure to monitor our *distance run,* noon to noon.

We get out the sextant and the stopwatch, go topside and make the shot, starting the stopwatch at the instant the lower rim of the sun is perched on the watery horizon—like an orange on a table. We go below and simultaneously read the chronometer and stop the stopwatch at a handy, round number of seconds of the chronometer (for instance, at a 10- or 15-second interval). Then we step to the chart table and write down our data while still holding the sextant.

Date   8 May 1978
Local Time   0838
Taffrail Log   3145
$H_s = 33°27.4'$
CT   11:36:10
SW   14 (sec.)

Now we put the sextant in its permanent stowage place and we're ready to work out our sight.

Before we put our answer on a chart as a sun LOP, I want to rewrite the previous problem as it appears in my sight book. Without the explanations and notes it's really a short exercise and is a realistic example of what we do with a sun shot when we're at sea.

And that's all there is to it! With some practice it's a five-minute operation.

So now take a look at Figure 4-10. I've drafted a plotting sheet that represents the sailing chart on which, at sea, we would actu-

Somewhat overnavigated, three sextants at work on Starbound, (left to right) Ernie, Ray Kukulski, and Gordon go for a sun sight.

Eyeball navigation from the spreaders as Starbound works her way through some reefs.

ally work. I've done this primarily because I can make the plot large enough for the reader to see where everything fits.

First we plot our *assumed position* (AP) from λ_a and L_a. Second, using our azimuth of 76.2 degrees, we draw a line from the AP toward the sun, shown on the chart as ☉. Third, we pick off 17.9 nautical miles, that is, 17.9 minutes, from the latitude scale at either edge of the chart and lay it off on the line from the AP toward the sun. Fourth, we draw a perpendicular to the first line at that point. That perpendicular is our line of position, our short segment of the circle of equal altitude as shown in Figure 4-1. *Our ship is on that line.* We label the LOP *0838 SUN.* Where it intersects with the line of our assumed course is our *estimated position* (EP). Our actual position might be a little north or south of this EP, depending on how much leeway we made during the night—or perhaps because of a current set.

Our next navigational job as our day at sea progresses is to obtain a noon sight of the sun, also called a *noon latitude* or *noon lat.* If we shoot the sun at *local apparent noon* (LAN), which means at its *meridian passage* (as high as it will get on this particular day), our LOP will be a horizontal east and west line, that is, our latitude.

A noon latitude is an easy calculation because we don't need the sight reduction tables to work it. However, we do need to find the declination of the sun at local apparent noon, the quickest way being with the *Nautical Almanac.*

Some sailors shoot a noon altitude by going on deck with the sextant several minutes before they estimate the meridian passage will take place. They "drop" the sun to the horizon with the sextant and then watch it continue to "rise" above the horizon and adjust it back "down." When the sun appears to pause in the scope and sit on the horizon without rising further, meridian passage has been obtained and no further adjustment of the sextant is required. The altitude reading is taken at that point and the GMT is obtained from the ship's chronometer. In this case, since GMT is only needed for declination (from the almanac), the time is not too critical: Within one minute of the actual time of LAN is satisfactory for the purpose of a noon latitude, since the sun's declination changes relatively slowly.

An easier method, and the one I prefer, involves an understanding of time zones and the ship's estimated longitude. A look at Figure 4-5 will show a boxed area in the lower right-hand corner of the almanac page displayed. I have circled SUN and MER. PASS. and 11h56m, for 8 May. This means that the sun's meridian passage occurs at 1156 hours on the central meridian of each of the 24 time zones around the world (0°, 15°, 30°, 45°, 60°, etc., and back to the *prime meridian* at Greenwich. So if our ship were *on* one of the 24 central meridians on 8 May, our LAN would occur at 1156 hours *our local time*. And, of course, it occurs also on the prime meridian at 1156 GMT, which is their local time.

But our ship will not be located right *on* a time-zone central meridian. We, for the purposes of these problems, are between the time-zone meridians of 45°W and 60°W and our LAN must be calculated from what our estimated longitude will be at the time of our shot. Here's how we go about it:

From our EP at 0838, we extend our course by the assumed distance we will make in the next three hours. Since our speed is about 6 knots, we'll make approximately 18 nautical miles. From Figure 4-9, it can be seen that our estimated longitude *at meridian passage* will be about 53°35'W. Now, since our ship is in the time zone whose meridian is 60°W (the +4 zone), our wristwatch will show that zone's local time—or it should. (It is a good idea to keep local time on at least one of the ship's timepieces, changing it as the ship progresses from zone to zone.)

Since LAN at 60°W is 1156 hours—but we will be at 53°35'W— we know that the ship's LAN will arrive earlier on our timepiece than 1156 by the time it takes the sun to move 6.25' (60°00' minus 53°35'). And since the sun "moves" across the ocean 1 degree of longitude in 4 minutes of time, we need to subtract 25 minutes, 40 seconds from 1156. But we don't need to be accurate to the second, so we'll say the ship's LAN will arrive 26 minutes earlier than the time zone meridian's LAN, rounding off on the safe side (being on deck with the sextant sooner rather than later). We subtract 26 minutes from 1156 and get 1130, our LAN.

Now we're ready to shoot our noon lat. We go on deck with our sextant at 1129, having made sure of our local timepiece's accuracy by checking it against the chronometer. We shoot the sun at 1130 sharp and assure ourselves that it has indeed "paused," which it will appear to do for several seconds as it attains its *zenith* (its highest point overhead). Since we will, properly, be a few seconds early when we start the shot, some small adjustment of the sextant will be necessary until the sun has settled. Then we take the sextant reading, write it down, and put the sextant away. We also take a reading from the *taffrail log*.

Our noon-latitude calculation looks like this:

MONDAY 8 MAY   NOON LAT/LAN 1130/GMT 1530/LOG 3163

H_s 83° 17.8   N. LAT = N. DEC − (90° − H_o)

IE   0

HE   − 2.8   90° = 89° 60.0

H_a 83° 15.0 H_o = 83° 30.8

AC   + 15.8   ─────────────

                            6° 29.2

H_o 83° 30.8

                     DEC = N 17° 05.9   + 0.3 (d = 0.7)

                         = N 17° 06.2

                       (−) 6° 29.2

                     LAT. = 10° 37.0

And so we have our noon latitude. It's just another LOP but one that runs due east and west. We put it on our chart (see Figure 4-9) and "advance" our morning LOP to cross it and so obtain a noon *running fix* (R. Fix).

Advancing an LOP is simple. Just carry forward a second line parallel to the 0838 LOP and in the direction of our course (in this case, 291° true) for the distance we have traveled since 0838, a distance we know from our log readings taken at the time of our shots.

Log at 1130 = 3163
Log at 0838 = 3145

18 nautical miles

(shown on Figure 4-9)

The work just completed, advancing a morning sun LOP to a noon latitude and thus obtaining a noon R.Fix is the primary method of navigation most cruising sailors use to cross oceans. The mathematics are simple and a knowledge of navigational theory may be minimal. The sun is in the sky every day, and even when a great deal of cloud cover is present, a few shots can generally be made. A small thin spot in the clouds is enough if a sharp-edged disk can be seen. At sea one generally has enough time to sit top-side with the sextant lanyard around one's neck and wait for a temporary brightening of the sky. I can think of only two or three days at sea during our circumnavigation when the sun didn't show itself at all.

If a noon-latitude shot is missed because of cloud cover during LAN, it is not a problem; one simply takes a sun shot later on and works out an LOP as is done for the morning sun shot. Then the morning LOP is advanced to cross the latest LOP, using the same method as that illustrated in Figure 4-9.

Star shots are easy! Most sailors I know find them as simple as sun shots. Of course, timing is important because both star and horizon must be visible, and then one must know which star he is shooting.

Once the star shot is made, the calculation is performed in just the same manner as that for the sun, except: the *altitude correction* comes from a different column (see Figure 4-3) and the GHA of Aries (our reference point in the sky) is first calculated and then added to the *sidereal hour angle* (SHA) of our star to obtain the GHA of the star.

Declinations of stars are tabulated in the almanac directly beside their SHAs. The declinations of stars change slowly, so the almanac values are used directly, without adjustments.

ELECTRONIC NAVIGATIONAL AIDS

I am not an advocate of navigational electronics for deep-water cruising boats; perhaps because 90 percent of these systems, which I have seen on cruising boats in foreign ports, were not in working order. Those systems that I have seen operating satisfactorily were primarily on boats owned by people who are very well versed in electronics. In other words they had the tools, spares, and know-how to fix them. Let's take a look at these systems.

Radar for small craft is readily available on the market. For a good system a sailor can expect to pay $2000—and the price tag can go much higher. If you expect to cruise in areas with a high incidence of fog, radar might be cost effective. Remember that *range* is line of sight and is thus limited by antenna height.

Loran-C can locate your vessel's position within 1000 feet—or better with repeated fixes. Basically what the Loran receiver does is receive signals from two or three Loran shore stations and determine location by measuring the *time distance of arrival* (TDA) of the signals. The best sets are automatic and the price ranges from $2500 on up. Manual receivers are less expensive but less accurate. It is important to remember that Loran coverage is not worldwide.

OMEGA is the latest and best toy of the moneyed sailor. Its price tag starts at $5000, but hopefully it will descend within reach of more of us as more manufacturers get into the act. It is a *very low frequency* (VLF), hyperbolic navigation system with a high accuracy of fix at a range as great as 5000 miles. Someday I would like to put an OMEGA system on *Starbound,* but it is so far down on my list of priorities it has become an unnoticed item. I consider it a luxury—not a necessity.

The *programmable calculator* for navigation is small, relatively inexpensive, and a lot of fun to use if you're inclined that way. It also is not a necessary tool for navigation, but it is faster than a pencil—how much faster depends on the operator. It can be programmed to do other jobs also: Speed curves, magnetic deviation, set and drift, fixes from bearings on known objects, and great circle calculations are all within its capabilities. It will *not* turn a novice into an accomplished navigator and pilot. What it will do is save some time (if you want it saved) and cut down on drudgery (if you consider piloting and navigation drudgery).

At the time of this writing, there are three programmable calculators worth considering: Texas Instruments' TI-59 at about $300, Hewlett-Packard's HP-67 at about $450, and National Semiconductor's NS-7100 for which I have no price but will probably sell for more than the other two.

None of these gadgets will make a good pilot/navigator out of a landlubber. Anyone who wishes to cruise his boat deep-water must pay his dues by learning piloting and seamanship in the broadest sense of those words and how to use a sextant and the navigational tables to find his position at sea. Sole dependence on electronics is foolishness in the extreme.

To preclude being attacked by electronics buffs bearing volt-ohm meters, I will go on record stating that there are various pieces of electronic gear that I consider highly desirable to have on board the deep-water cruising yacht. These are the *shortwave radio receiver,* the *radio direction finder* (RDF), the *radiotelephone* (preferably both VHF/FM and SSB) and the *depth sounder.* I've listed them in what I feel is their order of importance.

The *short wave multiband radio receiver* is needed for time, weather reports, entertainment, and news.

The *RDF* is a very practical and inexpensive means of determining the ship's bearing from any received radio signal within frequency range. If two such signals can be received, the ship's position can be determined, that is, if the source of those signals is shown on a chart. Since most landfalls that a deep-water cruiser will make put the ship within range of such signal sources (radio beacons and/or radio broadcasting stations), the RDF is a handy tool with which to make an accurate approach and avoid navigational hazards. Its value off a foggy coast is obvious.

Radiotelephones are not mandatory for a cruising yacht, but personally, I will not put to sea without one, or maybe two—a VHF/FM *(Very High Frequency/Frequency Modulated)* for short-range and *single-sideband* (SSB) for long-range communications. The prime functions of the radio telephone, as deep-water cruising boats use it, are: securing weather data, reporting the ship's position and arrival time to port officials in countries where this is standard operating procedure, asking for assistance in case of an emergency, and friendly communications with other yachts. (Details on communications gear are in the following chapter.)

A *depth sounder* is nice to have, primarily as a piloting aid, for matching the depth shown against chart soundings when approaching a coastline. It is also sometimes handy when anchoring, as an indication of scope needed on the anchor rode. It can be a help when trying to stay in the deepest part of a tight channel. A depth sounder is not worth a damn when conning a ship through a bunch of coral heads. Nearly always on a yacht the transducer is located on the hull somewhere aft. By the time the helmsman has an indication of danger, the ship's bow has already struck. A "Mark I Eyeball" up the mast and a good hand with a sounding line on the foredeck beat the hell out of a depth sounder in most deep-water cruising situations.

5

"Very Unusual Weather for This Time of Year"

A meterologist friend, speaking of the assets of his career, came up with a funny line—unintentionally, I'm sure. He said, seriously, "Weather is what makes the world go 'round."

Now that's amusing because the world going 'round is what makes the weather. And carrying it one step further—using weather is how the sailor goes 'round the world.

What does a sailor planning a deep-water cruise really want to know about weather? First of all he wants to know how to avoid the worst of it: the big destructive storms called tropical cyclones. Second he wants to know when and where his ship might get socked by the secondary stuff: the extratropical cyclones with their active fronts, the line squalls, the fog. Third he wants to know how to make the best use of the seasonal winds to get him from point A to point B, safety always preempting utility.

Basically our weather is caused by the effect of the sun on the earth and on its lower atmosphere. Since the earth rotates once on its axis every 24 hours, the section of the earth heated by the sun continually changes. In addition the surface of the earth is not uni-

A squall hits Starbound *off the coast of Florida.*

form. Although 71 percent is covered by oceans, land masses of varying heights are irregularly distributed over the remaining 29 percent.

The continually changing differences in atmospheric temperature (the heating and cooling) cause differences in *atmospheric pressure,* and these continual pressure changes produce a large-scale motion of air that we call wind and that always tends to blow *from* a high-pressure area *to* a low-pressure area. A very simplified circulation pattern of the earth's wind systems is shown in Figure 5-1. Notice how the winds are deflected: to the right in the northern hemisphere and to the left in the southern. The force producing this *wind deflection* is known as the *Coriolis force* and is caused by the earth's rotation.

Keep in mind that the illustration of the *wind patterns* shown in Figure 5-1 is oversimplified and that in actuality the direction of wind is skewed by the earth's land masses. Further, the rotational axis of the earth is tilted in relation to the earth's orbit about the sun so that *seasonal changes* add their complications to the wind patterns. Take a look at Figures 5-2 and 5-3 to see the generalized pattern of *actual* surface winds during the northern hemisphere winter and summer (opposite seasons occur in the southern hemisphere). At first glance these wind patterns seem a real mess. However, some study shows that to a large degree they do tend toward the simplified pattern of Figure 5-1.

When I first saw these patterns, I thought, "My God, how will I ever figure out a proper course!" Then I discovered that most of the work has already been done for us. Remember the *Pilot Charts* discussed in Chapter 3? Many years of research in navigation, oceanography, and meteorology have been combined to produce these charts. They are absolutely paramount in assisting the mariner to select the safest, most timely sailing routes. During our circumnavigation we plotted our course not only on the ocean sailing chart but also on the pilot charts for the appropriate month. We found them to be very accurate and our faith in them was commensurately strengthened.

Most dangerous for the cruising sailor is the *tropical cyclone,* the

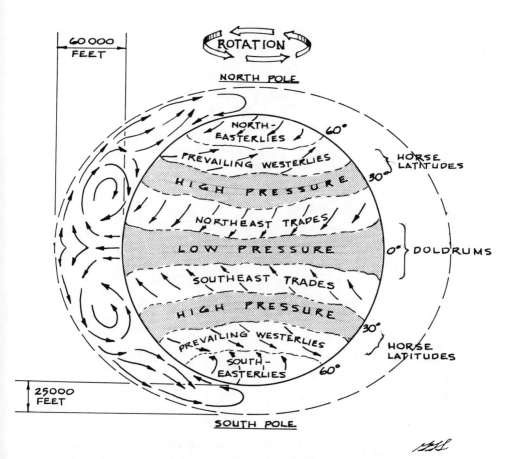

FIG. 5-1 — GENERAL CIRCULATION
OF THE ATMOSPHERE

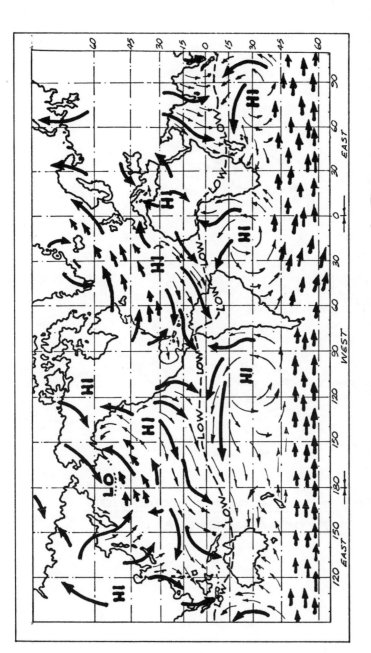

FIG. 5-2 ~ GENERALIZED PATTERN OF ACTUAL AIR MASSES & SURFACE WINDS IN JANUARY & FEBRUARY (DIAGRAM DEVELOPED FROM BOWDITCH)

AIR MASS MOVEMENT

WIND 20+ KNOTS

WIND <20 KNOTS

LENGTH OF ARROW INDICATES DEGREE OF CONSTANCY OF DIRECTION.

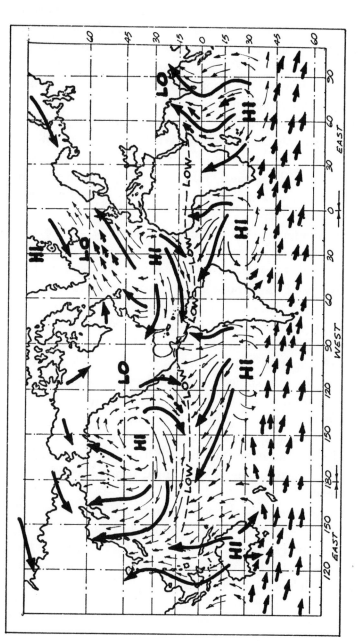

FIG. 5-3 – GENERALIZED PATTERN OF ACTUAL AIR MASSES & SURFACE WINDS IN JULY & AUGUST
(DIAGRAM DEVELOPED FROM BOWDITCH)

AIR MASS MOVEMENT

WIND 20+ KNOTS

WIND <20 KNOTS

LENGTH OF ARROW INDICATES DEGREE OF CONSTANCY OF DIRECTION.

violent cyclone that originates in the tropics. The word *cyclone* indicates the circular formation of the atmosphere in the vicinity of a low-pressure area. When the word *tropical* precedes it, it means that a large amount of energy is gathered into a relatively small area and that the weather in its vicinity will be extremely unhealthy for ships at sea.

Americans generally call the tropical cyclone a *hurricane*. In the Far East it is called a *typhoon*. In northwestern Australia they name it *willy-willy*. And in the Philippines, a *baguio*. In some other places it is simply called *cyclone*. Whatever they are called, the important thing is to avoid them. Any cruising sailor who puts his ship into the area of a tropical cyclone has made a basic error in planning—one that may result in the loss of his ship and perhaps his life.

Tropical cyclones form in low latitudes, just north or south of the equator, drift westward, then curve poleward and, sometimes, eventually eastward. They tend to be primarily oceanic storms, but when they strike land, they cause much damage but tend to dissipate there at a much faster rate than they do at sea.

Figure 5-4 shows the areas and frequency of occurrence of tropical cyclones and their approximate tracks. It becomes rather obvious, and very important, to plan the voyage to ensure that the vessel is not in an area subject to tropical cyclones during the months of their occurrence. Of course, all deep-water cruising yachts will eventually pass through one or more of these areas—but the smart cruising sailor does so only during the months of most reduced risk. And even then he will have his ear cocked to the air waves for early warnings of forming tropical depressions that may intensify.

A *tropical depression* can deepen and intensify into a *tropical storm* that can further intensify and become a *hurricane*. Meteorologically these related storms resemble one another. But while the true hurricane is relatively rare, the tropical depression and tropical storm are much less so, and they carry winds of enough velocity to really shake up a sailor. This related group has been classified according to intensity as follows: *tropical depression:* winds up to

FIGURE 5-4

TROPICAL CYCLONES: AREAS, TRACKS, SEASONS AND FREQUENCIES

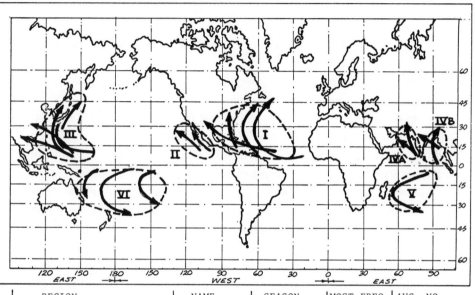

	REGION	NAME	SEASON	MOST FREQ.	AVG. NO.
I	Caribbean, Gulf of Mexico, East Coast U.S.	Hurricane	Jun-mid Nov	Aug-Oct	7
II	Southeast North Pacific	Hurricane	Jun-Nov	Aug-Oct	2
III	Far East	Typhoon/ Baguio	All Months	Jul-Oct	19
IVA	Arabian Sea	Cyclone	Apr-Jan	Jun, Oct, & Nov	2
IVB	Bay of Bengal	Cyclone	May-Dec	Sep	2
V	S. Indian Ocean	Cyclone	Oct-Jun	Dec-Apr	6
VI	Aust./W. South Pacific	WillyWilly/ Hurricane	Dec-Apr	Jan-Mar	2

34 knots (39 mph), *tropical storm:* winds 35 to 63 knots (40–72 mph), *hurricane* or *typhoon:* winds of 64 knots (73 mph) or higher.

All the cruising sailor can do, when in the low-latitude breeding grounds of these whirly-girls, is Watch Out!

(Chapter 13 includes some general rules for locating the storm center, avoiding it, and also leaving the storm area.)

SOME FACTS ABOUT FRONTS

A *front* or *weather front*, specifically, is the boundary of or the separation between, *air masses.*

Cold northern air masses are called *polar air masses.* Warm air masses originate in low latitudes and are called *tropical air masses.* There are two more subdivisions for air types: Air masses that form over land are relatively dry and are called *continental air masses;* those that form over water are relatively humid and are known as *maritime air masses.* So, the air masses we generally hear meteorologists talk about are classified as follows: *polar continental, polar maritime, tropical continental,* and *tropical maritime.* There are two other classifications that we hear about less frequently: *arctic* and *equatorial* air masses that form in the far north and in the equatorial regions respectively.

The factor that allows for the development of these six types of air masses is the general air circulation of the world. This factor also starts these masses in motion. In general they move away from their source regions: In the northern hemisphere polar air underlaps southward and tropical air overlaps northward. Note that areas within the more or less permanent boundaries of the source regions experience more or less uniform weather conditions. But areas outside the source regions, in the middle latitudes, will undergo continual changes resulting both from the passage of the different masses and from the effects of their meeting. What this all means is that the areas of the world that we sailors most generally frequent are beset with continual weather changes that are heralded by *weather fronts*. Remember, they are the boundary of, or separation between, air masses.

Although fronts differ as to type, they have many common weather properties: The *temperature* across a front can vary through a wide range, either abruptly or slowly, depending on the temperature contrasts of the air masses involved. A pronounced difference in *atmospheric pressure* occurs between adjacent points on either side of a front. An abrupt *wind shift* always takes place at a front. And finally, fronts always exhibit characteristic *cloudiness* and *precipitation*.

There are four types of fronts, each having its own particular properties aside from those mentioned above that are common to all. These four types are: *warm fronts, cold fronts, occluded fronts,* and *stationary fronts* (Figure 5-5).

A *warm front* is fascinating. A very extensive cloud sheet of fibrous *cirrus* first appears from 500 to 1000 miles ahead of the warm front. The mariner will see a large ring, or *halo,* around the sun or moon. Light rain will begin 12 to 18 hours later, winter and summer respectively. Cold air sinks and warm air rises, so warm air slides up the face of the cool air mass and condenses. Voilà—drizzle! And sometimes, fog.

Wind change caused by a warm front is generally not a matter for serious concern. In the northern hemisphere (southern hemisphere: opposite) the wind ahead of a warm front may be southeasterly while the cloud sheet of cirrus is overhead, and before any rain. Behind the frontal zone, the wind may be from a direction of more than 45 degrees clockwise, becoming south or even southwesterly. But the veering is generally slow and the deep-water sailor should not be too concerned (except for the rain running down his neck under his foul weather gear); sudden gusts are rare in a warm-front area.

An approaching *cold front* should be of concern to the mariner because it is the most active type of front. A cold front is the leading edge of a cold, dense air mass that is underrunning and lifting the relatively warm air ahead of it. As the warm air lifts (much

FIG. 5-5 ~ <u>FRONTAL TYPES ~ DIAGRAMMED</u>

COLD FRONT

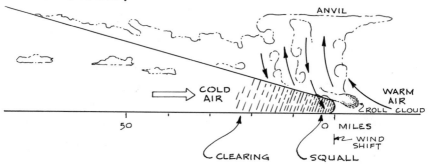

ANVIL

COLD
AIR

WARM
AIR

ROLL CLOUD

50

0 MILES

WIND
SHIFT

CLEARING

SQUALL

WARM FRONT

INCREASED
CLOUD LAYER

CLOUD SHEET

WARM
AIR

COLD
AIR

FOG

DRIZZLE

600

300

0 MILES

TRANSITION
ZONE

OCCLUDED FRONT

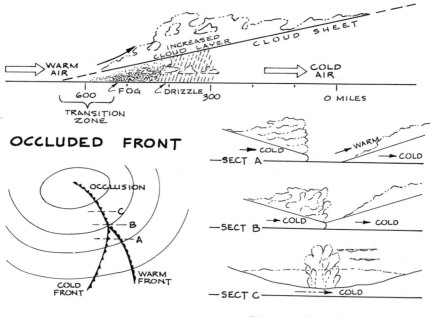

OCCLUSION

C

B

A

WARM
FRONT

COLD
FRONT

SECT A

COLD

WARM

COLD

SECT B

COLD

COLD

SECT C

COLD

<u>DEVELOPMENT CYCLE</u>

more rapidly than with a warm front), cumulous clouds and often severe thunderstorms develop along the cold front. The approaching cloud bank is relatively precipitous and is generally visible well in advance of its arrival. The arrival of the active front will be marked by a squall wind just under the advancing edge of clouds. Sometimes this advancing edge shows a fairly low, dark, and turbulent roll of cloud that sharply marks the under-running wedge of cold air. This is called, naturally enough, the *roll cloud* or *roller*.

The *strength* and *shift* of the squall wind is the primary concern of the sailor. The gusts are of short duration but can approach hurricane force in very active fronts. And the wind-shift can be as much as 90 degrees (clockwise in the Northern Hemisphere, counterclockwise in the Southern). To complicate matters, as the cold front approaches, the prevailing wind, which is generally from the southerly quadrant (in the Northern Hemisphere), blowing parallel to the front's "face," will begin to blow into the front—feeding it, so to speak. Then, just minutes before the squall line strikes, the wind on the surface will fall flat as the feeding wind rises from the surface of the sea and leaves the sailor in a wedge of still air. This is the "last chance" calm. The prudent mariner will be reefed down with everything secured.

On our ship we generally drop all sail and go on auxiliary power or raise a storm sail only. Although the squall gusts can be very heavy, the duration of the maximum wind is too short to raise a big sea. But all the same, we like to turn *Starbound* off from the expected wind shift and let her run with her stern to it. Generally, we are back on course within one to two hours after the frontal squall has hit. And, as usual with the advent of the cold air mass, we will have a cool breeze from poleward and clearing skies as a reward for our diligence.

An *occluded* front occurs when a cold front overruns the warm front preceding it. This happens because cold fronts generally move faster than warm fronts. The result is that the warm air supply to the warm front is cut off and shoved aloft. The cold air of the cold front merges with the cold air preceding the original warm front and the resulting front is said to be occluded. With this front there is a trough of cloudy air aloft that usually produces precipitation and possibly some thunderstorms. But there is generally no wind shift involved and since a *difference* in air masses is no longer present, the occluded front tends to dissipate rapidly and gives the sailor weak, variable winds.

A *stationary front* is essentially a stationary warm front, since no other type of front can be stationary. In other words the air masses are not in motion and the weather conditions are similar to a warm front. Stationary fronts generally do not present a problem to the mariner unless the cold air mass develops a movement toward the warm, in which case the frontal system buckles, steepens, and develops cold-front characteristics.

LOWS AND HIGHS

The word *cyclone*, as used by meteorologists, only indicates the circular formation of the atmosphere in the vicinity of a low-pressure area. The word *anticyclone* is similarly used to define the same atmospheric circulation, only in the opposite direction, around a high pressure area. Most sailors just call them *lows* and *highs*. In the Northern Hemisphere the air circulation around a low is counterclockwise and is clockwise around a high. The circulation is opposite in the Southern Hemisphere: clockwise around a low and counterclockwise around a high. I am not going to expound on the development of highs and lows; the important thing to know is where they are and how they will affect our weather when we are at sea—mostly because the midlatitude low-pressure areas with steep *pressure gradients* (the rate of change in atmospheric pressure) can develop some fairly hefty winds, even gale force or better.

It is important to know that the *trade wind zones* are fairly free of the variable weather these systems can generate. Figure 5-6 shows a generalized picture of world cyclone paths, the most common paths of the world's low-pressure systems. Notice the absence of paths in the trade wind zones.

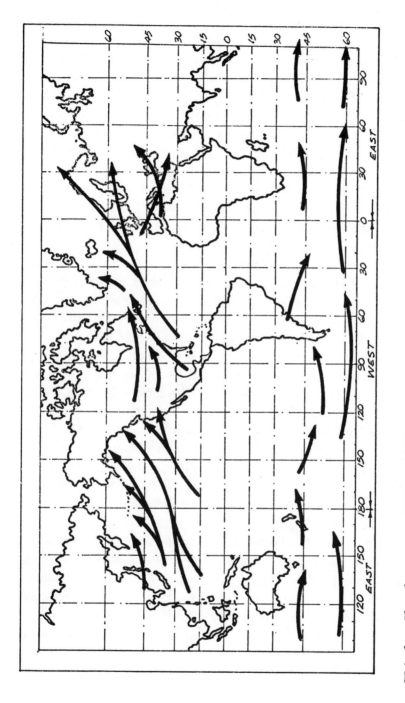

FIG. 5-6 ~ <u>GENERALIZED WORLD-CYCLONE PATHS</u>

Figure 5-7 presents a picture of a mature Northern Hemisphere low. It is composed of two well-defined air masses, one cold and one warm—with the cold predominating on the ocean's surface. Notice the angle the winds in each sector make with the *isobars* (the lines of equal atmospheric pressure).

A mature low has an average speed of 20 to 30 miles per hour or 480 to 720 miles per day. It should be easy to see how the wind will change for the sailor who has one of these troublemakers pass near him.

Please keep firmly in mind that a mature low in the Southern Hemisphere is a mirror image of that shown in Figure 5-7. It is also important to know that these systems move parallel to the isobars of their warm sectors.

Now I can almost hear the next question: How can I find out where these lows and their accompanying fronts are, and how soon might I expect a weather change that may cause me some trouble?

A good weather eye is the sailor's personal radar. An experienced sailor can almost smell a weather change. Cirrus coming in from the west practically shouts an impending front. Keeping a close watch on the barometer helps: The pressure will drop significantly as a big low approaches. But the most valuable aid is an accurate weather forecast based on satellite photos of oceanic areas and associated hydrographic and meteorologic data compiled from many sources. The way the cruising sailor obtains this aid is by *radio*. There is a worldwide network of radio stations offering forecasts. But the sailor must be able to understand them, interpret them, and then take any corrective action he deems necessary for his ship's safety.

The most useful radio receiver for obtaining weather data is a fine-tuning, full-band coverage, *shortwave transoceanic receiver* such as those produced by Zenith, Panasonic, Sony, and Heathkit. Ham-operation receivers are also very useful. The receiver should cover all bands from at least 4 to 20 mHz, but one covering an extended range from 2 to 30 mHz can be a help. The really good receivers will have a longwave band from 150 to 400 kHz, a medium wave band from 525 to 1650 kHz, a series of shortwave bands

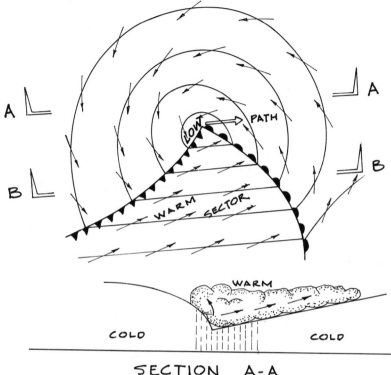

SECTION A-A

SECTION B-B

FIG. 5-7 ~ MATURE LOW OF THE
NORTHERN HEMISPHERE

ranging from 1.6 to 30 mHz, and a separate FM band from 76 to 108 mHz.

A good receiver is fairly expensive. One should plan on paying over $500 for the best of them and less than the best should not be considered for deep-water cruising.

Since weather warnings and communications are tied together (you have to have the equipment), a word about communications electronics is important here. *VHF/FM radiotelephones* are the most useful rig for short-range communications. They provide reliable service in the 20 to 50 mile range. Their cost is from $200 to $2000, but a really decent rig can be obtained for about $400. The three considerations that contribute to overall range performance are the *type of radio* (the higher sensitivity, the better "listening power"), the *antenna* (the higher the *gain*, the greater the "talk power" but, conversely, the greater susceptibility to ship motion), and the *antenna height* above water. Therefore many cruising boats like the 3 decibel (db) antenna with a mast top-mounting hooked up to a fairly sensitive radio. I say "fairly" because you get what you pay for—greater sensitivity calls for a greater price. It has been suggested by a friend who is expert in these matters that a sensitivity of "0.35 microvolts for 20 db quieting" should be the least a deep-water cruiser's radio should use.

VHF/FM is in wide use around the world. Contact with port authorities is required before entering the port in most parts of the world and that contact is usually made through VHF/FM.

For high seas long-range service the deep-water yachtsman might want a *single-sideband radiotelephone.* I say "might" because not every sailor feels that long-range communication is a requirement or even desirable. In addition SSB is expensive: $1500 is about the minimum a sailor will pay for a decent rig—and the price tag can get up to $5000. So what do you get for your money? The ability to communicate almost any time under *good* conditions up to 1000 miles during the day and 2000 miles or so during the night. And the 12 and 16 mHz long-distance bands on SSB, when they are operational, can allow communications up to 6000 miles!

But I guess the most important advantage SSB gives is the ability to contact the high seas radiotelephone network to get the weather forecasts put out by KMI, KQM, WOM, WOO, etc. Of course, the set must have the correct crystals for the frequencies.

Single-sideband ham radio is really coming into its own with cruising sailors. Nowadays I think about one out of every five boats cruising deep-water has a ham rig aboard. When propagation is good, a ham radio can provide the same ranges as mentioned earlier for other SSB rigs. But an amateur ham SSB transceiver costs a lot less than does the SSB, which uses *commercial* frequencies. The ham transceiver uses the 7mHz (40-meter) band for medium-range contacts—up to 1000 miles in daytime and more at night—the 14 mHz (20-meter band for long-range worldwide work, and the 21 mHz (15-meter) band, also for long-range daytime work. The 28 mHz (10-meter) band is not that useful, allowing only occasional daytime long-range communication. The 80-meter amateur band is prohibited for maritime mobile operation. Other ham bands are not of much use at sea.

A solid-state ham receiver is about one half the size of an electric typewriter and a good one can be obtained for about $800. It is legal to install a ham transceiver on your boat before getting a license, but it is illegal to transmit without one. The best way to obtain a license is to get *The Radio Amateur's License Manual* from a local store that deals with radio. Study hard and try to pass the *General* exam. A General license allows voice privileges. There are sample exams in the manual. If the General exam appears too heavy for you, then try to pass the *Novice* exam. This exam is easy; to qualify for novice, you must be able to send and receive code at five words per minute. However, the Novice license permits you to use only code and restricts frequencies and power. So the idea is to get a General license as soon as possible.

More specific information on ham radio for boats can be had by contacting the *Maritime Mobile Amateur Club*, W5CXM, 5672 Tiffany Drive, Houston, Texas 77045.

Table 2, pp. 32–36, are a compilation of weather forecast

sources for the oceans of the world. We are including them to give the reader an idea of the many sources available to the sailor who has a good receiver and the knowledge to use it.

A valuable publication to have aboard is *Worldwide Marine Weather Broadcasts,* which comes out annually from the National Weather Service. It can be ordered from the Superintendent of Documents, Government Printing Office, Washington, D.C. 20402.

WIND SYSTEMS

We've discussed the types of weather and weather systems that cause trouble of one kind or another for the cruising sailor. It seems fitting to close this chapter with a discussion of the wind systems that help us on our way. Prevailing wind systems, sometimes called *planetary wind systems,* are shown in an idealized fashion in Figure 5-1. The patterns of actual surface winds in summer and winter are generalized in Figures 5-2 and 5-3. A restudy of these figures makes it obvious that the wind systems that help the sailor the most are the *northeast* and *southeast trades*—that is, if your cruising course is generally to the west. But there are other planetary wind systems: the *prevailing westerlies* and the *monsoons.* Let's look at the trades first.

The trade winds blow from the belts of high pressure (located with the tropics) toward the equatorial belt of low pressure and are deflected to the west by the rotation of the earth. They are considered the most constant of all winds, but at times they weaken and the general pattern is disrupted. In the island groups of the South Pacific during January and February they tend to fall very light. The trades have an average speed of 10 to 15 knots. Area-wise they are the largest of the planetary wind groups, yet they are relatively free of cyclones (mature lows) whose paths mark the higher latitudes (see Figure 5-6).

As trade winds are caused by air moving from the high-pressure belt of the *horse latitudes* toward the equator, so are the *prevailing westerlies* caused by air moving from that same high-pressure belt poleward, toward the subpolar low. Again, the rotation of the earth "bends" the wind—but in this case to the east. In the Northern Hemisphere the prevailing westerlies are often variable, being affected by prominent circulation around the low- and high-pressure areas that continually invade their territory. However, in the Southern Hemisphere, owing to the uniform conditions of its broad ocean areas, the westerlies are steady and strong year round, with an average force of 17 to 27 knots. Owing to this wind strength, which increases with southerly latitude, the progressive "zones" have been called "the roaring forties, the furious fifties, and the screaming sixties."

Monsoons are winds whose direction reverses with the seasons due to a reversal of the primary *pressure gradient* that causes them to blow. The monsoon we usually read about is the most widespread: the Indian monsoon. During Northern Hemisphere winter the winds blow from the northeast, generated by the high-pressure system that establishes itself over Asia. But in the summer, when the high has dissipated and a low is established in its place, the winds completely reverse and blow from the southwest as shown in Figure 5-8. The winter monsoon is cold and dry, but when it switches direction and becomes the summer monsoon, it picks up moisture from the tropical ocean and becomes warm and humid. When it hits the high country of India, the air ascends, cools below its *dew point* (the temperature at which condensation begins) and propagates the rainy season of India's summer. And it rains for weeks on end.

Other monsoons exist but are not so widespread and pronounced as the Indian monsoon. The most obvious of these secondary monsoons is the one that exists west and southwest of the African "bulge" into the Atlantic. In the winter months this area is covered by the northeast trades. But during the summer, owing to the northerly migration of the doldrums belt, the southeast trades take over—but in a peculiar fashion: They hook in from the south and southwest.

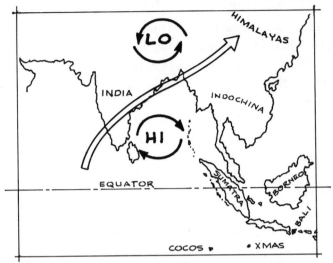

SUMMER MONSOON: MAY-SEPT ~
FLUKEY WINDS, SQUALLS, RAIN

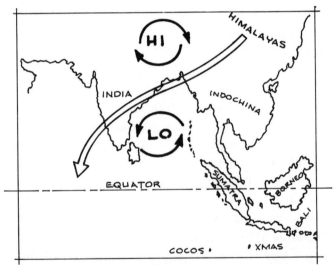

WINTER MONSOON: OCT-APRIL ~
STEADY WINDS, CLEAR, DRY

FIG. 5-8 ~ THE INDIAN MONSOON

All the winds we have talked about so far are winds of general circulation and those associated with lows and highs. But many *local winds* have such definite characteristics that many of them have been given colloquial names. The U.S. Weather Bureau supplied the following brief definitions:

bora: a cold wind of the northern Adriatic that blows down from the high plateaus in the north. A similar wind occurs on the northeastern coast of the Black Sea.

Chinook: a moist southwesterly wind from the Pacific Ocean, on the west coast of the United States, that is warm in winter and cool in summer

chubasco: a violent squall on the west coast of tropical and subtropical North America

cordonazo: a hurricane wind that blows from a southerly quadrant on the west coast of Mexico as a result of a hurricane passing off the coast

etesians: northerly winds that blow in summer over the eastern Mediterranean

gregale: a stormy northeast wind on the Mediterranean

harmattan: a dry, dusty wind of the west coast of Africa that blows from the deserts

katabatic: the cold, sometimes gale-force wind that may blow outward from a cold icecap as a result of intense cooling, subsidence, and spreading of the air

leste: a hot, dry, easterly wind of the Madeira and Canary islands

levanter: a strong, easterly wind of the Mediterranean, especially in the Straits of Gibraltar, associated with damp, foggy weather

mistral: a stormy, cold, northerly wind that blows down from the mouth of the Ebro in Spain to the Gulf of Genoa

norther: a stormy, northerly wind of sudden onset, occurring during the colder half of the year over the region from Texas southward, across the Gulf of Mexico and the western Caribbean. These winds are dependent on the strengthening of the cold-weather high-pressure area prevailing over the southern United States.

pampero:　　　a northwest squall that blows over or from the pampas of South America. Off the coast of Argentina, it is most prevalent from July to September.

Papagayo:　　　a strong to violent northeast wind that blows during the colder months in the Gulf of Papagayo, along the northwest coast of Costa Rica, and over adjacent Pacific coastal waters

Santa Ana:　　　a strong wind that starts suddenly and blows through the pass and valley of the same name in Southern California and then out to sea. Its force has capsized small craft off the coast.

shamal:　　　a northeast wind of Mesopotamia and the Persian Gulf.

sirocco:　　　this name is applied to various warm winds in the Mediterranean area, particularly in North Africa.

Tehuantepecer:　　　a strong to violent northerly wind of the Pacific waters off southern Mexico and northern Central America that is confined mostly to the Gulf of Tehuantepec and occurs during the colder months

williwaw:　　　a fall wind of the Aleutian coast. It should be noted that fall winds are cold winds that blow down an incline. They occur when cold air is dammed up in huge quantities on the windward side of a mountain ridge and then spills over suddenly and surges down the other side. These winds can be quite violent. The Tehuantepecer, pampero, mistral, and bora also are examples of a fall wind.

No chapter about weather would be complete without some mention of *fog*. There are four general categories of these minute water droplets that are suspended in air: *advection fog, radiation fog, frontal fog,* and *upslope fog.* The last two categories are continental types of fog and not of much interest to the sailor.

Radiation fog tends to form in harbors on clear nights with a slight wind. It is sometimes known as *ground fog* because it is thickest near the low points of ground—and of course it lays right on top of the water. As the sun comes up, it burns off. All the sailor has to do is wait. Radiation fog is not a problem at sea.

Advection fog is the stuff most commonly encountered at sea. It can be very thick and persist for long periods. Two processes are responsible for this kind of fog: cold air blowing across a warmer sea surface or warm air blowing across a colder sea surface.

The first case occurs frequently at the major warm ocean currents, such as the Gulf Stream, the northern part of the Japan Current, and the southern part of the Agulhas current. The fog formed is a shallow *steam fog*. In arctic areas, where the waters are warmer in winter than their continental surroundings, the same stuff forms and is called *arctic smoke*.

The second case, warm moist air blowing across colder water, is the kind that gives sailors the most trouble. It has been estimated that 80 percent of all maritime fog is originated by this process. A wind force of 4 to 15 mph is required for full development of this fog. If the wind is less, the fog is shallow and hovers near the surface. If greater, the fog lifts and becomes a low overcast.

The cruising sailor should be aware of the favorite hangouts of these thick, long-lasting advection fog formations. They occur over the Grand Banks and Newfoundland waters whenever the wind is southerly or easterly. This happens one in three days during winter months and two in three days during the summer.

Further east, the warm air blowing off the remnants of the Gulf Stream produces the pea-soup fogs of the English Isles.

The frequent dense fogs of northern Japan and the Aleutians are caused by the warm air traveling northeast with the Japan Current encountering the cold water flowing south through the Bering Straits (Figure 5-9).

Prevailing westerly winds off California meet the cold shore currents of that coast and produce the well-known California fog.

For the sailor who encounters fog while at sea, there is generally little cause for concern unless he is approaching land. The principal danger at sea is one of possible collision with other vessels. Usually, the navigator just waits for the fog to lift while proceeding on his compass course.

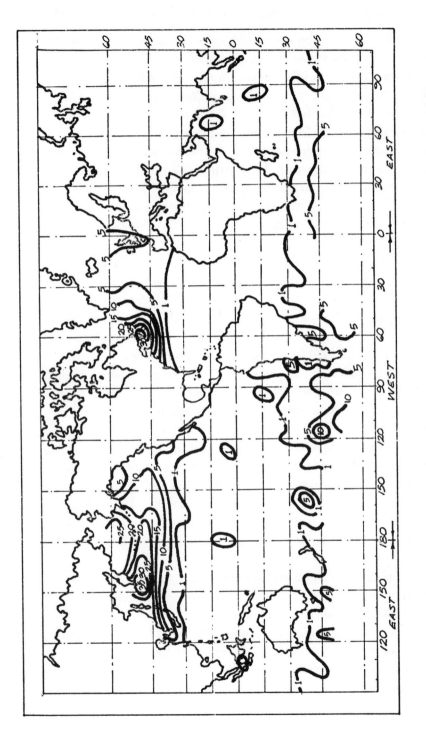

FIG. 5-9 ~ PERCENTAGE AVERAGE FREQUENCY OF FOG FOR JUNE TO AUGUST

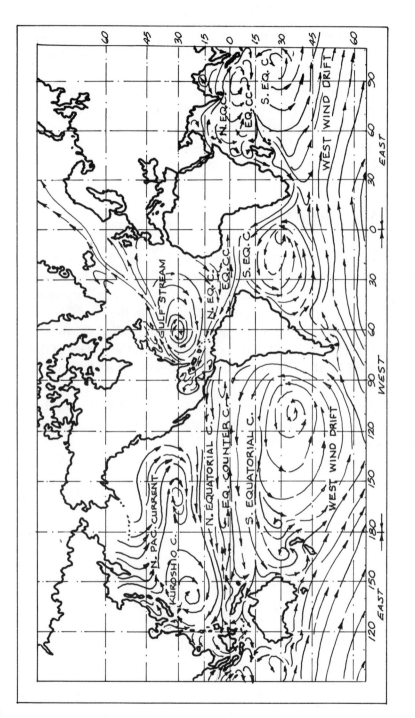

FIG. 5-10 ~ OCEAN CURRENTS OF THE WORLD, - GENERAL FLOW PATTERN

Fog has no affect on electronic aids to navigation. The best assistance a sailor can get is from radar and RDF—and a depth sounder if his ship is on soundings.

Frankly I would not attempt to take any ship into a fogbound coastal harbor unless I knew it very well indeed—and maybe not then. I think that if a cruising boat intends to sail waters known for fog, then radar is mandatory. All deep-water cruising boats should have an RDF and depth sounder on board.

OCEAN CURRENTS

When planning your cruise, it is necessary only to know that *ocean currents* must be taken into account. Practically all the information needed about them can be found in *Bowditch, Sailing Directions* (aka *Pilots*), *Coast Pilots,* and most particularly, in the *Pilot Charts.*

The horizontal and patterned motion of water called ocean currents is primarily the result of the wind's effect on the surface of the sea, modified by the Coriolis deflection (discussed earlier in this chapter). Secondary influences from deep-ocean currents also prevail but are of less importance than wind. Current is responsible for more boats being in a different location than planned than perhaps any other single factor. (Figure 5-10).

TWO

PREPARATION

A fox, finding a boar sharpening his tusks upon a tree, asks why he is doing that when there is no danger. "When danger comes," the boar answers, "it will behoove me not to sharpen my tusks, *but to use them.*"

"The Wild Boar and the Fox"
An Aesop's Fable (c.570 B.C.)

6

Health, Wealth, Love— and Time to Enjoy All Three

Now that we've gotten this far, let's make the following assumptions that—

—You now own or plan to own a well-constructed deep-water cruising yacht.

—you have your crew well in hand and you know who is going with you and are satisfied with your choice.

—your planning book is getting fat and heavy and additions are more frequent. Your cruise course is well laid out and you're happy with it.

—you've learned to find your position at sea by the use of celestial navigation. More important, you have become an adequate pilot and seaman.

—you understand weather and, although you have achieved a properly cautious attitude toward it, are not afraid of it.

Now it is time to set a sailing date. Your departure might be planned for a year hence, or earlier than that, or later, But by now you are very aware of the *right* time of year for your departure and that must be your target date.

Considerations for preparing your ship are rattling your brain. A quick thumb through the planning book reveals so many undone tasks you are numbed. But first considerations must be personal ones: job problems, health problems, what to do with the house, apartment, or condominium. What about the kids? What teaching aids will be required and who will be teacher?

Pets must be given serious consideration, also. Do they go or stay? Frankly, no matter how much you love them, pets can be much more trouble on a boat than a surplus crew member.

WEALTH—OR THE LACK OF IT

Remember, *cruising costs money,* not necessarily a lot of money—just "enough." How much enough is depends on you, your crew, your boat, and your cruising philosophy regarding in-port pleasures and boat maintenance.

Nina and I, and our son, Ernie, took *Starbound* around the world from 1973 to 1976 on an average of $400 per month. This sum was calculated to cover food for the three of us, plus fuel, parts, repairs, and port expenses. Friends who joined us kicked in an additional $250 per month, which we found worked out about right, considering the added formality given to meals aboard and the generally longer port stays required. Like it or not, a guest will increase cruising expenses in a disproportionate manner.

We had an absolutely fine time during our circumnavigation, even though we stayed out of restaurants, were careful of what we spent in bars, spent as little time as possible in tourist-frequented areas, bought stores of food in wholesale lots, and did virtually all the ship's maintenance ourselves.

Our next cruise is being planned on the basis of $600 per month—not just because of inflation but because we want to do more exploring of the countries we visit than we did our first time around.

We've met cruising people at the extreme ends of the cost spectrum, too. A wealthy New York couple, cruising with their two children and a hired crew of three on a 65-foot ketch, were spending about $4,000 per month (as near as we could estimate). Interestingly enough, they weren't having a very good time. The owner's insistence on treating the crew as servants engendered crew changes in every port. These people weren't cruising, they were "yachting"—and not doing a very good job of that either.

We also met Jan and Pete Kurst, and their son, Nick, who became friends of ours. They cruised their 30-foot Tahiti Ketch, *Dulciana*, on about $200 per month. They had to be damned careful of what they spent—but, after all, don't we all? It is simply a question of how careful we want to be.

Basic costs of cruising are expended in food, fuel, and maintaining the ship. If the ship is kept in good shape (and she must be) and has a full complement of spares (and she must have), then expenditures for the ship itself can be kept to the replenishment of spares and the bills for haulouts, which can be held to a minimum if you do your own bottom work and carry your own paint (which you should). Port charges, generally, are not a big item. Our total port charges around the world came to less than $500. Some places cost more than others. If it pleases you to secure to a dock, then get set to spend some extra money. All the cruising people we know much prefer to lay out to their anchors: Privacy, security, and economy being the three prime reasons for doing so.

Based on our experiences, we believe that an economy-minded couple with two children can cruise a well-found 40-foot boat in deep water, over an extended period of time and in relative luxury, for about $500 per month, average operating costs. We realize that the foregoing statement is much qualified, but it is a base on which to estimate cruising costs. A couple alone can cruise on a bit less. Two couples will find the cost greater. If restaurants, bars, and tourist-frequented spas are included in your port agendas, then we can only envy your bank account.

What to do about jobs is so much an individual problem that we hesitate to give advice that may seem obvious. Some examples of how various cruising friends of ours handled it follows, but we'll start with us:

We resigned our jobs with the U.S. government and cashed in our retirement funds. That pot of money, about $15,000, was just enough to finance our cruise. We returned to Chesapeake Bay, after two years and ten months of delightful sailing, with five dollars in our pockets. Having maintained correspondence with friends in the government and having forwarded employment forms to them a few months before our return, we were fortunate enough to be rehired within a few days after putting *Starbound* back on her old dock in Annapolis. When we left, there were no promises that we would be rehired—we had to take our chances. But we're both good at what we do and luck was with us.

We know several couples who simply retired from their jobs and now cruise on their relatively small retirement incomes, working here and there at this and that to supplement what they get from home—which, in most cases, isn't a lot.

Another friend, who was fortunate enough to make a lot of money in a relatively short time, simply invested it and now lives on the income. He also supplements this by working when he can. He is now building a larger boat and is planning another cruise.

Several people, mostly couples, sold their businesses at a high enough profit to finance a few years of sailing. Their future plans, however, were somewhat nebulous. A few returned and started other businesses; one young couple stayed in New Zealand, another in Australia—both with an idea toward immigration; and some are still cruising.

Several cruising couples cruise and write—a humbling business at best. One has to be very good to make money at it, and every writer we know has a folder full of rejection slips.

A couple we greatly admire are on their fourth world cruise. No one except their close cruising friends knows just how much water has gone under the keel of their Carol ketch because they don't write or lecture—they just sail and enjoy themselves thoroughly. Once every three years they spend a long winter—about six to eight months—working. They stay on their boat and spend all their spare hours refitting her. Then, with their strongbox replenished, they have the extreme pleasure of watching the land over the stern fade from sight once again.

And we know a few young single people—and also young married couples—who don't really have a cruising fund at all. They manage, with some difficulty, to cruise until they're nearly broke and then manage to make enough money, wherever they are, to carry on. But that's a tough way to cruise! It is hard to enjoy yourself when wondering where the next load of stores is coming from. We noticed that their boats are always kept in good repair, though.

Most cruising people have their future plans fairly well thought out. There is usually a job or a business to return to or to reestablish somewhere else—and always another cruise in mind.

Remember the ancient toast that covers everything? "Here's to health, wealth, love—and time to enjoy all three!" Notice in the order given that health comes first. And that's how it is with cruising. A physical checkup is as important for the crew as it is for the boat. Too many people neglect themselves in the rush to get the ship ready.

A general physical exam is the first order of business. A thorough dental and periodontal check should be next. And if your eyes haven't been checked lately, now is the time. We say "now" even though your departure date might be one year away. Then, if a hitherto unknown problem is turned up by the physical exam, you'll have a year to square it away. Dental and optical exams should be scheduled periodically in any case, so do it now—and again just before departure.

Many times we have heard people say, "We'd just love to take our boat on a long cruise—but with the kids in school, it will just have to wait."

Wait for what, we'd like to ask? Until they're in high school? Or college? Take them with you! Teach them yourself with the assistance of a good correspondence course. We think this is good advice for anyone with children in grade school, or even in high school.

It has been our experience that children on a cruise learn more from a parent-taught correspondence course in two hours per day than do their contemporaries going full time to the average public school. The children of two cruising families, known to us personally, took placement exams on their return to the United States after a two-year cruise. Scholastically those children were all graded one year beyond their contemporaries. And it was enlightening to see how much more mature they seemed to be.

To learn what correspondence programs are available, we suggest first asking the principal of your children's school for help. Your local library should also have a listing of correspondence schools. The Board of Education of your city, county, or state will be able to help you, too. And state universities generally have high school equivalency correspondence programs.

Because we have lived in the state of Maryland for some years, we have become familiar with the Calvert School, a nonprofit organization approved by the state that offers correspondence courses for grades through the eighth. The tuition charge for each school year includes *all* of the constantly updated course materials and books. And there is a teacher's advisory service available, a very handy item for the perhaps inexperienced parent/teacher.

The cost for a kindergarten course is $80. For grades one through seven, $140—and for grade 8, $150. The teacher's advisory service is $70 on top of the base charge. The Calvert School is located at 105 Tuscany Road, Baltimore, Maryland 21210, and their telephone number is (301) 243-6030. Upon application the school will arrange with you to have your child take a standardized placement exam that will help them to choose the optimum program. If your intent is to reenroll your child in the same school district after completing your cruise, it may also be necessary to obtain acceptance of the correspondence program from your district superintendent of schools before your departure.

Pets are a big problem on a cruise. They take up time better spent for the welfare of the crew and the boat. Food and medicines must be carried for pets. Their waste must be cleaned up. They're underfoot when below and in danger of going overboard when topside. They do no useful work. Virtually all foreign countries have extremely strict rules regarding animals. Generally, a bond must be posted to insure that the pet stays aboard at all times. In British Commonwealth countries that bond is equal to US $500. If the animal puts one paw ashore, it is destroyed *and* the bond is forfeited. Rabies and distemper do not exist in many countries and they want to keep it that way. So, consider carefully the complications of including a pet on your cruise. We strongly recommend leaving them with relatives or other friends (which may not make you too popular with them either).

Now we can almost hear a certain number of dismayed wails. O.K., we agree it's a personal decision—but remember, that animal can't be put in the backyard and ignored. It is going to be right there on that boat, living in close quarters with you. I'll admit that cats are easier to cruise with than dogs, but not much. The big problems with a cat are fur, odor, and the damn "cat box." Nearly all animals shed fur constantly and it is impossible to keep the stuff out of the bilge. Every single boat with a cat in residence smells like cat. If a litter box is not provided, the cat will deposit its waste in odd corners below decks. If a litter box is provided, it must be installed somewhere out of the way and secured. If it is below, it will smell. If it is topside, it is going to get wet and be strewn on the decks—and someone will step in it. Animals are lovable, but lovableness cannot offset the disproportionate number of problems they bring with them to a deep-water cruising boat.

We sold our house to buy *Starbound* and moved aboard the same day the papers were signed. We put our furniture—all the "good" stuff—in storage, and it remains there to this day, thirteen years later. Sometimes we think about selling it or giving it away, but neither of us can quite bring ourselves to that final point of total severance from our "things." Perhaps just knowing that those favorite pieces—the solid walnut coffee table, the king-size bed, the heavy old sideboards, the golden oak table—are still available to us, acts as an emotional crutch of sorts, a tenuous tie to the land.

We totally enjoy living aboard and cannot really envision another house in our future. Still, the furniture remains in storage.

If you have an apartment and a deep-water cruise in mind, the problem is easily resolved. Put the furniture in storage and give up the apartment. Or, if you can stand parting with the furniture, sell it. But be aware that used furniture will bring only a fraction of its market or sentimental value.

A house is a different kind of problem. It can be sold or rented. If you have strong reasons for holding on to the place and can afford it, why then, put it in the hands of a very reputable rental agent and go cruising. Frankly, not very many cruising sailors do this unless their plans are for a cruise of relatively short duration, perhaps one year. And it is a rare sailor who can afford a cruising sailboat, a nice house, and the time and expense of a cruise, all sans employment. Nearly all the deep-water sailors we know have severed their primary ties to the land. They have only their ship and "enough" money. And they're all surpassingly happy.

7

Ship's Business

When contemplating a deep-water cruise of extended duration, it is perhaps human nature to slip some of the more boring aspects of preparation to the bitter end of the lists. We caution against this and urge you to at least begin to consider some of the financial and legal logistics involved in moving your ship and its crew from one country to another.

Traveling around one's own country is not a financial problem as long as the checkbook and credit cards are available. And the very cautious can always obtain traveler's checks, their cost not a big item for a vacation-type trip. But how does the yachtsman make sure he will have enough cash, where and when he wants it, without carrying his whole pot of gold around with him? A safe? A locked box? A hiding place aboard? What about fire, theft, or shipwreck? Will the checking account back home be of use? What about those traveler's checks—or will a letter of credit be more worthwhile?

Looking at the last first, *traveler's checks* are negotiable almost anywhere and can be replaced if lost. However, it costs one percent to buy them and, in some countries, a fee is charged to cash them. And cash tied up in traveler's checks earns no interest.

A *letter of credit* is a handy way to have quick access to a large amount of money. The purchaser "buys" a letter of credit from his bank, then draws against it from various banks in other parts of the world. Of course, an initial fee is charged at home and subsequent fees are charged whenever the document is used. Letters of credit can be obtained from the international department of major banks and from large district offices of American Express.

Carrying a large sum of cash aboard is just plain foolish. It is exactly the case of "all the eggs in one basket." No yachtsman ever really thinks that the boat will be robbed or burnt or sunk—but if any one of these things should happen, even though the crew might escape, they'll be stranded with no resources at all—and in a foreign country.

We feel that the best way to cruise is with a small pot of *working cash* aboard, which can be replenished from the big pot at home. Replenishment funds can be wired for as they are needed. But now the problem becomes one of logistics. First, how much working cash should you keep on board and how long will it last? Second, where are you going to wire from and how long will it take to get the money? Third, who at home is going to do the honors for you?

Actually the solutions are interrelated. The amount of cash kept on board should be at least 50 percent in excess of the amount needed to get to the next major supply port, which will be the proper place to wire for more money. It will also be a port in which you must plan to spend 10 to 14 days, since that is approximately how long it will take to receive money after you've wired for it. Of course, you can make the request by wire from one port that funds be sent to the next. But that can get to be a complicated procedure at best, implying a prior knowledge of available banks at the next port and the receipt of a notice from home telling you to which bank the money was sent. And too, bad weather or other problems may force you to miss that port and you might find yourself two islands downwind from your badly needed money.

So plan on a two-week stay in any port from which you plan to wire for money. Make sure you arrive there with enough money to operate. Then work on the boat, see the country, and line up sources for the stores and spares you'll need to buy.

Now, who at home will handle these financial matters for you? If you have a business manager, attorney, or agent, the problem is simplified. Otherwise it will have to be a member of your family, a *very* good friend or, as we did it, the bank. In any of these cases, you will have to give them power of attorney.

We found that our bank handled the matter to our complete satisfaction. We dumped 90 percent of our funds in a savings account, which earned some interest for us, and put the rest in our checking account just to take care of the occasional bill that would eventually catch up to us.

The aforementioned bills were usually from American Express or BankAmericard (now VISA), which brings up the next point: Internationally known credit cards are not mandatory for cruising but can be very handy indeed! Especially when the wired-for money doesn't arrive when it should, and you find yourself with two bucks in the kitty. If there is an American Express office in port, your card will buy traveler's checks at least. Also, a chat with the manager of any bank will usually allow you to write a personal check on your account at home, with your credit card and passport as references. (We thought this amusing since not a single bank at home will do as much for you unless you have an account there.) We found Barclay's Bank of England to be particularly helpful, wherever we found one.

It is a perhaps surprising fact that many people have never had occasion to travel outside their country to the extent that a passport is required and have only a very general idea of what a passport or a visa actually is.

A *passport* is a formal document issued by a government to a citizen of that nation certifying his citizenship, and requesting protection for him while abroad. In the U.S. a passport is in the form of a small, bound pamphlet that is issued by the State Department upon application. Application forms can be obtained from the U.S. Passport Agency in large cities or from the authorized government office in smaller towns (usually the U.S. Post Office).

A *visa* is something else again; it is an endorsement (usually in the form of a stamped seal, which is signed and dated) made *on a passport* by the proper authorities of whatever country you are visiting, denoting that the passport has been examined and that the bearer may proceed.

Every crew member of a small ship going foreign must have a passport. Children under 12 may be included on one or the other of their parent's passports, but if the cruise duration should extend past a child's twelfth birthday, a lot of hassle might be saved by initially getting them their own passport.

Leaving the United States is simple—for a U.S. citizen. One may merely leave, passport in hand. But entering *or* leaving a foreign country can be a surprise to the uninitiated—at least to those people uninitiated to travel in a small ship.

Most of today's travelers fly in and out of various countries whose airports are geared to dealing with the formalities of exit and entry in just minutes. To those accustomed to such procedures, we say, when sailing deep water, be prepared for a large step back in time. After anchoring in a foreign port, the captain of a yacht must be prepared to deal with from one to six officials—with tact and diplomacy.

The method by which visa endorsements get stamped into your passports will vary with the country. Initially we would suggest that you write a letter to the nearest embassy of each country you intend to enter during your cruise. (A list of embassies and their addresses is included at the end of this chapter.) A polite, brief, typed request for information, outlining your cruise plans and detailing your timetable as closely as possible, will generally induce an immediate response forwarding visa requirements as well as other very desirable information about that country.

Some countries require visas *prior* to entry. Others do not and the visas are obtained upon arrival. In most countries there are time restrictions placed on visas and consequently they must be obtained along the way. This was characteristic of Australia and South Africa during the time of our circumnavigation and we had to obtain those visas while we were in New Zealand.

When requesting a visa, always ask if there is a period within which it must be used, whether it can be dated for your approximate arrival time or whether it will become effective upon arrival. If a visa must be used within a certain period of time after issue, one obtained too far in advance may not be valid, particularly if you are delayed for some reason. *But the rules change constantly,* so we advise you to write those letters. The wording can be almost identical, except for your proposed dates of entry into each country.

If your plans include touring by land or sea from one country to another and then returning to the first, you should request a *multiple-entry visa.* We failed to do so when obtaining our South African visas and this omission caused us problems when we went from South Africa to Rhodesia and back. We arranged for our South African visas while in New Zealand and were asked whether we wanted multiple-entry or *single-entry visas.* Not knowing the difference and being in too big a rush to stop and think, we replied that single-entry visas would be sufficient. What a mistake that was! A fair amount of time and personal diplomacy were used before we could leave South Africa and be assured of reentry. In the future we will always request multiple-entry visas for any country with borders adjoining places we may wish to visit. We recommend the same procedure to all cruising yachtsmen.

Visas are always issued for a finite length of time, the duration of which changes from country to country. If your planned visit is going to extend beyond the visa expiration date, you will have to arrange for an extension. This can be a hassle—and not particularly in just the smaller countries. So be aware of visa durations and plan accordingly. Make sure that the country in question will allow an extension (some don't) and find out the procedure for obtaining one.

Some extremely interesting cruising waters require special per-

REPUBLIC OF INDONESIA

CLEARANCE APPROVAL FOR INDONESIAN TERRITORY

No. D.F.A. : *41/1975*   *5-2-75*
No. D.D.S. : *HK/342 L/II/75*   *19-2-75*
No. D.S.C. : *DM 160/14/16*   **4 MAR 1975**

The following non-scheduled shipping has been approved by the Indonesian Government :

1. SHIP :
    a. Owner of ship : Gordon G. Stuermer & Nina R. Stuermer
    b. Name of ship : " STARBOUND "
    c. Nationality : U.S.A.
    d. Type : Auxiliary Ketch
    e. Dimensions :
    f. Displacement : 35 tons
    g. Call-sign : WJ 5529

2. CAPTAIN : Gordon G. Stuermer

3. CREW : Nina R. Stuermer and Ernest G. Stuermer

4. PASSENGERS/CARGO : None, only Mr. Thomas Hoff (Mr. Stuermer's cousin) may fly to join them for a holiday, in which case he may be living on board the yacht for a short time.

5. a. Last port of call before entering Indonesia : Darwin, Australia
    b. Next port of call after leaving Indonesia : Cocos Islands

6. Dates/ports of call in Indonesia : June to October 1975: Roti, Timor, Savu, Flores, Sumbawa, Lombok, Bali and Java.

7. PURPOSE : Pleasure.

APPROVED BY

(a) Department of Foreign Affairs :

(Signature & Name)

(b) Department of Defence & Security :
A.N. KE-G CPS. HANKAM
PABAK DJUS.

(Signature & Name)
R. KASENDA
KOLONEL LAUT (P) NRP. 759/P.
M. PARTAWIATA
MAL LAUT (P) Nrp. 1820

(c) Directorate General of Sea Communications :
Directorate of Sea Transport

Drs. F. Soemarko
(Secretary)

Applicant :

(Signature and Name)
Laura A. Clerici
Vice Consul of the United States of America

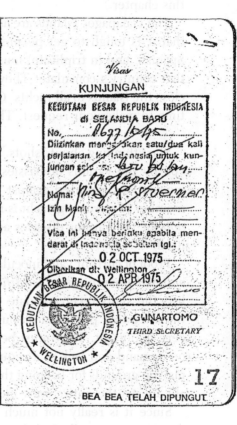

WARNING.-

FOR ALL VISITORS TO BALI.

WE WOULD LIKE TO INFORM YOU OF
THE FOLLOWING :

1. IT IS ILLEGAL TO DRESS IMPROPERLY
WHEN IN A PUBLIC AREA.

2. PUBLIC BATHING WITHOUT COMPLETE
SWIM SUITS FOR MEN OR WOMEN IS
STRICTLY PROHIBITED.
THIS APPLIES TO ALL BEACH AREAS
AS WELL AS OTHER PLACES.

3. IT IS ILLEGAL TO PARTAKE IN THE
USE OF HARMFUL DRUGS, SUCH AS
MARIJUANA, MORPHENE, AMPHETAMINES,
ETC.

4. ANY WILLFUL VIOLATION OF THE ABOVE
LAWS AND REGULATIONS WILL SUBJECT
THE OFFENDER TO PROSECUTION.

THANK YOU FOR
YOUR COOPERATION

IMIGRASI
DENPASAR

Visas
KUNJUNGAN

KEDUTAAN BESAR REPUBLIK INDONESIA
di SELANDIA BARU
No. 8627/6/75
Diizinkan mengadakan satu/dua kali
perjalanan ke Indonesia untuk kun-
jungan selama
Nama:
Izin Meni:

Visa ini hanya berlaku apabila men-
darat di Indonesia sebelum tgl.:
0 2 OCT 1975
Diberikan di: Wellington
0 2 APR 1975

GUNARTOMO
THIRD SECRETARY

KEDUTAAN BESAR REPUBLIK INDONESIA
WELLINGTON

17

BEA BEA TELAH DIPUNGUT

mits. Indonesia and Ecuador's Galapagos Islands are peculiar in this regard. To sail Indonesian waters a yacht must be in possession of a *sailing permit*. This is obtained by making application to the U.S. consulate in Djakarta, who obtains the permit for you. (We've included copies of our application, and the permit, at the end of this chapter.)

The Galapagos Islands are absolutely fascinating. But be advised that it is tough to get permission to visit. A *solicitud* (typed, in Spanish, and in triplicate) must be submitted to Ecuador through that country's consulate. They discourage visitors and sometimes close the islands to all yachts. *One year* in advance is not too short a time to make your request. The Galapagos are worth the trouble.

Start thinking about "shots." Included in the information sent to you by the various embassies and consulates will be the various inoculations required against disease in that country. Each crew member of a cruising yacht is required to furnish *proof of inoculation* for the various diseases against which a country is protecting itself.

Proof of current valid inoculation is given by an individual *International Immunization Certificate:* a yellow folder-type card that lists the shots received, date of inoculation, and the signature of the attending physician or public health official. These cards are very important. They must be presented to the health authorities on demand and lack of a required inoculation of one of the crew may be grounds for keeping the yacht in quarantine, which generally means the entire crew must stay on board.

Since it is really not much trouble to keep inoculations up to date, it seems really foolish not to do so. But there were still two instances during our circumnavigation when we heard about a yacht being quarantined for out-of-date inoculations.

I think the biggest problem lies in the fact that it is easy to forget to check those certificates—particularly if you are staying in one country for an extended period. The cards are checked only upon entry and in the flux of port activity, they are easy to overlook.

Write to the National Center for Disease Control, Atlanta, Georgia 30333 to obtain your certificates as well as a booklet that outlines what inoculations are required for each country you intend to visit. Verify the requirements against the information sent to you by the various consulates and embassies. You should also phone the local division of the U.S. Public Health Service and obtain information on where to get a card and the required shots. But cross-check your sources of information. Disease areas change, and a country that last year did not require immunization against cholera might require them this year.

The very real and very personal and very best reason for keeping your immunization shots up to date is to preclude illness aboard your vessel.

Every official you contact while entering or clearing every port is going to want a *crew list*. Crew lists are quite simple to prepare and should be made up before your arrival in port. It can be hand printed, but a typed list looks better. And they must be signed by the skipper. If your crew remains intact throughout the cruise, you may choose to make up a bunch of them ahead of time. But sign them with the officials present; it is not necessary but it creates a better impression.

CREW LIST YACHT *STARBOUND*

United States Documentation No. 261706

Captain:	Gordon G. Stuermer	U.S.A. D 2235549
Crew:	Nina R. Stuermer	U.S.A. D 2228314
Crew:	Ernest G. Stuermer	U.S.A. D 2228315
Crew:	Raymond J. Kukulski	U.S.A. F 1921435

GORDON G. STUERMER, Captain

Gordon G. Stuermer
Yacht STARBOUND
c/o General Delivery
Auckland, New Zealand

20 January, 1975

The American Embassy
Medan Merdeka, Selatan 5
Djakarta,
Indonesia

Dear Sirs,

My wife and I and our son are sailing around the world in our yacht STARBOUND and are at present in New Zealand awaiting the termination of the hurricane season. We will commence our trip about April 1975. On our route we hope to cruise through Indonesia and the Indonesian Embassy in New Zealand has advised me to contact you so that we may obtain a sailing permit/security clearance for our yacht from the Indonesian authorities.

I understand that you require the following information:

1. Owners: Gordon G. Stuermer and Nina R. Stuermer

2. Name of boat: STARBOUND. Port of Registry: Baltimore (Annapolis), Maryland, U.S.A. Registration (documentation number): 261706

3. Type of boat: Auxiliary ketch

4. Displacement: 35 tons

5. Net tonnage: 30. Gross tonnage: 31

6. Call sign: WJ 5529

7. Captain: Gordon G. Stuermer, United States citizen, Passport No. D2235549

8. Crew: Nina R. Stuermer, United States citizen, Passport No. D2228314; Ernest G. Stuermer, United States citizen, Passport No. D2228315

9. Last port before entering Indonesia: Darwin, Australia

10. First port after leaving Indonesia: Cocos Islands

11. Dates and ports to be called at: It is extremely difficult for a sailing vessel to give an accurate itinerary for months in advance, but we would expect to enter Indonesian territory during the second half of June 1975 and cruise through the following islands: Roti, Timor, Savu, Flores, Sumbawa, Lombok, Bali, and Java.

    We would plan to leave Indonesia about the end of September to commence our crossing of the Indian Ocean.

12. Passengers and cargo: None

13. Purpose of voyage to Indonesia: A desire to visit Indonesia during the course of our circumnavigation and learn something of the customs of the people. In addition we are writing a book about our voyage for the David McKay Publishing Co., New York, N.Y., U.S.A.

It is possible that my cousin, Mr. Thomas Hoff, may fly out to join us for a holiday, in which case he may be living on board the yacht for a short time.

As we are hoping to leave Auckland about the end of March, 1975, and since we understand it takes at least a month to obtain our visas from the Embassy of Indonesia in Wellington, we would be very grateful if this matter could receive your prompt attention.

Very truly yours,

Gordon G. Stuermer

There are a few other pieces of paper you must have for deep-water cruising. The documentation or *registration papers proving ownership* of your yacht should always be available. And the *clearance documents* from your last port are always going to be asked for. Keep them in order, preferably in a folder of some kind with the last one on top. You'll be referring to them constantly while filling out various papers in countries with the more complicated procedures.

Proof of financial solvency is required in many countries. Usually they don't push the issue to the point of requiring proof in tangible forms such as visible cash or bank statements. However, they have the option of doing so.

What is to be done with all this "software," as the Navy calls it? These are documents that you cannot afford to lose under any circumstances—not by theft, fire, shipwreck, or sinking. They can all be replaced eventually, but their loss would effectively terminate the cruise for a long spell—perhaps permanently.

When starting our circumnavigation on *Starbound*, and not really having thought about the problem, we kept all this precious stuff in an old, blue plastic, zippered briefcase that we wedged in the bookcase at the front of our bunk. If we left the boat totally vacated while in port, we would hide the briefcase. And we squirreled our pot of cash away in a separate hidey-hole. Looking back, this procedure was not smart. Even if a thief couldn't find our cash or passports, they could have been lost by fire. And since they weren't in a waterproof container, we would have lost them by shipwreck or sinking. It is easy to think that those things will never happen—but they do!

What we recommend is the following: Buy a Halliburton-type camera case, one of the streamlined, aluminum kind that looks like a dispatch case. Make sure it is the type with a double-lip closure that has a rubber gasket running all the way around it. There should be a feel of resistance when closing it to ensure the opening seals well. Line the case with closed-cell, fire-resistant foam, at least one inch thick. Fit a folder for papers into one side of it and spaces for passports, checks, and cash into the other side. Build the separators out of foam so there will be as few voids as possible.

Find a good hiding place or build one for the case—one that a thief couldn't easily find but one that allows fast access in case you have to grab the goodies and bail out.

When officialdom comes to visit, simply remove the necessary papers from the case ahead of their arrival and put them back when they leave.

A friend of ours built a nice case out of marine plywood. It had a gasket all around the top and the lid clamped down with six cam-type fasteners. Many coats of varnish preserved it against moisture and it would float very nicely. He built a hidden storage for it in the side of a locker and unless you know it is there, you'd never find it.

We heard about one boat that had a built-in, fireproof barrel safe. A very nice job, but the boat was robbed while the owners were ashore and the thieves merely chopped the safe out of the bulkhead and took the whole damn thing away to open at their leisure. Also, if the boat is sinking, there is no time to open a safe.

There is one last piece of ship's business to begin thinking about: the receiving of *mail*. The "where" of it is obvious: your mail drops should be those major ports where you intend to supply the boat and wire for money. The "how" of it is an individual problem. A home address is needed, along with a conscientious handler. This will most likely be a member of your family—parents, brother, or sister—but a business manager or agent might also take care of it.

Your bank might provide this service for a small fee—some do. It is nice, though, to have someone with a close, personal interest in you managing the posting. Then they can weed out the junk before they send the important mail. And they can track down needed spare parts and post them at the same time. And they can receive film for developing as well as send fresh film back with the next batch of mail.

Our parents did all of this for us during our long cruise, and a very warm feeling it gave us to know we had someone who *cared* taking care of things.

List of Embassies*

Embassy of Argentina Chancery 1600 New Hampshire Ave., N.W. Washington, D.C.	387-0705
Embassy of Australia 1601 Massachusetts Ave., N.W. Washington, D.C. (Visa Consular & Immigration)	797-3000 797-3159
Embassy of Bahamas 600 New Hampshire Ave., N.W. Washington, D.C.	338-3940
Embassy of Barbados 2144 Wyoming Ave., N.W. Washington D.C.	387-7373
Embassy of Bolivia Chancery 1625 Massachusetts Ave., N.W. Washington, D.C.	483-4410
Embassy of Brazil Consular Section 3006 Massachusetts Ave., N.W. Washington, D.C.	797-0100

*All area codes 202; consult zip code directory for zips.

Embassy of Canada 785-1400
Chancery
1746 Massachusetts Ave., N.W.
Washington, D.C.

Embassy of Chile 785-1746
Chancery
1736 Massachusetts Ave., N.W.
Washington, D.C.

Embassy of Costa Rica 234-2945
Chancery
2112 S. St., N.W.
Washington, D.C.

Embassy of Cyprus 462-5772
Chancery
2211 R. St., N.W.
Washington, D.C.

Embassy of Czechoslovakia 363-6307, 363-6308
3099 Linnean Ave., N.W.
Washington, D.C.

Embassy of Denmark 234-4300
Chancery
3200 Whitehaven St., N.W.
Washington, D.C.

Embassy of Dominican Republic 332-6280
Chancery
1715 22nd St., N.W.
Washington, D.C.

Embassy of Ecuador 234-7166
Consular Division
1470 Euclid St., N.W.
Washington, D.C.

Embassy of Egypt 232-5400
Chancery
2310 Decatur Place, N.W.
Washington, D.C.

Embassy of Finland   462-0556
Chancery
1900 24th St., N.W.
Washington, D.C.

Embassy of France   234-0990
Chancery
2325 Belmont Road, N.W.
Washington, D.C.

Embassy of Greece   667-3168
Chancery
2221 Massachusetts Ave., N.W.
Washington, D.C.

Embassy of Grenada   347-3198
927 15th St., N.W.
Washington, D.C.

Embassy of Guatemala   332-2865
Chancery
2220 R. St., N.W.
Washington, D.C.

Consulate of Haiti   723-0116
4400 17th St., N.W.
Washington, D.C.

Embassy of Honduras   966-7700
4301 Connecticut Ave., N.W.
Washington, D.C.

Embassy of Iceland   265-6653
2022 Connecticut Ave., N.W.
Washington, D.C.

Embassy of India   265-5050
Chancery
2107 Massachusetts Ave., N.W.
Washington, D.C.

Embassy of Iran   797-6500
Chancery
3005 Massachusetts Ave., N.W.
Washington, D.C.

Embassy of Iraq Chancery 1801 P. St., N.W. Washington, D.C.	483-7500
Embassy of Ireland Chancery 2234 Massachusetts Ave., N.W. Washington, D.C.	483-7639
Embassy of Israel 1621 22nd St., N.W. Washington, D.C.	483-4100
Embassy of Jamaica Chancery 1666 Connecticut Ave., N.W. Washington, D.C.	387-1010
Embassy of Japan Chancery 2520 Massachusetts Ave., N.W. Washington, D.C.	234-2266
Embassy of Lebanon Chancery 2560 28th St., N.W. Washington, D.C.	332-0300
Embassy of Liberia 5201 16th St., N.W. Washington, D.C.	723-0437
Embassy of Libya 1118 22nd St., N.W. Washington, D.C.	452-1290
Embassy of Madagascar 2374 Massachusetts Ave., N.W. Washington, D.C.	265-5525
Embassy of Malaysia 2401 Massachusetts Ave., N.W. Washington, D.C.	234-7600

Embassy of Malta   462-3611
2017 Connecticut Ave., N.W.
Washington, D.C.

Embassy of Maritus   244-1491
4301 Connecticut Ave., N.W.
Washington, D.C.

Embassy of Morocco   461-7979
Chancery
1601 21st St., N.W.
Washington, D.C.

Embassy of New Zealand   265-1721
(New Zealand Embassy)
Chancery
1746 Massachusetts Ave., N.W.
Washington, D.C.

Embassy of Nicaragua   387-4371
Chancery
1627 New Hampshire Ave., N.W.
Washington, D.C.

Embassy of Norway   266-9550
4200 Wisconsin Ave., N.W.
Washington, D.C.

Embassy of Pakistan   332-8330
Consular Division
2315 Massachusetts Ave., N.W.
Washington, D.C.

Embassy of Pakistan Annex   265-9666
2735 Connecticut Ave., N.W.
Washington, D.C.

Embassy of Panama   483-1407
2862 McGill Terrace, N.W.
Washington, D.C.

Embassy of Paraguay   483-6960
2400 Massachusetts Ave., N.W.
Washington, D.C.

Embassy of Peru   833-9860
(Peruvian Embassy)
Chancery
1700 Massachusetts Ave., N.W.
Washington, D.C.

Embassy of Portugal   265-1643
Chancery
2125 Kalorama Road, N.W.
Washington, D.C.

Embassy of Spain   265-0190
Chancery
2700 15th St., N.W.
Washington, D.C.

Embassy of Sri Lanka   483-4025
2148 Wyoming Ave., N.W.
Washington, D.C.

Embassy of Sweden   965-4100
600 New Hampshire Ave., N.W.
Washington, D.C.

Embassy of Switzerland   462-1811
Chancery
2900 Cathedral Ave., N.W.
Washington, D.C.

Embassy of Thailand   667-1446
(Royal Thai Embassy)
Chancery
2300 Kalorama Road, N.W.
Washington, D.C.

Embassy of The Federation of Malaysia   234-7600
2401 Massachusetts Ave., N.W.
Washington, D.C.

Embassy of The Netherlands   244-5300
4200 Linnean Ave., N.W.
Washington, D.C.

Embassy of the Philippines　　　　　　　483-1020
Labor Attaché Office
1617 Massachusetts Ave., N.W.
Washington, D.C.

Embassy of the Republic of Cape Verde　659-3148
1120 Connecticut Ave., N.W.
Washington, D.C.

Embassy of the Republic of Indonesia　293-1745
2020 Massachusetts Ave., N.W.
Washington, D.C.

Embassy of the Republic of Singapore　667-7555
1824 R. St., N.W.
Washington, D.C.

Embassy of Trinidad & Tobago　　　　　467-6490
Chancery
1708 Massachusetts Ave., N.W.
Washington, D.C.

Embassy of Turkey　　　　　　　　　　667-6400
1606 23rd St., N.W.
Washington, D.C.

Embassy of Uruguay　　　　　　　　　331-1313
Chancery
1918 F. St., N.W.
Washington, D.C.

Embassy of Venezuela　　　　　　　　265-9600
Chancery
2445 Massachusetts Ave., N.W.
Washington, D.C.

8

The Vessel;
A Hull Survey

The first consideration given to the preparation of a boat for deep-water cruising, is that of *safety.* There are times when a small ship will be called upon—usually by the elements, but sometimes abetted by momentary mishandling—to take on a sea. When this happens, the ship actually can be mostly underwater, resulting in hydraulic forces being exerted on its structure, both hull and rig, the magnitude of which the landsman can only imagine. I do not intend this statement to be a scare phrase. It is simply a fact that every deep-water yacht of which we know has, at one time or another, been hit with a really big sea that has washed her completely. However if the ship has been designed and built properly, maintained well, and prepared for sea conscientiously, her crew can embark on a passage with a sense of security in knowing that the ship, even if caught in an extreme situation such as a knockdown or a broach, will come through safely.

So let's assume that your ship's design and construction is adequate. And let's also assume that you've maintained her well. What we recommend is that you now accomplish a *complete safety sur-*

vey of the yacht. And we also recommend that you do the survey yourself, although you may require, or desire, professional help.

If you feel a certain lack of confidence regarding your abilities to do the job without missing something important, it will be natural. But look at it this way: If anything goes wrong while you're at sea, you'll have to fix it yourself anyway—and how much easier it will be when you know your ship intimately.

So if you presently don't have the knowledge required, hire a reputable marine surveyor—but hire him to help and advise you. While the survey is being done have him teach you what you'll need to know about the ship's hull, rig, and machinery. The surveyor you hire should have firsthand knowledge of deep-water cruising and be familiar with your yacht's type of construction. To locate a good surveyor check with respected boat builders and repair yards, other yacht owners, and perhaps banks that do marine financing. A proper survey will take at least a full day, probably more. Prepare for it: The boat must be hauled and scrubbed and every locker in her must be open and empty.

The following are some important points to consider during your survey of the hull:

For *fiberglass hulls* consider the overall appearance of the gel coat first. Aside from giving the hull a uniform, slick, attractive finish, the gel coat acts as a moisture barrier to keep water out of the laminates. Look for signs of impact damage and *crazing* (small radial cracks) particularly at the leading edge of the bow (the cutwater), the boot top areas, the keel, and the garboards. Look for *air bubbles,* which can form behind the gel coat in flat areas. If your boat is hard chined, check particularly for air bubbles right at the chine. Check the entire bottom for blisters and small craters, which look like blisters with the skin pulled off (which is what they are). Be particularly careful to check the bottom of the keel for grounding damage. All breaks in the gel coat should be repaired. And while she's out, paint the bottom and boot top and wax the topsides.

An internal hull inspection will consist primarily of a close inspection of the longitudinal stringers often used in the bilge and where large flat areas are stiffened against flexing. These stringers are usually preformed fiberglass shapes that are glassed directly to the inside surface of the hull skin. Check the bond to make sure they haven't pulled loose and at the same time make sure that no structural failures in the stringers themselves have occurred. Carry this inspection right up into the chain locker. Flake the chain out onto a canvas placed on the foredeck.

To do a thorough check means you will have the boat pretty well torn up inside. That's fine, because it'll give you the opportunity to check the chain plate attachments as well as the joint between deck and hull. Also, when your inspection is complete, it's a perfect time to scrub the bilge.

For *wooden hulls* look at the paint system first. This coating protects the hull materials from deteriorating and should be kept in good shape. Check the hood ends of the planking where they enter into the rabbets at bow and stern, and all planking butts. There should be no splits, particularly at fasteners. Check out fasteners: The plugs covering them should be tight and flush with the planking. If they protrude a bit or show traces of rust around them, they should be chipped out and the fasteners themselves examined for deterioration. They may have to be reset, dried out, and represerved under the plug—or replaced.

Seams should be smooth and tight. But it is very hard to maintain an unbroken paint surface at the seams of a carvel-planked boat—much easier with a strip-planked boat. All boats *work*. Carvel-planked wooden boats, particularly the larger, heavier, older ones, are notorious for cracking their paint at the seams. *Starbound* does it constantly, particularly amidship. As long as the seam itself is tight and smooth, we don't worry too much about it. We've been tending toward the elastomeric seam compounds more and more. Their rubberlike consistency has enough give to keep the seams tight despite the working.

Take a hard look at the areas around the garboard seams, the rudder shaft, and any scarf joints in the keel timber and stem. Check for rot by tapping with a small hammer—lightly. If the wood

Maintenance never ends. Nina works on bulwark.

is bad, it will sound dead: a "thump" instead of the "thock" of healthy wood. Verification of wood rot can be made using a knife. If the blade can be inserted into the wood easily *across the grain*, the wood has deteriorated.

Check to make sure there is no gap between the ballast keel, be it lead or iron, and the keel timber—nor should there be any sign of working between them. These usually indicate a problem with the keel bolts and will call for tightening or even replacing them.

Checking the hull from the inside is much tougher and more important than the outside check. Generally more problems can be found when crawling around in the bilge than are evidenced by the outside check.

Using the hammer-and-knife technique, check the stem, keel, deadwood, shaft log, horn timber, frames, knees, and floors. Inspect all the fastenings holding these pieces together. If they're loose, tighten them. If they're rusted, clean and preserve them. If they're deteriorated badly, replace them.

Once again, while you're at it, check the clamp and shelf at the junction of hull and deck, the chain plates and their fastenings, and all of the structure in the chain locker and lazaret. Then scrub the bilge, let it dry well, and treat the entire interior surface of the hull with Woodlife or some other good wood perservative/rot spore killer. We found that a pump-type rose sprayer, with the nozzle set to project a stream, rather than a mist, works very well for this job. But ventilate well and wear protective gear for your skin and eyes as well as a breathing mask. In general anything that will kill rot is also poisonous to people.

When checking out a *steel hull* there are two problems to be concerned with—galvanic corrosion and chemical corrosion, more commonly called *electrolysis* and *rust*.

Rust is the surface oxidation of steel. This "iron" oxide is porous and, contrary to popular belief, after the first rust layer is formed, the rust does not stop; it keeps on going, although it is slowed down as less oxygen reaches the parent metal. The only way to protect against rust is to employ conscientious preventive maintenance: Keep an *intact* protective barrier over the parent metal.

This is not as easy as it sounds—unless you know exactly what is on the hull of your steel boat. Materials compatible with the existing system should be used. If you did not put the existing protective barrier on the boat yourself, it will be worth your trouble to find out exactly what it is so that you can match it.

While in Australia we watched some of the procedures involved in renewing the paint system on a steel yacht. The hull was taken down to bright metal by sand blasting and a new barrier built up from scratch, starting with a molten zinc spray job put on with a special gun. This was followed by special primers and many coats of plastic paint.

The bottom antifouling job interested us. Virtually all metal boat owners have gone to the organo-tin bottom paints, the active ingredient usually being tributyltinoxide—called TBTO. They have done this because copper-based bottom paints react galvanically with the parent metal, so several barrier coats of an insulating paint are necessary before the antifouling layer can be put on. Barrier coats are still necessary under TBTO paints, but only one or two coats in lieu of the six or seven used under copper-based paints.

Aluminum hulls do not suffer from oxidation as steel hulls do—at least not since the advent of the new aluminum alloys, particularly the 5000 series and the 6000 series. These alloys are strong, ductile, and very corrosion resistant in sea water. Despite this fact nearly all owners of aluminum boats paint their topsides because they look better than with the raw aluminum surface. Of course, bottom paint is a must for *any* boat to prevent marine growth. A TBTO bottom paint should be used for the same reason it is used for steel boats: the prevention of galvanic corrosion. Copper bottom paint on an aluminum hull can cause even worse problems than it does on a steel hull because aluminum is more galvanically active than steel. Even if many barrier coats are used, just one scratch through to the parent metal produces a nice little battery, with the sea water acting as the electrolyte as the aluminum starts "giving" metal particles to the copper in the paint.

With any metal boat hulls, make sure the paint system is intact,

The propeller tip exhibits cavitation corrosion. Note the "flake" electrolytic corrosion on the shaft.

both topsides and bottom. Look for rust (steel boats) and grayish white aluminum oxide (aluminum boats). Check all joints and crevices especially carefully.

Metals dissimilar to the hull *must* be insulated from the hull material. Look at the ballast keel and its fastenings, the through-hull fittings, the propeller and rudder shaft bearings, the chain plate attachments. These are choice spots for electrolytic corrosion to occur.

The interior of a metal boat can be very difficult to survey. If the hull skin inside has been foamed or otherwise treated to prevent "drumming" and condensation, it is usually impossible to check trouble spots without stripping away parts of the treatment. And it is the rule rather than the exception for a cruising metal boat to be so treated. All I can recommend is to try and get the material peeled off at the critical spots and put it back when you are satisfied with your inspection. Once again, what you will be looking for are signs of corrosion—electrolytic and otherwise.

Ferro-cement hulls can be surveyed in much the same way as the hulls just discussed as far as through-hull penetrations are concerned. Look for signs of corrosion that might indicate that hull fittings are in contact with a part of the reinforcing steel. If the ballast keel is bolted on, make sure it is tight. And again, the paint system should be intact.

We've seen a few ferro-cement boats on which the paint, both above and below the waterline, was peeling off in sheets. This is generally caused by improper preparation of the raw surface or, in at least one case, by using a finish paint that was not compatible with the undercoat. The protective coating of any boat must be a system with full compatibility between all the elements.

The interior survey of a ferro-cement hull usually calls for tearing half the joiner work down because of the propensity of the builders to cover up the "rock" with wood ceiling and paneling. But again, any boat should have easy access to all through-hull fittings as well as the chainplate attachment points. Also, all of the interior structure will be attached to metal clips, which are welded to the reinforcing system prior to the hull being plastered. These clips, especially any below the waterline, should be checked for corrosion.

ELECTROLYSIS AND CORROSION

This subject is too vast to cover here in complete detail, so with the permission of the author, Jerry Kirschenbaum, and the publisher, I have excerpted some of the primary points from the three-part article "Electrolysis and Corrosion" published in the July, September, and November, 1978 issues of *Woodenboat* Magazine, P.O. Box 78, Brooklin, Maine 04616.

My recommendation is to obtain a copy of the article and study it. It is relatively technical but quite comprehensive.

Electrolytic corrosion is a boat's social disease.

There are many types of corrosion—electrolytic and otherwise. There's the classic *galvanic corrosion* (usually called electrolysis); *stray-current corrosion; crevice corrosion* caused by oxygen imbalance in a metal corner; *cavitation erosion corrosion* at the stern; *stress corrosion* brought on by excessive vibration; *alloy intergranular attack*, or *dezincification*, or *impingement attack*, or *graphization*.

Because the most serious and common types of electrochemical corrosion in boats are the first two mentioned, galvanic and stray-current corrosion, I have primarily chosen excerpts dealing with these.

. . . the amount of energy in a metal and the tendency of that metal to give up that energy is called *potential* (usually measured in volts at a given temperature). The actual giving up of that energy and the decay from a metal back to an ore is called *corrosion*.

If you arrange metals according to their potential for energy release, a simple table can be created—with those metals that easily give up energy at one end and those that do not at the other. This table is the Electromotive Series (which corresponds closely to what we call the Galvanic Series) (see Table 8-1).

The metals which let energy flow out easily (and metal particles with it) are called *anodic* or *less noble*. These are metals like zinc (Zn) and magnesium (Mg) and are termed *active*. The metals which do not give up energy easily but tend to receive energy flow are called *cathodic* or *more noble;* these are termed *passive*. (As in all things, there are Givers and the Takers.)

Thus, the whole measure of whether a metal will give up energy in favor of another is determined by the *relative difference and position in their potentials* for energy release. The greater the difference, the more intense the corrosion process. A quick glance at the Galvanic Table can establish these relationships for you.

Remember this key concept: a difference in potentials will cause electric current to move (through sea water) from anodic to cathodic surfaces.

So, in order to have galvanic corrosion you need four things:

1. *Two metal areas* with significantly *different potentials* for energy release.
2. The metal areas have to be in *electrical contact* with each other.
3. Both metal areas must be immersed in a solution that will conduct current (an electrolyte, usually sea water).
4. And, finally, there must be a supply of oxygen.

Now, to the most serious and the most common kind of corrosion: *stray-current corrosion.*

Today, most well-built boats are constructed with considerable care for the materials used. And, usually, one starts out with a fairly corrosion-resistant vessel. However, once she rolls down the ways, experiences the stresses of sailing or

TABLE 8-1

The Galvanic Series

Recommended Maximum Allowable Potential Difference
Exposed Position — 0.2V
Interior Position — 0.25V

Givers
Anodic End
Least Noble

Potential (volts)	Metal
1.73	Magnesium (Mn)
1.58	Magnesium — 9% Aluminum (Al), 1% Mn, 1.5% Zinc
	Aluminum Anode Alloy
1.14	Galvanized Iron (hot dipped)
1.13	Zinc Plating (electro-plated)
1.12	Cadmium (Cd) Zinc solder
1.09	Zinc Based Alloy
1.05	Zinc (Zn)
	Aluminum Rivet Alloy
	Beryllium
1.02	Aluminum — 4% Zinc
0.96	Aluminum — 1% Zinc
0.91	Aluminum Alloy (12.5% Zinc, 2.5% Copper, 0.8% Iron, 0.7% Silicon
0.86	Cadmium Plated Steel (0.001 in)
0.85	Aluminum
0.79	Steel, non-stainless — (0.5% Mn, 0.20% Si, 0.12% C)
0.78	Grey Cast Iron
0.74	Tinned Steel, (hot-dipped)
0.73	Forged Aluminum Alloys
0.61	Mild Steel (at 75.2 deg. F)
0.61	Chromium plate on Nickel on Steel (Ni 0.0005 in)
0.56	Tinman's Solder
0.55	Tin, electro-plated on Steel
	Some "Active" Stainless Steels (Passive stainless steels can go "Active" under certain conditions. And when they do, they can be Anodic. Hence, they would fall here on the series.)

Active Zone

Metal (Electron) Flow ↓

Potential	Metal
0.55	Lead (Pb)
0.53	Chromium Plate on Nickel on Steel (Cr 0.005 in)
0.50	Silver Lead Solder
0.50	Tin
	Wrought Iron
0.47	Cast Iron Alloy (at 57.2 deg. F)
0.45	Steel, Stainless (12% Chromium)
	Manganese Bronze
	Naval Brass (60% Copper — 39% Zinc)
	Yellow Brass
0.36	Admiralty Brass
0.35	Steel, Stainless, high Chrome
0.33	Brass (60/40)
0.31	Gun Metal
0.29	Copper/Nickel/Iron (at 64.4 deg. F)
0.26	Silicon (Si)
0.26	Cupro-Nickel
	Silicon Bronze (containing Nickel, Zinc, Copper & Silicone)
0.25	Brass (70/30)
0.22	Copper (Cu)
0.14	Nickel (Ni)
	Nickel, Passive (containing Iron, Chrome & Stainless Steel)
0.11	Monel Alloy (at 71.6 deg. F)
0.10	Titanium (at 80.6 deg. F)
0.08	Tin Bronze (5% Sn)
0.08	Silver
+ 0.25	Graphite (at 75.2 deg. F)
+ 0.26	Platinum (at 65.4 deg. F)
	Gold

Passive Zone

Takers
Cathodic End
Most Noble

Notes:
All Temperatures are at approximately 77 deg. F unless otherwise noted. All potentials are negative (unless noted). Potentials are shown only to illustrate relative position of materials in the series.

powering through heavy seas, lives with bad marina wiring, sloppy housekeeping, and new (and poor) installations of equipment, then things get moving . . . and when they move, you have a real monster aboard!

We've discussed galvanic corrosion in terms of an electrical driving force of a few volts created by a difference in potential between two metals in contact. Imagine what this galvanic couple would be like if you dropped 12, 24, 32, or 110 volts into the equation. You can make up for a lot of distance on the galvanic scale by raising the input voltage. No more fractions of a volt. Now, two metals, previously not too far apart on the scale, can really take off when one of them receives a truly powerful charge.

You do not even need different metals. Just send the current in and it will take off through the metal, carrying electron particles with it on the way to ground (in the water). Where do these powerful stray currents come from? A variety of places. Consider these:

- Crossed grounds on equipment or new installations.
- Leaks in the circuits causing voltage drops.
- Leakage from loose or broken terminal connections.
- Frayed or broken wires.
- Shore power connections, improperly grounded, isolated, or shorted.
- Battery chargers not rated or protected for marine use.
- Polarity warning devices not sufficiently protected.
- Faults to ground in boat wiring.
- The boat moored alongside—or even elsewhere in the boatyard or marina, but using the same shore circuit you are on.
- The boatyard or marina's wiring or protection devices.

Some of these sources are obvious. Others are subtle. What is not subtle is what these stray currents can do, and how fast they do it.

Damage from galvanic corrosion and almost all of the other

types is usually measured in months or years. Damage from stray-current corrosion can be measured in days or hours. . . .

And here are some of Mr. Kirschenbaum's general solutions to the problems of galvanic and stray-current corrosion. His articles, of course, contain much more detailed information.

The entire problem of galvanic corrosion could be solved if you could guarantee absolutely that there were no dissimilar metals either on board or close by. And that's virtually impossible. Even if you fastened completely with bronze, used bronze thru-hull fittings throughout, a bronze prop, and a bronze shaft, the minute you put the boat's engine or pumps aboard you will have lost the battle. Engines are steel. Parts of them (big chunks, too) are alloys: aluminum, iron, chrome, mild steel, and some bronze.

The real answer is to avoid dissimilar metals and contact between them as much as you can, and when you have reduced the problem to a minimum, plan on dealing effectively with what's left.

Here is an absolutely key concept: Since you must assume that however hard you try you are going to have some amount of dissimilar metal potentials aboard, *use the galvanic corrosion and electrolytic process to work for you.** Electrically tie together all the metals you want to save and create one big potential number. Then, aim this multi-metal collection at some poor hapless metal which is at the less noble end of the galvanic scale—a metal you will not mind losing: A Sacrificial Anode.

That is called *bonding* your boat.

Just remember that it will be the metal on the end of the galvanic chain that will be zapped. So, if your zinc anode finally wastes away and you don't replace it, and the next noble

*Italics mine.

A new heat exchanger for the main engine. Note the provision for a zinc pencil missing from the old exchanger (top).

metal piece, galvanically speaking, is the prop or the rudder pintles, then you will have a new sacrificial anode (with you making a very real sacrifice).

So *bonding* is the first and primary method that should be used to protect your boat. The second method that may be used is that of *impressed current:*

You can use the power from your boat's batteries to pass a current through special, chemically inert anodes. This current is constantly metered by a controller device, and kept in balance by a reference electrode. In this way, a proper polarity relationship can be maintained so that the vital metal parts of the boat do not give up particles.

By far, pleasure craft use bonding and sacrificial anodes for protection, * leaving the impressed current systems to the larger vessels with generating systems aboard.

There are five nuts and bolts reasons to bond your boat:

• To collect all the various metal potentials into one *boat potential* and make a final connection to a less noble, sacrificial anode.

• To create a low-resistance path to carry off any *stray current* or potentials on the surface of metals or equipment, thus helping to prevent highly dangerous electro-chemical corrosion.

• To provide a back-up to the boat's grounding system and prevent *shock hazard.* This also backs up the system for ground faults.

• To bond the boat for *lightning protection.*

• To reduce *electronic interference* aboard.

Many details of the article, particularly the well-illustrated method for planning and implementing a bonding system for a boat, are outside the scope of our text. But the article has given me

*Italics mine.

so much food for thought that I intend to start analyzing the sum total of my own vessel's systems. While we do not seem to have any gross problems with electrolytic corrosion, I can easily think of a few questionable areas, especially when I consider the 12-volt starting system, the 32-volt ship's service system, and the 115-volt shore/generator system that we have aboard. I now think our lack of any real problems of the kind described has been due to good original construction and good luck with consequent installations of the various gear aboard.

Crevice-related corrosion is the third most serious and prevailing of the types of corrosion found on boats. Briefly, what happens is that the surfaces within a crevice of a metal gets less oxygen than the outer surfaces, which causes the interior surface to go anodic and give electrons to the outer surface. So the metal essentially feeds on itself. Crevice corrosion can occur under heads of fasteners, under struts and chainplates, and—dangerously—in the interior of end fittings of standing rigging, particularly the lower ends. Since salt deposits grossly accelerate crevice corrosion, flushing these fittings with fresh water will help.

9

The Vessel; Deck, Deckhouse, and Rig

The deck of a yacht is not a "lid" plunked down on a hull just to keep the wave tops and rain on the outside. A deck is the top flange of the hull girder and it is a prime component of the basic structural system.

The cabin, or deckhouse, is actually a part of the deck proper in some yachts. In most yachts the main deck is stoutly framed out with beams and carlins around the perimeter of the cabin, allowing the transition of diaphragm stresses in the deck. The cabin has its own deck or house-top, which also receives its share of stress.

These stresses are not uniform, nor of one kind: There are compressive, tensile, and even torsional stresses involved, and their magnitudes change constantly as the ship is subjected to wind and wave forces. There are large local loads taken by the foredeck when a ship is being driven to weather—and even larger loads imposed during a knockdown or broach. The arrangement and strength of the total deck structure must combine to withstand these stresses, and not on a short-term basis—but for the life of the ship.

Stress cracks from poor fiberglass construction show around a winch pedestal and on the side of a deckhouse where it joins the main deck.

Here is a generalized list of the functions of that aforementioned "lid":

•Performs as the upper flange of the structural hull girder as mentioned above.

•Absorbs the lateral deflection of the mast(s) at the partners.

•Acts as the *base* for the primary propulsion system when under sail. (Remember, most sheets lead to winches bolted through the decks, which means that in effect the vessel is being pulled along by her decks!)

•Houses the control center (the cockpit), and all the associated gear: tracks, winches, padeyes, cleats, steering pedestal, engine controls, and a host of additional stuff.

•Forms the foundation for ground-tackle machinery and provides the working platform for handling ground tackle and the stowage for anchors.

•Acts as a stowage area for dinghy, raft, propane, other fuel, extra water, life rings, boat hooks, and everything else that won't fit below.

•Performs as the support and framing elements for those devices allowing the passage of crew, air and light, fuel and water: hatches, portlights, doghouses, ventilators, Charley Nobles, and filler plates.

•Functions as a primary living area/backyard/work area/sundeck; the majority of sea time and port time is spent topside. And so there are all those devices to keep the crew aboard: lifelines, taffrails, toerails, and handrails—all supported by the deck.

•Should not "sweat" or "drum" below. The crew circulation paths should not be too slippery or too rough. It should be washable. Additional fittings should be relatively easy to attach and still be strong enough for their purpose.

•*Must be watertight*—even in a storm at sea.

Isn't it surprising to review a list like the foregoing and realize what a deck must really do? It still surprises me—I suppose be-

A sturdy companionway hatch on a Rafiki 37. Note the high coaming.

cause a deck as such is generally taken for granted. Bear in mind that the functions listed are only general ones—there are many more.

To efficiently act as an integral part of the ship's structure, the deck must be attached to the hull in a fashion which makes it so. Fiberglass hulls are particularly notorious for having a weak *hull/ deck joints*. It is common practice for production builders of fiberglass boats to slop a little resin or other sealer along the joint, sock on the lid, and screw in a bunch of mechanical fasteners around the perimeter. Then they cover the joint with an extruded piece of aluminum laughingly called a "rubrail" and snap a piece of extruded rubber into the middle of the aluminum.

Look for the sign of a reputable builder: He will lay up several layers of fiberglass and resin across the joint on the inside of the hull and actually form a *clamp and shelf* longitudinal strength member at the sheer. This should bring the joint up to more than the strength of either the hull or the deck. Usually, mechanical fasteners are also used, prior to the glassing work. The joint on the outside should be completely sealed with no passage for water allowed.

The hull/deck joint of ships constructed of steel, aluminum, wood, or ferro-cement are inherently better made. Wooden vessels always have a solid shelf and clamp, with the frame heads and deck beams tied into them with heavy bolts. Metal hulls have longitudinal angles, performing the same shelf-and-clamp function, irrevocably welded into place. If the deck beams of a metal ship are of wood they are through-bolted to the metal shelf.

I've seen just one ferro-cement boat with a weak hull/deck joint: Small clips were welded to the reinforcing steel at intervals and wood deck beams were bolted to these. Most well built ferro-cement boats with wood decks will have a steel angle that acts as a longitudinal shelf and clamp running the full length of the sheer. This angle is welded to all the primary reinforcing steel prior to plastering. Then the wood deck beams are through-bolted to the shelf. If the deck is also ferro-cement (rather unusual because of the weight involved as well as the difficulty of attaching the nu-

FIG. 9-1 ~ SOME STURDY HULL-DECK SECTIONS
NOT TO SCALE

TEAK RAIL CAP

TEAK BULWARK CAPS

FILLER

TEAK TOE-RAIL OVER JOIN

BONDING LAMINATIONS

HALF OVAL ON OAK RUB-STRIP

LAMINATIONS OVER BOND

OAK RUB-STRIP OVER JOIN

FIBERGLASS SECTIONS

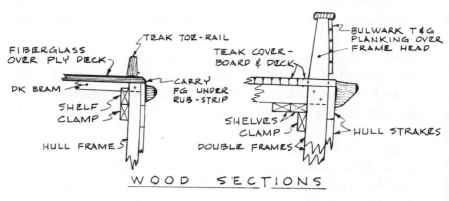

FIBERGLASS OVER PLY DECK

TEAK TOE-RAIL

TEAK COVER-BOARD & DECK

BULWARK T&G PLANKING OVER FRAME HEAD

DK BEAM

CARRY FG UNDER RUB-STRIP

SHELF CLAMP

SHELVES CLAMP

HULL STRAKES

HULL FRAME

DOUBLE FRAMES

WOOD SECTIONS

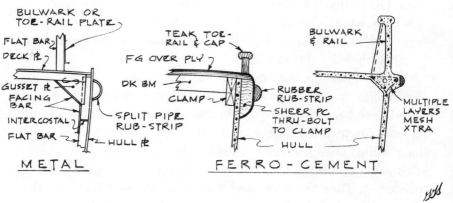

BULWARK OR TOE-RAIL PLATE

FLAT BAR

DECK PL

TEAK TOE-RAIL & CAP

BULWARK & RAIL

FG OVER PLY

GUSSET PL FACING BAR

DK BM

CLAMP

RUBBER RUB-STRIP

MULTIPLE LAYERS MESH XTRA

INTERCOSTAL

FLAT BAR

SPLIT PIPE RUB-STRIP

HULL PL

SHEER PC THRU-BOLT TO CLAMP

HULL

METAL   FERRO-CEMENT

Fig. 9-1 Some sturdy hull-deck connections (not to scale).

merous fittings required), then the clamp and shelf are formed as part of the reinforcing and become a very strong part of the monocoque construction.

A few words about *rubstrips, rubbing-strakes, rubrails, guard-strakes,* or whatever you care to call them. They must be strong enough, deep enough, and wide enough to transmit the energy of an impact force from the point of impact through enough of the ship's integral structure to absorb the energy without structural damage. This means the *guardrail,* as we on *Starbound* call hers, has to be a hefty, tough piece of structure fastened directly or indirectly to the ship's framing structure. Then when you goof up a docking and your ship swings her whole weight into a piling, the only thing that'll be hurt will be your pride.

The part of the rail intended for impact should be metal. *Starbound* has a 6-inch wide by 8-inch deep white oak guardrail, nearly flat on top for footing and tapered from the hull out at the bottom to a 2½-inch bearing area that is capped with a 1½-inch wide rubstrip of half-oval bronze. The rail is bolted right through her hull and frame heads, and it has protected her hull for 30 years. It has saved us from expensive grief countless times. We can tie up to creosoted pilings and just let her ride on them. A bit of diesel oil on a rag cleans the creosote off the bronze. I'm placing a lot of stress on the importance of a good guardrail because of the number of yachts I've seen with damaged topsides for lack of adequate protection in this area. Take a hard critical look at yours!

The term *mast partners* denotes that heavily built-up structural area of the deck immediately surrounding the mast. The partners act to distribute the lateral forces exerted by the mast. The mast should be carefully fit to the partners. This is usually accomplished by *mast wedges.* The fit of the wedges is critical: They should be just snug between mast and partners and should never have to be driven or otherwise forced into place.

Carefully examine all fittings bolted through your decks for signs of inadequacy, wear, and deterioration. Make certain that tracks, padeyes and winch bases are really through-bolted. If your decks are fiberglass, examine the areas subject to the most stress for signs

Forward hatch on the same Rafikiis, with a heavy plexiglass light.

of cracking and crazing. The bases of the sheet-winch pedestals, anchor windlass, and mooring cleats and chocks are particularly subjected to heavy stresses. And all fittings should be *bedded* to prevent leakage. If your decks are metal, remember that all fittings of a dissimilar metal should be insulated from the deck.

The *cockpit* should be comfortable but not too large. It is advantageous for the helmsman to have a full field of vision while comfortably seated. He should also be able to brace himself on the opposite seat. Engine controls must be instantly accessible. The instrument panel must be visible from the helmsman's position and should have a watertight cover over it. Cockpit and cockpit drains and their relative size have always been a subject for contention. A large, comfortable cockpit is very desirable for deep-water cruising. However, a deep-water boat is bound, sooner or later, to have her cockpit flooded. If the weight of water is such that the cockpit sole sinks below the waterline level, then the drains won't work. This is an unusual circumstance but has happened to boats with low freeboard aft.

A lot of criteria has been published about *cockpit size and drainage*. Racing regulations state the cockpit volume below the *lowest* coaming point should not exceed .06 × LWL × beam × freeboard aft, with the cockpit sole at least .02 × LOA above the waterline, and that the drains should be sized so that when the cockpit is filled with a volume of water equal to three-quarters up the footwell *plus* one-half the additional volume up to the lowest coaming, the cockpit will drain completely in under three minutes!

Frankly I think three minutes is too long. I'd like to see water gone almost instantly—but certainly in less than one minute. However, this is limited by the size of the drains you're able to install. The best installation I've seen is in a Hinckley 41 belonging to a friend. The boat has four 3-inch drains, one in each corner of the sole. They *crossdrain* to the opposite side of the hull under the cockpit with almost straight sections of heavy exhaust-type hose that are fitted to through-hull sea cocks. The interior dimensions of the hose and sea cocks are 2 inches. The 3-inch diameter drains are

Starbound's *main companionway hatch. The cover and door are made for heavy weather.*

fitted with only tic-tac-toe grates to minimize flow resistance. The cockpit, filled with water to seat level, drains in less than one minute. An installation like this is costly—and worth it.

The most common faults I've seen with cockpit drains are: (1) They are too small; (2) there are not enough of them; (3) the drain hose size is mismatched to the grate size; and (4) the grates are constricting.

Stowage on deck must be provided for those items too bulky to stow below or in cockpit lockers. These stowages should incorporate chocks and lashings of a suitable size to withstand the force of a green sea.

A *self-inflating life raft* and its emergency equipment should be stowed in the usual cannister on deck.

A *rigid dinghy* should be stowed upside down, preferably under the main boom. Smaller boats sometime stow them on the foredeck over the hatch, with the dinghy transom up against the mast, but they do get in the way there. *Inflatable dinghies* are best kept inflated and stowed the same way if the room is available. Small cruisers with limited deck area usually deflate them and stow them below for long passages.

Whisker poles, spinnaker poles, reaching struts, and *boat hooks* should be fitted to chocks with housed ends to prevent their being snagged by the sheets.

The *flanges* of portlights should be bedded and bolted to the house. If they are larger than two square feet, they should have storm covers: ½-inch tempered plexiglass works well for this.

Many production boat builders today use a snap-in type of "window" that looks like it belongs on a bus. A good sea will snap them right into the cabin. The U. S. Navy designs to 1000 lbs per square foot for "wave slap," with good reason.

Ventilators should have a 6-inch diameter cowl or bigger. Their deck openings, whether in a Dorade-box or not, should have deck plates provided. You'll hardly ever use them, but they are inexpensive insurance.

All *hatches* must be very sturdy. Sliding companionway hatches must have an interlocking system to prevent the possibility of their being carried away. We have seen this happen more than once—on other people's boats—and have heard of similar incidents many times. A solid overcover protecting part of the sides and forward end is a good design being used on many fiberglass hatches.

Hinged hatches must have a gasket all around and a strong method of securing that will actually compress the gasket. Fabric covers or dodgers will give added protection. A dodger over the main companionway hatch that will allow the hatch to be opened or to remain open when it is raining is worth having, especially in the tropics.

Some thoughts about *awnings:* There are few pieces of cruising gear that are so cost effective. A full *harbor awning*, one you can walk under, is very desirable. But one over the cockpit area is damn near mandatory. It protects the crew against the direct sun as well as the rain. The cockpit awning should be large enough so that all seating positions are shaded and, hopefully, with full standing room under it—at least when on the cockpit sole. White Acrilan is my favorite awning material. It is sun and water resistant, and dries and folds easily. It seems to outlast cotton by four to one and nylon or Dacron by two to one. The white color reflects most of the heat and I would caution against the darker colors that are also available. We have heard from other yachties that Dacron awnings allow the sun to penetrate so much that they have been sunburned while sitting in their shade, but they're still better than none!

As much as we all love the sun, it can do more insidious damage to a boat *and* its crew than any other environmental factor. It deteriorates plastic, paint, varnish, glue, wood, and caulking. It is a principal enemy of sails and lines. And overexposure will *kill* people. As far as the boat and its gear is concerned, the less sun the better. And that also goes for the crew—to a large extent. The cruising sailor gets so much sun on his skin—even when he's working at protecting it—that to actually *try* to get more is just stupid. Deep-water people wear as little as possible because of the lack of laundry facilities, and for comfort in tropic heat and humidity. But a white T-shirt will save your back the worst of the sun—and long hair will save your ears and neck (if you dislike hats as much as I

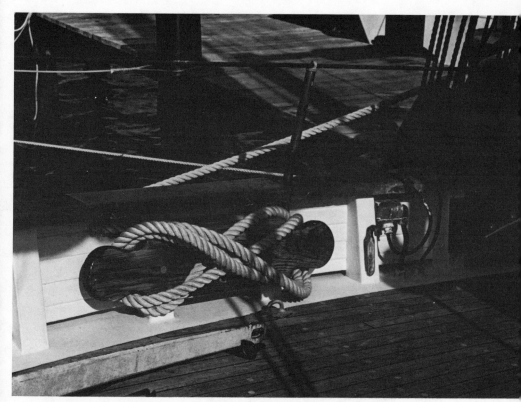

Starbound's *bulwark is a solid foundation for many components.*

*Aluminum mainmast on a Gulfstar 50. Note the whisker pole instal-
lation.*

do). So the cockpit awning is really necessary; it allows you to wear less and still be protected. If you need any more convincing, check with your local dermatologist about the prevalence of sun-caused skin cancer.

Make sure the deck has a form of *anti-skid* on all traffic and working areas. Good sized *toe rails, coamings,* and *bulwarks* are a necessity for deep-water cruising. They help keep the crew and the gear on board and they are good foundations for jib sheet, and vang tracks, and padeyes.

Pulpits and *stanchions,* provided with taut *double* lifelines, are needed around the deck perimeter. The stanchions should be through-bolted to the deck and toerail and be spaced not more than 6 feet on center. The upper lifeline should hit your leg at least 6 inches above the knee—about 24 inches above the deck as a minimum. It would be safer if they were 30 inches up. Aboard *Starbound,* every time we go offshore we put an extra safety line of ¾-inch nylon clear around the deck, from bowsprit–end right to the after davits. It's at chest level and has saved me from going overboard on two occasions, once at night in a gale.

The final item of the deck survey should be to *check for leaks.* A leaking deck is worse than a leaking hull because you have to deal with the water twice. First, you must get it out of your bunk, clothes, books, and electronics gear, because (face it) a deck leak never drips on the cabin sole. Second, you must pump the run-off out of the bilge (where it is rusting your canned goods with each roll of the boat). A leaking deck can do more to make life miserable aboard than almost anything. Even a storm at sea can be handled with a certain amount of equanimity if you can go below to a warm, dry cabin on occasion. Every penetration of the deck must be bedded and gasketed and booted and baffled and caulked and seamed—and maintained that way. There is always much more maintenance on the deck than there is on the hull—and that goes for fiberglass boats too!

Turn a high-pressure water hose on all those cracks and crevices and fittings while someone below checks it out. I dare you.

Aluminum spars depend solely on the standing rigging for lateral strength.

MASTS AND RIGGING

Spars on all cruising yachts used to be made of wood—sometimes solid pine but usually hollow spruce. Nowadays, most of them are aluminum alloy—including the booms.

Spar-section size, wood or metal, is based on estimated loads that are calculated using several factors—but primarily the stability of the hull, the distance between chainplates, and the fore triangle height. Appropriate factors of safety are cranked in and the right section is selected. But many cruising boats today are ex-racers and these boats may have cut down on the section of both spars and rigging to reduce weight and windage. Do some comparison studies of your rig against some successful cruising rigs. Most authors of cruising books include diagrams and photos of their rigs and discuss them to some extent. Perhaps you might want to add an additional lower shroud, or even replace the shrouds with heavier wire. If you have a ketch or schooner with the masts' support dependent upon one another, some thought might be given to staying them independently.

I find that the cruising fraternity in general is not in favor of *masts stepped on deck*—unless they are supported by heavy tabernacles explicitly for the purpose of lowering the rig for canal and bridge work. *Masts stepped on the keel* provide a more secure rig because of the additional lateral support at the deck. If a deck-supported mast loses even one piece of rigging, the mast is prone to collapse. We've seen this happen twice. One of those times the mast, made of hollow spruce, seemed to jump over the side of the boat, trailing rigging. On the second occasion the mast was aluminum. A lower shroud-fitting failed and the mast slowly folded just at the spreader and then fell over the side. Conversely, several times we've seen rigging fail on *masts stepped through the deck* (once on *Starbound*) with no serious consequences. One rigging failure, which occurred on a sloop with an aluminum mast, resulted in the mast having a surprisingly severe curve permanently set into it. The mast managed to resist folding completely and jury rigging got the sloop into port.

Wooden spars require more maintenance.

Standing rigging should all be 1 by 19 stainless, although there is nothing at all wrong with galvanized wire except the constant fight to keep the zinc coating intact. If it starts rusting, it is almost impossible to correct the condition. Most traditionalists simply replace it often. In the long run stainless rigging is much more cost effective.

Wire end fittings should be of a mechanical type, usually called *swageless terminals*, such as Norseman or Electroline. Their extra weight doesn't make any difference on a deep-water cruiser and while they are not as pretty as a *swaged terminal*, they can be made up on board and checked (via an inspection hole) to verify the installation.

Swaged terminals are installed on wire ends with a specialized machine, usually employing hydraulic force. Enormous pressure is involved to cold flow the metal of the fitting around the wire. The problem with these fittings is that, sooner or later, longitudinal cracks can appear in the stressed portion of the barrel and will lead to eventual failure. This does not occur 100 percent of the time, but it happens far too often for comfort—especially on a deep-water yacht. In fact I've noticed the condition more often on deep-water yachts than on those sailing around the bay. Perhaps this is because of the greater stresses imposed by deep-water sailing and certainly the salt air will propagate crack growth. The experts tell me that this cracking is initiated by intergranular and possibly pit corrosion of the stainless material, which is accelerated by the locked-in swaging stresses and helped along famously by a salt atmosphere.

To summarize the principal prejudices against swaged terminals: (1) their failure rate is too high; (2) they cannot be made up on board without the aid of heavy and expensive machinery; and (3) if they require replacement, the fitting must be cut off, leaving the wire too short for its job unless an extra toggle is inserted between the chainplate and the rigging screw (turnbuckle).

Make sure all *rigging screws* are secured against turning by the use of cotter pins, locking wires, or other locking devices. Then tape all protrusions to avoid damage to sails, line, and your own hide. If your rigging screws are the closed barrel-type, check for

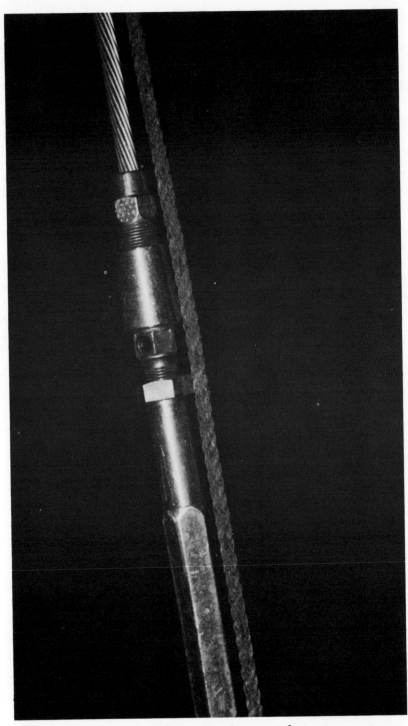

An example of a swageless terminal on standing wire rigging.

sufficient thread "bury" on one of them by unscrewing it all the way and measuring the length of total thread. The rest of the rigging screws can then be checked by simply measuring the unengaged thread length.

See that all lower ends of rigging are fitted with toggles. They ensure the angular freedom that provides the required exact alignment of rigging screw to wire-end fitting to wire.

Tang fittings on the mast must also be in exact alignment with the wire. Any misalignment between the standing rigging wire and its end fittings will promote fatigue failure through constant flexing.

Chainplates should be in very close alignment with the rigging attached to it. Toggles will take care of a slight misalignment but will not make up for a sloppy installation.

The *pins* that connect all of your rigging elements together should come in for a close inspection. If a pin is too small for the hole, it will not develop its full bearing strength. Most pins are oversized for their associated gear, incorporating a large factor of safety. This is good and as it should be, but if one of the rigging elements has too small a hole for the pin of the next element, the temptation to drill it out is strong. Resist that temptation unless you can assure yourself without doubt that you will not reduce the tensile strength of the fitting below that of the wire.

To sum it up: All of your rigging fittings should have a breaking strength equal to or greater than that of the wire. All fittings should be of the same material. All pins should be oversized (as most manufacturers make them) and match their holes.

Lubricate all of your rigging fittings while you're checking them. Anhydrous lanolin is recommended for the job. Pay particular attention to rigging screw threads and pin bearing surfaces.

While you're up in a bosun's chair checking the masthead fittings, take a look at the *masthead sheaves.* If the halyards are of wire, the sheave diameter at the center should be sixteen times the wire diameter; that is, a 4-inch diameter at the bottom of the "score" for ¼-inch wire—and a bigger diameter is better. And make sure the score is sized to the wire.

Lubricate the sheave pin and all the rigging pins. A worthwhile

suggestion: Take some close-up photos of your masthead gear. Measure the sizes of all parts and write them directly on the prints after they're developed. Put the photos in the rigging section of your planning book; then you'll always have a ready reference to the upper fittings without going aloft. We found that searching for parts in a foreign port was much simplified by showing the part or a photo of it—another point for Polaroid.

Many cruising sailors have switched over to *low-stretch rope* for all running rigging, including halyards. This is much nicer stuff to handle than rope/wire combinations or wire alone and is much more kind to winch drums—and masts.

It is very advantageous to have virtually all of the lines on board of one kind and size. Replacement is obviously simplified as well as more economical since you can buy a 600-foot reel of rope for much less per foot than you would otherwise pay. Stow the reel in the lazaret and use it for everything. And measure and record the length of all running rigging. It's easier than remeasuring each time you want to replace a piece.

A deep-water cruising yacht should carry enough rope to replace all running rigging *at least* twice. And if wire halyards are used, at least one spare set should be in the bosun's locker.

Everyone seems to agree that it is important to match rope characteristics to the job intended. That's a fine thought, as far as it goes, but *line* should also match the blocks through which it is reeved and should be large enough so the human hands can take a hard strain on it. (Rope is called rope until put in service and is then called *line*.)

The perfect line is very strong, abrasion resistant, will not age, is light in weight, and inexpensive. There is no such line, but the best of it comes close.

Synthetic fiber rope, particularly *nylon* and *polyester,* is so much better than the old natural fiber stuff (manila, hemp, cotton, jute, and sisal) that it is now used almost universally on boats.

Sunlight used to play hell with synthetic line seven or eight years ago, but the formulas have been changed so that now nylon and polyester line suffers very little degradation from ultraviolet light. There is a small amount: ¼-inch line will lose about 15 per-

Nina shows off Starbound's *new staysail.*

cent of its working strength with a one-year exposure to sunlight, but the larger the size, the less percentage of degradation. For all practical purposes and allowing for the factors of safety usually employed when sizing line for marine use, I think it is safe to say that before ultraviolet has much effect on it, a nylon or polyester line will be discarded because of abrasion or some other kind of wear.

Choosing the right kind of line is easy. If you want to resist some type of shock loading, choose a stretchy line like nylon. It's good for anchor rodes, topping lifts, dock lines, tow lines, and mooring pennants. If stretchiness is not a requirement, and perhaps a liability, then use polyester rope; halyards and sheets, outhauls, and downhauls should be of polyester.

There are a few other synthetics worth discussing. *Polypropylene line* will float, which makes it sound good for dock lines and tow lines—in fact water skiers use it almost exclusively. However, polypropylene line has no resistance to sunlight unless it is black in color. Lampblack is added for this purpose and stops the penetration of ultraviolet rays. We use black polypropylene on *Starbound* for our shroud lanyards, bowsprit basket, dinghy painters, and danbuoy line to the life ring. Every bit of brightly colored polypropylene line we've tried to use has turned to straw in less than one year. Only the black stuff works out—and then only in certain applications.

There are basically three kinds of rope construction: laid, braided, and plaited. *Laid line* is almost always three-strand nowadays, four-strand being outmoded. *Braided rope* can be constructed in several ways but most common is the two-part double braid: a braided core covered with a braided sleeve. *Plaited rope* is of eight-strand construction, four double strands woven as in a four-strand sennit; Columbian's Intrepid line uses this type of construction.

Laid rope is a rotating type: Under strain it will actually tend to unwind and when quickly released can hockle. But it is very easy to splice and is less expensive than braided or plaited line, and easier to find.

Braided and plaited ropes are *nonrotating,* a highly desirable characteristic for tackles and anchor rodes. They are perhaps 15

Black poly-pro rope is used for lanyards aboard Starbound.

percent stronger than laid rope and stretch less. Both types render easily through blocks and both types resist tangling and hockling. They can be dumped in a pile and will still pay out easily. However, braided rope is really tedious to splice and special fids are necessary. Also, braided rope cannot be coiled—it must be made up in a flaked (figure 8) pattern. On the other hand plaited rope splices easily and coils well (a factor of its pliability) despite its nonrotating characteristic.

A cautionary note about double-braided rope, the stuff made of a braided core and braided cover: Eye splices in this line made in accordance with the manufacturer's older instructions have the core cut out at a position that leaves a portion near the throat of the eye, with only the cover for strength. If a disproportionate loading occurs in the two legs of the eye splice, the leg that has only the cover for strength will break at half the line's rated breaking strength. Such circumstances can occur when, for instance, a wet eye splice of a mooring line is passed over a rough and rusty bollard. A broken synthetic line snaps back in a whipping circular motion at a speed of 700 feet per second; a *lethal situation*. A new method of splicing double-braided line has been developed, but how much it will help to alleviate the reduction in breaking strength is not yet known. If you insist on using double-braided line, splice it according to the new instruction that allows for some of the core to be tucked down into the standing part of the line. Or, use a bowline instead of a splice, remembering that a bowline in dry nylon line will reduce its breaking strength by 38 percent.

We've used all kinds of rope aboard *Starbound* over the past thirteen years. Today practically every line aboard is eight-strand plait, in nylon or polyester as the application requires.

A final few words about rope: A man can exert, with just his two hands, a pulling force of about 100 pounds on a 1-inch diameter line. The amount he can pull drops off very quickly with smaller-sized lines because the surface area in contact with the hands becomes so small. I'm sure everyone has tried to pull hard on a small-sized line. Aboard *Starbound* the smallest line I have to really throw my weight into is ⅝-inch diameter. I can get a good grip on

Dinghy stowage on a cruising ketch.

Boat maintenance never ceases. Ernie works on Starbound's *bulwark.*

it. There are a few pieces of ½-inch line, which are downright un-comfortable to strain on even when my hands are calloused.

I recommend that you cast a critical look at all line aboard. Haul hard on some of the sheets and halyards; then imagine doing it 15 times each hour in a rough sea with everything soaking wet. Per-haps you'll want to change sizes to bigger stuff.

In any case, if your lines have been in use a few seasons—or perhaps you don't know just how long they have been aboard—renew them before leaving. It is inexpensive insurance when com-pared against the possible consequences of a halyard or sheet giv-ing way when under strain.

SAILS

Starbound carries 10-ounce Dacron *fore and aft sails* with triple-stitched 18-inch panels. They are red-brown (tanbark) in color be-cause they are easier on the eyes at sea than if they were white, they don't show stains, the dark color tends to resist ultraviolet degradation, they look traditional on my very traditional ship, and I like them. I keep them well covered when in port.

Her *square sail* and *raffee* are 8-ounce white fabric, an old nylon formula. They were aboard when we bought her and they now need replacing. We carry a spare white 8-ounce *mainsail* and two spare older *jibs* that are still serviceable. Her *storm sails* are 12-ounce red brown Dacron: a tiny *jib* and *storm trysail*, both roped all around.

The best advice I can give regarding cruising sails is: Build them tough, triple-stitch all seams, sew and line all cringles, use plenty of patches and leather chafing gear, and the toughest hanks and slides available.

10

Machinery Above and Below Decks

ABOVE DECKS

Two pieces of basic topside machinery bear discussing: the anchor windlass and wind vane steering.

An *anchor windlass* or *capstan* is a real necessity for deep-water cruising. Your primary anchor rode should be all chain and hauling chain by hand is out of the question, though it can be done at the expense of your hands and back. The windlass should have a *wildcat* (sometimes called a *gypsy*) for chain and a smooth *drum* for rope. It is best if both wildcat and drum can be activated independently. The windlass should be able to operate manually, even if its normal mode is electric or hydraulic. It should not be located right in the eyes of the ship but aft a bit (two or three feet), which will allow a chain stopper installation, give some leeway for examination of the chain as it comes aboard, and help with the pitching movement of your ship (heavy weight on the ends of a yacht increases its tendency to pitch).

Make sure the wildcat is provided with a *chain stripper:* a heavy piece of metal mounted under the wildcat that kicks the chain links out of the recesses of the wildcat and allows the chain to drop fairly into the chain locker.

Lastly, examine the foundation of the windlass, its bed and its fastenings. The deck structure must be very heavy in this area and constructed in such a way as to distribute the load into the remainder of the foredeck. (For more discussion of ground tackle, see the next chapter.)

A deep-water cruising yacht must have a form of *self-steering.* Hanging onto the helm for days on end is ridiculous when you can be reading, writing, playing cards, making love, or otherwise enjoying yourself. If you like to steer, fine. Take the wheel for a few hours, or minutes; then when the enjoyment palls, turn the helm back over to the automatic helmsman: the *wind vane* or the *auto pilot.* When sailing deep-water, you'll get more than enough time on the helm, even with self-steering.

Starbound has an auto pilot. The reason she has this electrically driven piece of gear instead of a wind vane is because her mizzen boom overhangs her transom by eight feet and her stern davits carry a 9-foot dinghy that we prefer to keep in that location. I might mention also that we were given the auto pilot—a very good one. It took quite a few dollars to put it in top shape, but they were well spent.

The auto pilot or wind vane seems to take on a personality very quickly. Most deep sea sailors name them for their characteristics: *Starbound's* is called Grumpy because he works in a cave (the lazaret) and just grunts once in a while and sometimes quits altogether unless you give him tender loving care.

If you own a large boat with a separate generator, you may choose to go with an auto pilot. This may also be true if you own a ketch rig with a mizzen that might interfere with wind vane steering. The vane needs clear air to operate well and unless the boom end is well inboard or quite high, it may be a waste of effort to install a vane.

Most deep-water cruising yachts have wind vane steering. I

most heartily recommend them with these reservations: Buy a good one and install it properly. The good ones are usually expensive and are made of materials such as monel, bronze, and reinforced plastics. The mechanical parts must be quite strong and well machined. Gear components must be especially tough. The best vanes are highly sensitive to any yawing rotation of the yacht and tend to counteract it instantly. This is known as *yaw damping*. The wind vane that does this best is the *servopendulum* type, the servopendulum acting to operate the ship's main rudder. It seems to be a fact of cruising economics that this is also the most complex and most expensive type of vane.

If your boat is inherently yaw resistant, you may be able to get good steering from the more simple *auxiliary rudder control* type of vane. With this gear the main rudder of the ship is fixed and the vane's rudder does all the steering. A large number of manufacturers make gears based on this system.

BELOW DECKS

To check the below-decks machinery let's start with the biggest first: the *auxiliary engine*. It should be a diesel. If it is a gasoline engine, start thinking about changing it. I say this because of the very real danger of carrying gasoline aboard, secondly because of the complicated, trouble-prone ignition system, and thirdly because of the greater economy and availability of diesel fuel. I intend the foregoing to be a hard-nosed condemnation of gasoline engines aboard deep-water yachts, and I believe all deep-water sailors will agree. During our circumnavigation I can remember just two yachts with gasoline engines: One skipper was already dickering for a small diesel to replace his (in New Zealand) and the skipper of the second boat was in the hospital with severe burns from a gasoline explosion aboard his yacht. This incident occurred at the dock of the Royal Cape Yacht Club in South Africa shortly before our arrival there.

So we'll assume that your engine is a diesel—the size doesn't

matter as far as the checkout procedure is concerned. However, the adequacy of your engine should be considered against its intended uses.

Propulsion is the primary function of an auxiliary engine and many times we've heard a cruising sailor voice a wish for more power, usually for the purpose of driving against weather, currents, and tidal flow.

Generally the auxiliary engine of a deep-water sailing yacht should be able to drive the boat at her hull speed in smooth water. An approximation of *hull speed* (V) can be obtained by the formula: $V = 1.2\sqrt{LWL}$. If your ship has a waterline length of 36 feet, her hull speed should be at least 7.2 knots.

Range will depend on the full capacity of your permanent tanks plus the amount you may want to carry as deck cargo. It will be wise to figure out how far this amount of fuel will take you and balance it against your cruising plans. If transiting canals are included in your agenda, find out if fuel will be generally available— and for what price.

The secondary function of an auxiliary engine, assuming your ship is too small to accommodate a separate electric plant, is *generating electricity* for the lighting systems above and below decks, the radiotelephone, any electronic navigation equipment you may decide to carry, and possibly an auto pilot.

A refrigeration compressor may also be driven electrically, but I've been seeing an increasing number of efficient freezer/refrigerators whose compressors were driven mechanically by front-end take-offs. A belt-driven compressor is engaged via an idler pulley and freezes eutectic plates in the refrigeration system. New designs, high K-factor insulation, and more efficient, magnetically driven compressors are putting a frozen food capability (and ice cubes) realistically and economically within reach of the deep-water sailor.

If you are satisfied that your auxiliary engine will push the ship at hull speed and at the same time do the other jobs you want it to do, then it is time to take a very critical look at the *maintenance of the engine.* I've listed these in no particular order because they're all important. Remember, you are going to be doing the maintenance:

•Make sure there is a complete, deep drip pan under the engine and transmission. Spilled or leaking engine oil, transmission fluid, or fuel slopping around in the bilge along with salt water will create a mess too horrible to contemplate.

•Provide a method to pump out your old engine oil easily. A neoprene hose attached to a fitting at the very bottom of the sump pan will make it easy to use a hand pump.

•The fuel and oil filters must be changed often. Make sure they're easily accessible, even to the extent of modifying the engine enclosure.

•Make sure the alternator and starting motor can be easily removed. The alternator is ususally quite simple, but I've seen a few starters that were nearly inaccessible—and in one case could only be removed by jacking up the engine. Ridiculous but true.

•The shaft coupling must be accessible. *Accessible* means you should be able to reach, dismantle, and reassemble it easily.

•Belt drives to the front-end take-off should be simple to adjust or replace.

•The raw water coolant pump impeller should be removable without unbolting the pump body from the engine. Those neoprene impellers have a nasty habit of wearing out or disintegrating at awkward times.

•If the engine is fresh water cooled, the heat exchangers must be fitted with sacrificial zinc "pencils," which will need to be changed often.

•See if the fuel pump can be fully serviced. Bosch-type pumps must have their lubricating oil changed frequently.

•The engine head should be removable with the engine in place. This is also true of the injectors. I make the point because some production boat builders have the unfortunate habit of shoe-horning the engine under the cockpit in a manner to almost preclude reaching the top of the engine.

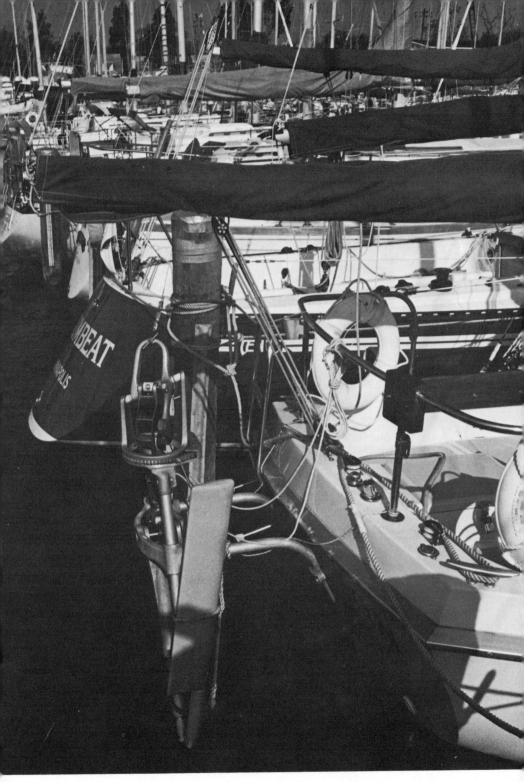

An Aries windvane with rudder up and sail removed while in port.

•The exhaust system must be designed to prevent sea water from getting into the engine via the exhaust manifold. The best design is a water lock system. The system should also be designed for replacement, which is called for from time to time due to the high corrosion factor caused by mixing exhaust gases with sea water.

These are the most important maintenance considerations. To summarize: The marine engine must be maintained faithfully if you intend it to run when you need it. *And to maintain it, you must be able to reach it!*

At sea on *Starbound*, we normally charge batteries about 1½ hours each day, usually after breakfast. We do this primarily for our electrical refrigeration, but since our Onan diesel generator puts out 3 kilowatts at 115 volts we have enough to charge our battery banks, light off the hot water boiler (diesel-fired with an electric ignition), and do any jobs aboard that require an electric drill or grinder. Nina also grinds coffee in the blender at this time and has been known to do some sewing of various types on her electric sewing machine (she has a hand crank type also). This is not to be construed as an endorsement to go deep-water cruising with all this stuff. It is simply that we own a fairly large cruising ketch that has a separate engine room, so we can carry the gear without too much penalty. Also, I like machinery and it seems to like me. If I owned a smaller ship, I could easily do without a lot of the machinery and the maintenance that goes with it.

It is important to have two heavy-duty *battery banks:* one for engine starting and one for ship's service. If the engine can also be started with a crank—a highly desirable feature—even better. But compression releases are necessary for hand cranking and not many marine diesels of 4 cylinders or more have them.

Calculate the normal cruising usage of electricity in a 24-hour period and ensure that the battery capacity is 150 percent of that usage.

Provide a master switching system so that either or both batteries can be used either for starting or for ship's service. The switch should have an off position to totally isolate both banks if the ship is left for a long period.

Batteries must be located as high above the bilge as possible. It is important to keep them dry and salt free. If possible they should have their own enclosures with vented lids to allow the escape of hydrogen (H_2). The enclosures, or other means of retention, must be hefty. Batteries are a heavy, concentrated weight containing corrosive acid and must not be able to break loose in any sea. The enclosures must provide good access for checking connections and maintaining electrolyte levels.

The *alternator* should be a heavy-duty marine type, which means the rotating field is encapsulated in epoxy. Its capacity should be such that it will easily replace the 24-hour normal cruising usage of electrical power in less than 2 hours. Automotive-type alternators are not normally capable of that much output. It would be wise to make a few trial runs to ensure its capabilities.

The ship's *wiring system* should be assessed carefully. If the yacht has some years on her, the insulation should be spot checked for deterioration. Be alert for sloppy installations made by previous owners. Watch out for one-wire common ground systems; a two-wire system is the way to go for all circuits.

If your ship is a relatively new production-type yacht, be on the lookout for skimpy, undersized wiring and "lowest-bidder" circuit boxes and switching panels. Some manufacturers will install the cheapest stuff available. *Caveat emptor!*

The wiring system should have several different circuits: two or more for cabin lights and one each for navigation lights, binnacle, pumps, windlass, radiotelephone, and other electrical equipment.

In general the heavier the wire size, the better. Heavier wire acts like a larger water pipe: It has less resistance so will carry more current flow with less current drop. The main leads from the batteries to the circuit box should be the heaviest available for the purpose.

Wire insulation should be heavy plastic. Old wire with rubber insulation should be checked carefully. Any break in the insulation is hazardous. All wiring must be protected against abrasion and should be supported by straps and clamps. It should not be allowed to move around with the ship's motion.

The terminations of all wiring should end in proper terminals or connectors that fit the wire properly and are mechanically crimped onto it. It is highly advisable to tin the wire end with solder before crimping on the terminal device, then solder the terminal after the crimp. The crimp makes a superior *mechanical* bond, but the solder makes a superior *electrical* bond.

Fuel tanks should be critically inspected. Because they are out of sight and seemingly basic in nature, they are too often overlooked. Many boat owners do not even know of what material their tanks are made.

Years ago *tin-lined copper* was touted as the very best material. This has been phased out because of cost and also because the tin lining eventually deteriorates, with resulting gummy deposits in the fuel caused by interaction with the copper.

Today *monel metal* makes the best material for all tanks used for gasoline, diesel oil, or water. But monel tanks cost about five times as much as tanks built of other materials.

Many manufacturers of fiberglass boats now make *integral tanks* of the same material, but *fiberglass* tanks have several drawbacks. First, diesel oil and gasoline molecules are very small and can penetrate the relatively porous resins used in fiberglass construction. Use of more dense resins means greater construction costs and because of competition, reduced profits, something which no boatbuilder is willing to accept. So "rainbows" continue to form on the water outside many fiberglass boats built with integral tanks, and you can smell the stuff in the bilges.

Integral fiberglass tanks are acceptable for fresh water because the larger water molecule generally precludes leakage, but many people complain about the water's resin taste, which seems to hang on for years. A friend successfully overcame this problem by coating the inside of his tanks with hot wax, working through the cleanout accesses in the tank tops.

Another problem can arise from integral tanks, primarily with fiberglass hulls but one that has also been found to exist with metal

Windlass and anchor arrangement at the bow of a fiberglass sloop.

hulls: The creation of a "hard spot." The bulkhead of an integral tank, if butted directly to the hull skin without benefit of a pad or thickened area acting to distribute the stress imposed by the edge of the tank bulkhead, will create a hard spot. Cracks will emanate from the reverse side (outside) and indicate the first signs of progressive failure. In all cases, separate (nonintegral) tanks are highly recommended for both fuel and water.

Black iron tanks used to be popular. Actually a form of hot-rolled steel, the material is still available today. However, it still has the problem it always did; although long-lived, scale builds up on the inner tank surface and eventually spalls off to clog the filters.

Starbound has heavy-gauge steel tanks that were installed 30 years ago. We just finished reconditioning them, which included steam-cleaning their interior, sand-blasting their exterior, and applying two coats of a cold-galvanizing preparation called Devcon-Z. This coating has an impressive track record.

Mild steel tanks are perhaps the most common today. Heavy-gauge mild steel tanks, galvanized on the outside only, are very satisfactory for diesel oil. They can also be galvanized on the inside if only gasoline is used. This will extend the life of the tank even further. But be cautioned that diesel fuel can contain acids that break down the zinc of the galvanized coating. This product will foul injectors on diesel engines. Acidic diesel fuel is more commonly found outside the United States, but a load can still be picked up here and there at home—for instance, when using home-heating oil for fuel in lieu of No. 2 diesel as many large boats do. So it is rather a moot point whether or not to galvanize the inner surface of a diesel tank; if you can ensure that only high-grade diesel is carried, then go ahead. But you'll have a tough time assuring the fuel quality—even in this country.

Stainless steel is not a suitable material for fuel tanks. It is subject to pit corrosion and pin hole leaks are a frequent occurrence. Stainless steel water tanks are fairly common and seem to hold up well. *Starbound* has four of them that have been in service for 30 years. My last inspection revealed no leaks.

Aluminum is the newest material being used for tanks. Boats with aluminum hulls have been using integral aluminum tanks for years. The 5000 series aluminum is highly corrosion resistant and is strong, light, and weldable if inert gas welding techniques are employed. Aluminum tanks must have a heavier wall thickness than steel tanks. Some of the marine standards recommended for aluminum tanks are: a plate thickness of .090 inches for tanks up to 80 gallons and .125 inches for tanks up to 150 gallons. I think this is much too light. I would recommend .125 and .250 respectively, as a minimum.

I also understand that the Coast Guard has approved aluminum tanks as the only ones that can be foamed in place, the foam being used to support the tanks. Again, I recommend *solid structure* to support a fuel tank, not foam. When tanks are full, they are heavy. Diesel fuel weighs 7.1 pounds per gallon, so a full 80-gallon tank weighs 568 pounds plus the weight of the tank itself. Remember the physical law: Force = mass × acceleration. If the mass of a full fuel tank is accelerated by the motion of a rolling ship at sea, one hell of a big force will result. Tanks must be carefully supported to distribute their weight into the framing structure of the ship, and they must be secured in place against any motion the sea might hand out, including "turning turtle." All clamps and straps should be padded to prevent chafe.

Avoid *terneplate* as a fuel tank material for a permanent installation. This is the stuff that 6-gallon outboard tanks are made of: a thin steel sheet coated with a lead-tin alloy. They corrode through quickly. Incidentally, to prolong the life of your outboard tanks, paint any outside scratches immediately (I use Nina's fingernail polish—it's always handy). And add a little "dri-gas" to the fuel if the tank is going to sit partly full for any length of time. Paint the bottom lip of the tank with a rubber compound—Whip-Dip works fine—that stuff nonsailors use to stop cowtails on the ends of lines instead of serving them.

Here are some things to look for when inspecting your tanks: You should be able to see them and reach them without tearing out permanent structure. Rub your hands over the outside of the tank. If you can smell fuel on your hands, investigate further. Filler hoses from deckplates to tank top fittings should be wire-wound neoprene, stoutly fastened with hose clamps. *Vents* must be installed in the tank top with copper tubing running from the fitting to topside. The topside vent opening should point down and be as high above the deck as is practicable (I've seen them carried part way up the mast). The copper vent tubing should be ½-inch diameter; ¼-inch doesn't allow air to escape fast enough when filling, and the fuel will blow back. Avoid plastic tubing for vents; it can deteriorate with age and will melt in case of a fire.

On a really first-class fuel tank the *fuel supply line* should come from the top of the tank. A pipe or tube will extend from the tank top fitting down inside to within an inch or two of the bottom. Below this suction point a *sump* should be located. The sump should look like a small upside down "fez," welded to the tank's bottom. It should be accessible and have a pipe plug in its bottom to drain off collected dirt and water. Copper tubing fuel lines leading from the tank to the primary filters are O.K. if they're secured properly, but make sure the section of fuel line leading from the primary filters to the engine itself is *armored flex hose* rated for fuel. Engine vibration can cause fatigue failure in tubing if the tubing is led directly to the filters on the engine.

If the fuel tanks are aluminum, use a short section of fuel-rated flex hose with coated steel or stainless steel fittings between the tank and the copper tubing running to the engine. The idea is to electrically isolate the aluminum tank from the copper tubing. Make sure the return line from the engine meets the same criteria as the supply line. Your tanks should have *cleanouts:* removable fuel-tight covers over tank openings that are big enough to allow inspection and cleaning of the tanks. The tanks should be baffled fore and/or aft to preclude noise, to reduce the chance of possible damage due to the hydraulic force of moving liquid, and to reduce the *free surface effect*, which can screw up the ship's stability. Forget about fuel gauges: They require extra tank penetrations and they're not dependable. Use a *calibrated dipstick*. Any tank whose quantity of fuel or water can't be measured directly should be modified accordingly.

Starbound's *Ford diesel is easily accessible from the galley.*

Tank tops should be rounded so that water cannot stand on them. The tanks should be located or protected so that bilge water can't splash on them. They should have good ventilation all around.

A good fuel system is an important factor in a deep-water yacht. I remember a few instances when, because the diesel engine started and ran at full power within just a few seconds, *Starbound* was able to pull herself out of serious difficulties.

11

Ground Tackle, Tenders, and Life Rafts

A cold January wind is blowing up our creek. *Starbound* is tugging at her dock lines and groaning against the pilings of the big tee-head. Snow is promised by morning. I've just finished a hot cup of coffee out on the afterdeck and watched the cirrostratus build up—and thought about anchoring.

GROUND TACKLE

When considering *ground tackle* for deep-water cruising, keep in mind that more yachts have been lost because of poor ground tackle and anchoring techniques than have been lost in storms at sea.

During our circumnavigation there were just eight ports where we did *not* use our ground tackle full time: Bermuda (St. George), Panama (Balboa), New Zealand (while in Auckland), three of the many ports inside the Australian Barrier Reef, Mauritius, and Capetown. In all other ports we were anchored, usually with two

229

anchors, a few times with three, and once with four. First-class ground tackle is a deep-water yacht's primary security in a foreign port. *Do not skimp on it.*

The size and type of ground tackle and how much rode is put out depends on several factors, the depth of water, and the kind of bottom not the least among them. But the first and biggest factor to take into consideration is the *windage* of your ship. *Wind drag* will account for most of the force the ground tackle must resist. There are two lesser forces, *current drag* and *wave action load,* which we'll discuss later, but for now here is an easy and relatively accurate way to measure it for a yacht, using an imaginary 40-foot ketch as an example.

The aerodynamic formula for *wind drag* is as follows:

$$D = C_d \frac{P}{2} V^2 S$$

C_d is the coefficient of drag, which varies with the shape of the object.

P (rho) is the air density.

V is the wind velocity.

S is the cross sectional or projected area the wind is blowing against.

Now this drag formula can be much simplified for our purposes. For cylindrical shapes $C_d = 1.00$; for flat rectangles $C_d = 1.28$ and for spheres, $C_d = 0.47$. For a streamlined shape like an airplane $C_d = 0.1$.

Generally for pleasure boats $C_d = 0.80$ would be a good consolidated figure to use—if the wind would stay directly on the bow. But boats yaw at anchor and the biggest forces on the ground tackle are always generated with the wind about 30 degrees off the bow. Also, cruising boats generally have a lot of oddly shaped gear secured topside, which gives the hull a considerably less streamlined form than the bay weekender. After considering all the parameters, I believe a C_d of 1.00 is proper for a cruising yacht.

For P we'll simply use the U. S. standard atmospheric air density. (For those interested, the value is 0.0023779 slugs per cubic foot at 59 degrees F and 29.92 inches H_g). By holding C_d and P at the aforementioned constants, corresponding values of wind drag can be found for various *wind velocities* as follows:

Wind Speed (knots)	Wind Drag* (pounds per square feet of projected area)
10	0.33
20	1.30
30	3.00
40	5.40
50	8.40
60	12.00
70	15.20
80	20.10

*Wind-drag values based on drag coefficient of 1.00 and U.S. Standard Air Density

Now all we have to do is calculate the projected cross-sectional area of the boat looking at it from 30 degrees off the bow and multiply this figure by the above wind-drag (per square foot) value for the maximum wind in which we might have to anchor.

Since the sine of 30 degrees is 0.5, we can handily compute the *horizontal dimensions* of hull and cabin by using half their value and multiplying by their height. We'll assume that the freeboard average as 3 feet and the cabin height as 2 feet above the main deck. We'll also assume the masts to have an average 7-inch diameter (about 0.6 feet) and the shrouds to be ⅜-inch diameter (about .03 feet). Let's say the main is 45 feet above the deck and the mizzen 35 feet.

	Feet × Feet	Square Feet (rounded off)
Hull:	(40/2) × 3.00 =	60
Cabin:	(25/2) × 2.00 =	25
Mainmast:	45 × 0.60 =	27
Mizzenmast:	35 × 0.60 =	21
Main Boom (w/furled sails):	(15/2) × 1.00 =	8
Mizzen Boom (w/furled sails):	(10/2) × 1.00 =	5
Liferaft (on deck):	3 × 1.50 =	5
Dinghy (on deck):	(10/2) × 1.50 =	8
Lifeline Stanchions (1-inch diameter):	25 × .083 =	2
Pulpit (1-inch diameter):	50 × .083 =	4
Lifelines (⅜-inch diameter):	(140/2) × .03 =	2
Shrouds and Stays (total length of all):	600 × .03 =	18
Running Rigging (use ⅝-inch diameter):	300 × .06 =	18
	Total =	203 sq. ft.

From this figure and the previous table we can figure what the total wind drag will be for various wind speeds. For example, if the wind is blowing 60 knots, the ground tackle must hold a force of 12 × 203 = 2436 pounds.

Current-drag forces are not appreciable. A 5-knot current running through the anchorage will probably add 300 pounds to the anchor load of our sample 40-foot ketch; a 2-knot current will be much less. Frankly we have had to consider current in anchorages only a few times in the thirteen years we've owned our ship, but it can be said that once is enough. To be realistic about it, I believe the addition of 300 pounds to the calculated wind-drag force will be sufficient to take into account any currents likely to be encountered, for yachts up to 45 feet. If your ship is appreciably larger—say 55 to 65 feet—use a 500-pound figure.

Wave-action loads are generally slight as long as the ship can oscillate with the waves without snubbing. Snubbing can occur when the ship is riding to an insufficient length of rode, or some-

Starbound's three primary anchors (from the top): 65-lb. Danforth, 130-lb. Herreshoff, and 100-lb. Navy lightweight with a 50° fluke angle for mud.

times when the rode material is too light in weight to provide a proper shock-absorbing catenary. When using proper ground tackle and anchoring techniques, wave-action loads do not present a problem.

ANCHORS AND ANCHORING

Before choosing the proper ground tackle for our sample 40-foot ketch, some additional points should be made. First, a deep-water cruising yacht should carry *at least three anchors*. Many only carry two—but remember, putting out two anchors is the *normal* procedure in many ports of the world—then what do you do if one is lost? We know of many instances of anchors lost by cruising boats. Unsecured shackle pins, broken shackles, parted chain, coral-chafed nylon rode, theft—these are some of the ways to lose an anchor. So carry three anchors, as a minimum. *Starbound* carries four; we've met boats with five!

The next point is that at least two of these anchors should each be able to develop a *horizontal holding power* equal to the yacht's wind drag at 60 knots, plus the current drag, as a factor of safety. For our sample yacht we found this total force to be 2436 + 300 pounds, so let's use 2750 pounds as a rounded-off value.

The reason that either of two anchors should hold the ship in a 60-knot wind is this: There may come a time when you find yourself locked into a harbor with high winds. A whole gale will have gusts to 70 and 80 knots—and a typhoon starts at 65 knots and winds up from there. We've met several yachts that have found themselves in just such a position. With good holding ground and good ground tackle, they managed to survive with all their anchors out. So if there are at least two good sets of ground tackle aboard, you might expect, ideally, for your ship to hold her ground in winds of over 100 knots. Many have done so.

The term *horizontal holding power* refers to the fact that any anchor will develop its maximum rated holding power for a particular bottom condition only when the pull on it is absolutely parallel

Stowage of a Danforth at the stemhead of a cruising yacht.

to that bottom. If the shank of the anchor is raised from the bottom even a small amount, the anchor's holding power is severely reduced (see Figure 11-5).

Face the fact that one anchor rode should be *all chain*. A prime advantage, as well as disadvantage, of chain is its weight. The weight is needed to keep the anchor shank *horizontal* and to maintain a deep catenary for the absorption of shock loads. On the other hand a large weight of chain when stacked up in a forward chain locker can induce an undesirable pitching movement in a seaway, unless your yacht is designed to carry it. One way out of this quandary is to locate the chain locker several feet aft of the bow and lead the chain down to it from the windlass with a large navel pipe set on an angle.

Another method, much more common, is to carry only 100 feet of chain forward and stow an additional 100 feet in a special locker farther aft. There won't be too many anchorages where you'll want to put out more than 100 feet of chain rode (and also, not many where you'll want less). With this method the weight in the bow is reduced and you will have the option of shackling on the second 100 feet to the first if it's needed. Or you can put out the second 100 feet on a second anchor. Or you can add a nylon rode to the first 100 feet and even a second nylon rode to the second 100 feet. If your cruising plans include really deep anchorages, a third 100 foot of chain can be carried amidship; a large amount of chain stows in a surprisingly small volume.

If the decision is made to carry one chain rode only and to employ nylon for the other anchor rode(s), it will be absolutely necessary to shackle a heavy chain lead to the anchor preceding the nylon. Once again, this will serve to keep the anchor shank horizontal and will aid the nylon is resisting shock or surge loads. But it will also resist the chafe from the bottom, something that nylon cannot do. *Chain leads* should be at least 20 feet long and one size heavier than the all-chain rode; that is, if the chain rode is ⅜-inch (trade size), use ⁷/₁₆-inch for the chain lead.

To many people, chain is chain and rope is rope. To the deep-water sailor, chain and rope are an integral part of his ship's security system. Most deep-water cruising boats spend the majority of their time at anchor. How odd then it would be to neglect the system that keeps one's ship safely at anchor, the system whose failure could easily mean the loss of home, transportation, possessions, money, dreams and, perhaps, life.

In Tables 1, 1A, 2 and 2A we have reproduced some of the pertinent specifications for chain and rope. They are worthy of some study.

The *chain specs* are published by the National Association of Chain Manufacturers (NACM) and cover the commercial grades of *welded* chain. The two chain grades of interest to deep-water sailors are No. 2001 High Test steel chain and No. 3002 Proof Coil steel chain.

The chain that people buy from their marine hardware store is usually No. 3002 Proof Coil. Actually it is hard to tell what you are buying unless you carefully measure one link and match it against the dimensions of Table 1A. This is because each chain manufacturer tends to use his own nomenclature for the chain he sells. So look for the *NACM spec number* on the chain's shipping container or ask to see the store's purchase order to see if it appears there. The manufacturer's catalog should be available too. A check there should reveal what you are buying. But measure the links anyway, for insurance. As stated in Table 1, the dimensions are subject to a tolerance of plus or minus 4 percent.

If at this point of your cruise preparations you must purchase chain, either to replace the existing chain or to make up a new all-chain rode, consider choosing No. 2001 High Test chain in lieu of No. 3002 Proof Coil chain. The difference in cost is relatively small and the working-load limit will be increased by about 75 percent. This does *not* mean that you should pick a smaller trade size; buy the same size as if you were selecting No. 3002, but select High Test chain instead. This will increase your factor of safety with no increase in weight. Recognize that the dimensions of the links are slightly different and may not fit your existing windlass wildcat. If

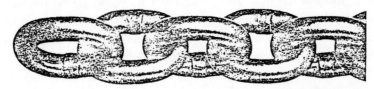

NO. 2001 **HIGH TEST STEEL CHAIN**

Trade Size, Inches	Material Size		Nominal Inside Link Dimensions, Inches		Maximum Length, 100 Links, Inches	Maximum Weight, 100 Feet, Lbs.	Working Load Limit, Lbs.	Minimum Proof Test Load, Lbs.	Minimum Break Test Load, Lbs.
	Inches	Decimal	Length	Width					
1/4	9/32	.281	.82	.39	86	80	2500	4100	7750
5/16	11/32	.343	1.01	.48	105	123	4000	6700	11500
3/8	13/32	.406	1.15	.56	121	175	5100	8500	16200
7/16	15/32	.468	1.29	.65	135	235	6600	11200	20700
1/2	17/32	.531	1.43	.75	150	300	8200	13700	26000
5/8	21/32	.656	1.79	.90	186	450	11500	19500	36900
3/4	25/32	.781	1.96	1.06	205	655	16200	27000	50400

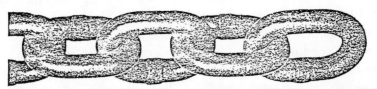

NO. 3002 **PROOF COIL STEEL CHAIN**

Trade Size, Inches	Material Size		Nominal Inside Link Dimensions, Inches		Maximum Length, 100 Links, Inches	Maximum Weight, 100 Feet, Lbs.	Working Load Limit, Lbs.	Minimum Proof Test Load, Lbs.	Minimum Break Test Load, Lbs.
	Inches	Decimal	Length	Width					
3/16	7/32	:218	0.95	0.40	99	42	700	1400	2800
1/4	9/32	.281	1.00	.50	104	76	1175	2350	4700
5/16	11/32	.343	1.10	.50	114	115	1750	3500	7000
3/8	13/32	.406	1.23	.62	128	166	2450	4900	9800
7/16	15/32	.468	1.37	.75	142	225	3250	6500	13000
1/2	17/32	.531	1.50	.81	156	286	4250	8500	17000
9/16	19/32	.593	1.75	.87	182	355	5250	10500	21000
5/8	21/32	.656	1.87	1.00	194	425	6375	12750	25500
3/4	25/32	.781	2.12	1.12	220	605	9125	18250	36500
7/8	29/32	.906	2.50	1.37	260	811	10750	21500	43000
1	1-1/32	1.031	2.75	1.50	286	1045	12400	24800	49600
1-1/8	1-5/32	1.156	3.12	1.75	324	1321	15600	31200	62400
1-1/4	1-9/32	1.281	3.25	1.87	338	1622	19200	38400	76800

WELDED CHAIN

SPECIFICATIONS

NATIONAL ASSOCIATION OF CHAIN MANUFACTURERS

1001	ALLOY STEEL CHAIN
2001	HIGH TEST STEEL CHAIN
3001	BBB COIL STEEL CHAIN
3002	PROOF COIL STEEL CHAIN
3003	MACHINE CHAIN
3004	COIL CHAIN

Adopted August, 1961

Scope

These manufacturing specifications cover Welded Chain in the commercial grades listed below. It should be noted that none of these grades is calibrated for use with pocket wheels; such applications require special processing beyond the scope of commercial standards. Application governs size and type of chain to be used.

No. 1001 Alloy Steel Chain High strength chain generally used for slinging, hoisting and load binding purposes.

No. 2001 High Test Steel Chain Better quality carbon steel general purpose chain suitable for ordinary applications such as on railroad cars, construction, industrial uses, load binding, towing, logging, etc.

No. 3001 BBB Coil Steel Chain General purpose carbon steel chain suitable for applications such as on railroad cars, construction, industrial uses, load binding, logging chains, tow chains, etc., other than overhead lifting.

No. 3002 Proof Coil Steel Chain General purpose carbon steel chain suitable for all ordinary applications such as on railroad cars, construction, industrial uses, load binding, etc., other than overhead lifting.

No. 3003 Machine Chain Straight link or twist link. General utility chain, made of carbon steel. Not used in overhead lifting.

No. 3004 Coil Chain Straight link or twist link. General utility chain, made of carbon steel. Not used in overhead lifting.

Definitions

"Working Load Limits"

The "Working Load Limit" is the maximum load in pounds which should ever be applied to chain even when chain is new and when the load is uniformly applied in direct tension to a straight length of chain.

"Proof Test"

The "Proof Test" is a term designating the tensile test applied to a chain during or subsequent to the process of manufacture for the sole purpose of detecting defects in the material or manufacture. It is the load in pounds which the chain has withstood, in the condition and at the time it left the factory, under a test in which the load has been applied in direct tension to a straight length of chain with a uniform rate of speed on a standard testing machine. The actual loads applied vary with the size of chain being tested but are sufficient to provide the necessary Proof Test.

When requested, the manufacturer shall furnish a certificate of Proof Test to the purchaser or his representative.

"Minimum Break Test"

"Minimum Break Load" is the minimum load in pounds at which chain, in the condition it would leave the factory, has been found by experience to break, under tests in which the load is applied in direct tension to a straight length of chain with a uniform rate of speed on a standard chain testing machine.

Weights and Dimensions

The weights and dimensions shall be as prescribed in Table I.

(A) (1) The diameter of the bar from which Alloy Steel Chain is made shall not be smaller than nominal size less commercial tolerance.

(2) The diameter of the material from which Proof Coil Steel Chain, BBB Coil Steel Chain, High Test Steel Chain, Machine Chain and Coil Chain is made shall not be less than the material size shown in the table, subject to normal commercial tolerance.

(B) Maximum weights and dimensions are subject to no further plus tolerances. Nominal weights and dimensions are subject to a plus or minus tolerance of 4%.

CORDAGE INSTITU

Three-Strand Lai
(Standa

CAUTION!
WORKING LOADS ARE GUIDELINES ONLY.
See Footnotes at bottom and reverse side.

NOMINAL SIZE		POLYPROPYLENE				POLYESTER			
Diameter	Circum-ference	Linear Density[1] (lbs./100 ft.)	New Rope Tensile Strength[2] (lbs.)	Safety Factor	Working Load[3] (lbs.)	Linear Density[1] (lbs./100 ft.)	New Rope Tensile Strength[2] (lbs.)	Safety Factor	
3/16	5/8	.70	720	10	72	1.20	900	10	
1/4	3/4	1.20	1,130	10	113	2.00	1,490	10	
5/16	1	1.80	1,710	10	171	3.10	2,300	10	
3/8	1-1/8	2.80	2,440	10	244	4.50	3,340	10	
7/16	1-1/4	3.80	3,160	9	352	6.20	4,500	9	
1/2	1-1/2	4.70	3,780	9	420	8.00	5,750	9	
9/16	1-3/4	6.10	4,600	8	575	10.2	7,200	8	
5/8	2	7.50	5,600	8	700	13.0	9,000	8	
3/4	2-1/4	10.7	7,650	7	1,090	17.5	11,300	7	
13/16	2-1/2	12.7	8,900	7	1,270	21.0	14,000	7	
7/8	2-3/4	15.0	10,400	7	1,490	25.0	16,200	7	
1	3	18.0	12,600	7	1,800	30.4	19,800	7	
1-1/16	3-1/4	20.4	14,400	7	2,060	34.4	23,000	7	
1-1/8	3-1/2	23.8	16,500	7	2,360	40.0	26,600	7	
1-1/4	3-3/4	27.0	18,900	7	2,700	46.2	29,800	7	
1-5/16	4	30.4	21,200	7	3,020	52.5	33,800	7	
1-1/2	4-1/2	38.4	26,800	7	3,820	67.0	42,200	7	
1-5/8	5	47.6	32,400	7	4,620	82.0	51,500	7	
1-3/4	5-1/2	59.0	38,800	7	5,550	98.0	61,000	7	
2	6	69.0	46,800	7	6,700	118.	72,000	7	
2-1/8	6-1/2	80.0	55,000	7	7,850	135.	83,000	7	
2-1/4	7	92.0	62,000	7	8,850	157.	96,500	7	
2-1/2	7-1/2	107.	72,000	7	10,300	181.	110,000	7	
2-5/8	8	120.	81,000	7	11,600	204.	123,000	7	
2-7/8	8-1/2	137.	91,000	7	13,000	230.	139,000	7	
3	9	153.	103,000	7	14,700	258.	157,000	7	
3-1/4	10	190.	123,000	7	17,600	318.	189,000	7	
3-1/2	11	232.	146,000	7	20,800	384.	228,000	7	
4	12	276.	171,000	7	24,400	454.	270,000	7	

[1]**LINEAR DENSITY**
Linear Density (pounds per 100 feet) shown is "average." Maximum is 5% higher.

[2]**NEW ROPE TENSILE STRENGTHS**
New Rope Tensile Strengths are based on tests of new and unused rope of standard construction in accordance with Cordage Institute Standard Test Methods.

[3]**WORKING LOADS** a
with appropriate
applications, and
conditions. Working
only with expert k
professional estima

E SPECIFICATIONS

ht-Strand Plaited
ruction)

Supersedes:
Cordage Institute Specifications for
Synthetic Rope, February 1974 and
Cordage Institute Specifications for
Composite Synthetic Rope, January 1975

NINAL ETER ches)	COMPOSITE[4]				NYLON				NOMINAL DIAMETER (inches)
	Linear Density[1] (lbs./100 ft.)	New Rope Tensile Strength[2] (lbs.)	Safety Factor	Working Load[3] (lbs.)	Linear Density[1] (lbs./100 ft.)	New Rope Tensile Strength[2] (lbs.)	Safety Factor	Working Load[3] (lbs.)	
16	.94	720	10	72	1.00	900	12	75	3/16
1/4	1.61	1,130	10	113	1.50	1,490	12	124	1/4
16	2.48	1,710	10	171	2.50	2,300	12	192	5/16
3/8	3.60	2,440	10	244	3.50	3,340	12	278	3/8
16	5.00	3,160	9	352	5.00	4,500	11	410	7/16
1/2	6.50	3,780	9	440	6.50	5,750	11	525	1/2
16	8.00	4,600	8	610	8.15	7,200	10	720	9/16
5/8	9.50	5,600	8	720	10.5	9,350	10	935	5/8
3/4	12.5	7,650	7	1,080	14.5	12,800	9	1,420	3/4
16	15.2	8,900	7	1,310	17.0	15,300	9	1,700	13/16
7/8	18.0	10,400	7	1,540	20.0	18,000	9	2,000	7/8
1	21.8	12,600	7	1,870	26.4	22,600	9	2,520	1
16	25.6	14,400	7	2,180	29.0	26,000	9	2,880	1-1/16
/8	29.0	16,500	7	2,490	34.0	29,800	9	3,320	1-1/8
1/4	33.4	18,900	7	2,820	40.0	33,800	9	3,760	1-1/4
16	35.6	21,200	7	3,020	45.0	38,800	9	4,320	1-5/16
/2	45.0	26,800	7	3,820	55.0	47,800	9	5,320	1-1/2
7/8	55.5	32,400	7	4,620	66.5	58,500	9	6,500	1-5/8
3/4	66.5	38,800	7	5,550	83.0	70,000	9	7,800	1-3/4
2	78.0	46,800	7	6,700	95.0	83,000	9	9,200	2
/8	92.0	55,000	7	7,850	109.	95,500	9	10,600	2-1/8
1/4	105	62,000	7	8,850	129.	113,000	9	12,600	2-1/4
/2	122	72,000	7	10,300	149.	126,000	9	14,000	2-1/2
5/8	138	81,000	7	11,600	168.	146,000	9	16,200	2-5/8
/8	155	91,000	7	13,000	189.	162,000	9	18,000	2-7/8
3	174	103,000	7	14,700	210.	180,000	9	20,000	3
3/4	210	123,000	7	17,600	264.	226,000	9	25,200	3-1/4
2	256	146,000	7	20,800	312.	270,000	9	30,000	3-1/2
4	300	171,000	7	24,400	380.	324,000	9	36,000	4

good condition non-critical rmal service d be exceeded conditions and Working loads should be reduced where life, limb, or valuable property are involved, or for exceptional service conditions such as shock loads, sustained loads, etc. SEE REVERSE SIDE FOR FURTHER INFORMATION AND ADDITIONAL FOOTNOTES.

[4]COMPOSITE ROPE. Materials and construction of this polyester/polypropylene composite rope conform to MIL-R-43942 and MIL-R-43952. For other composite ropes, consult the manufacturer.

CAUTION: USE OF WORKING LOADS

Because of the wide range of rope use, rope condition, exposure to the several factors affecting rope behavior, and the degree of risk to life and property involved, it is impossible to make blanket recommendations as to working loads. However, to provide guidelines, working loads are tabulated for rope in good condition with appropriate splices, in non-critical applications and under normal service conditions.

A higher working load may be selected only with expert knowledge of conditions and professional estimate of risk and if the rope has not been subject to dynamic loading or other excessive use, has been inspected and found to be in good condition and is to be used in the recommended manner, and the application does not involve elevated temperatures, extended periods under load, or obvious dynamic loading (see explanation below) such as sudden drops, snubs, or pickups. For all such applications and for applications involving more severe exposure conditions, or for recommendations on special applications, consult the manufacturer.

Many uses of rope involve serious risk of injury to personnel or damage to valuable property. This danger is often obvious, as when a heavy load is supported above one or more workmen. An equally dangerous situation occurs if personnel are in line with a rope under excessive tension. Should the rope fail, it may recoil with considerable force—especially if the rope is nylon. Persons should be warned against standing in line with the rope. IN ALL CASES WHERE ANY SUCH RISKS ARE PRESENT, OR THERE IS ANY QUESTION ABOUT THE LOADS INVOLVED OR THE CONDITIONS OF USE, THE WORKING LOAD SHOULD BE SUBSTAN-TIALLY REDUCED AND THE ROPE BE PROPERLY INSPECTED.

DYNAMIC LOADING VOIDS WORKING LOAD AS TABULATED ABOVE.

Working loads are not applicable when rope is subject to significant dynamic loading. Whenever a load is picked up, stopped, moved or swung there is an increased force due to dynamic loading. The more rapidly or suddenly such actions occur, the greater this increase will be. In extreme cases, the force put on the rope may be two, three, or even more times the normal load involved. Examples could be picking up a tow on a slack line or using a rope to stop a falling object. Therefore, in all such applications as towing lines, lifelines, safety lines, climbing ropes, etc., working loads as given **do not apply.**

Users should be aware that dynamic effects are greater on a low elongation rope such as manila than on a high elongation rope such as nylon, and greater on a shorter rope than on a longer one. The working load listed contains provision for very modest dynamic loads. This means, however, that when this working load has been used to select a rope, the load must be handled slowly and smoothly to minimize dynamic effects and avoid exceeding the provision for them.

Courtesy of

CORDAGE INSTITUTE

there is a mismatch, your windlass manufacturer may have a wild-cat that fits. If you have doubts, obtain a few sample links and check.

For example: To select chain for our aforementioned 40-foot ketch, which we found would impose a total drag force of 2750 pounds, I might choose ⅜-inch Proof Coil. From Table 1A, the working load limit is 2650 pounds, almost matching the force we must resist. But instead I would select High Test chain. The working load limit is increased to 5100 pounds, thereby enhancing safety and allowing me to sleep more peacefully on a blowy night.

There are a few additional points about chain. It is nearly impossible to find BBB chain anymore. I understand that chain manufacturers make it only to order. So what is being sold in marine hardware stores? Most outlets sell No. 3002 Proof Coil chain, which has a working load slightly lower than that specified for BBB chain, which is about 2750 pounds for the ⅜-inch trade size. So here's what a deep-water sailor in need of chain should do: Contact the nearest chain manufacturer and see if you can buy No. 2001 High Test chain directly from them or perhaps from one of their distributors. They can tell you who handles the type you want. Specify the length; ⅜-inch chain comes in drums of 500 feet each! A distributor should sell it in shorter lengths.

Rope anchor rodes should be of nylon because of its shock absorbing quality. I highly recommend eight-strand plaited construction for them. This construction produces a rope that is nonrotating (so it cannot unlay), does not hockle or even tangle if reasonable care is taken, splices easily, and produces a highly grippable surface.

Table 2 is a reproduction of part of the rope specifications—the part covering synthetic rope. Note that the specs are for three-strand laid and eight-strand plaited construction only. These specs were published in August, 1978, and supercede all previous specs put out by The Cordage Institute. They come as a shock to people who use a lot of rope because of the high safety factors and consequent recommend low working loads.

The Cordage Institute is a group formed by, from, and for the

A plow (CQR) anchor in its home at the bow of another cruising yacht.

various rope manufacturers in this country. The data is established by the chief design engineers of all the companies working in common. The reason for the high safety factors and the many cautionary notes and caveats in the new specs are to protect the rope companies from the multitude of product liability suits from which they have been suffering in recent years.

Because of the ultraconservatism of the specs, notice that the size of nylon rope needed to hold our sample ketch against the calculated drag force is 1 $\frac{1}{16}$-inch diameter—that is, if we were to adhere strictly to the published working-load limitations. However—and this is carefully considered—since I, personally, do not intend suing the Cordage company if my anchor line parts, I would rather refer to the words in Footnote 3 of Table 2: *Working loads should be exceeded only with expert knowledge of conditions and professional estimates of risk.*

U. S. Navy specifications state that working loads should never exceed 40 percent of the rope's tensile strength. Applying my own more conservative seat-of-the-pants safety factor, I use a working load limit never exceeding 30 percent of the tensile strength. Please note that this is *not* a recommendation—I don't need lawsuits, either. It is simply what I use on *Starbound* and what I believe is a quite conservative use of synthetic rope.

Based on the foregoing, I would choose ¾-inch diameter line for our sample 40-foot ketch. A quick calculation shows me that ⅝-inch line also falls within my personal guidelines—that is, 0.30 × 9350 = 2805 pounds, greater than the drag force of 2750 pounds. But there are other considerations. The tensile strength figures of Table 2 are based on new and unused rope (Footnote 2). Also, although not stated in Table 2, nylon absorbs water to a small degree, so its tensile strength is reduced by 10 percent when the rope is wet. This is not a characteristic of polyester rope (Dacron), but polyester rope makes poor anchor line because of its low stretch. Again, everything is a compromise.

Figure 11-1 shows six anchors, the top row of which are the most common ones in use on deep-water yachts: the *Danforth* (lightweight), the *CQR* (plow), and the *Herreshoff* (kedge). The para-

DANFORTH

Developed by R. S. Danforth in 1939, this anchor provides excellent holding power in sand and <u>firm</u> mud with a 32° fluke angle. Its holding power is poor in soft mud & the flukes tend to "skate" over shingle, clay and weed.

PLOW OR COR

A British development, patented by G. I. Taylor in 1933, this anchor is a cruising favorite. Its holding power is almost the same as the Danforth & it will tend to penetrate the harder bottoms. It is not very efficient in rock and coral.

yachtsman,
Kedge,
Herreshoff,
Fisherman

The illustration is of a Herreshoff type, with broad tapered palms. A good all-around anchor, but needs a much heavier weight in proportion to its holding power than the others shown. Very good in coral, rock & weed.

NORTHILL

A modern version of an ancient Chinese design, this anchor is generally underrated. its shape makes it hard to retrieve & stow, but it has good hold-power in most bottoms. With a folding stock it will stow neatly.

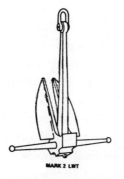

MARK 2 LWT

A U.S. Navy development: heavier for its size than the Danforth, its holding power is nearly comparable and its drawbacks similar except its heavier weight promotes easier bottom penetration.

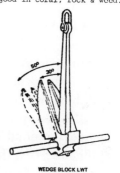

WEDGE BLOCK LWT

A subsequent Navy development to the Mark 2 Lightweight, this anchor allows changing the fluke angle to suit bottom conditions. 30° is ideal for sand 50° is ideal for mud. A good anchor, but not available to the public.

Fig. 11-1 Common anchor types.

graph of information below each anchor is intended to be very general.

The bottom group of anchors on Figure 11-1 contains some that are not seen too often, but they should be—they are all good anchors. Particularly, I admire the *Northill*. It is my belief that it will do everything a plow anchor will do and more besides. It has always been good in rock and coral, and its sharp flukes will penetrate weed. It is true that it is hard to get a Northill back aboard without scarring the hull, but techniques can be developed for that.

The *Mark II lightweight anchors* are widely used by the U. S. Navy and are good anchors. I have never seen this anchor for sale commercially, but they might be obtainable through surplus outlets.

Based on obtainability, I recommend one each of the top row for deep-water cruising. If a good-sized Northill can be located, I would not hesitate to substitute it for any one of the three.

Here are some important points to know about anchors:

•A heavy anchor is better than a light anchor of the same type.

•*Fluke area* is important in sand and mud, but *fluke angle* is more important: 34 degrees is an ideal angle for sand, but 50 degrees is an ideal angle for mud. An intermediate angle is poor in both bottoms. See Figures 11-3 and 4.

•U. S. Navy tests have shown that to develop their maximum holding power all anchors must drag about 50 feet to achieve their optimum set on the bottom. See Figures 11-3, 4, and 5.

•The same tests have shown that the shank must be *parallel* with the ground to realize the maximum holding power. See Figure 11-5.

•Weight of ground tackle and length of rode are the two primary factors acting to keep the shank horizontal, as well as to mitigate shock loading from wave action and wind gusts.

•No single type of anchor is ideal for all applications, but I believe a relatively heavy Northill might be the best compromise.

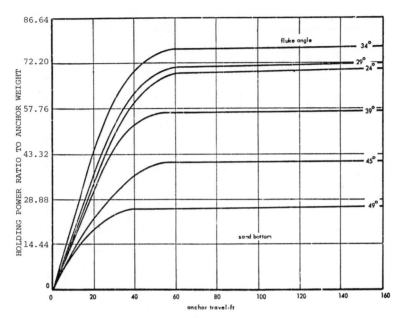

Figure II-3- Graph of fluke angle tests in sand bottom

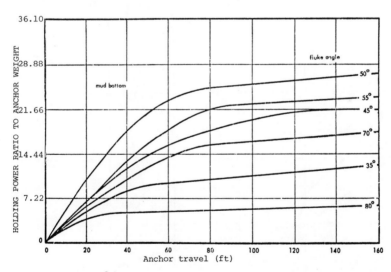

Figure II-4 Graph of fluke angle tests in mud bottom

DATA DERIVED FROM U.S. NAVY TECHNICAL REPORT M-044; "NEW AND MODIFIED ANCHORS FOR MOORINGS" by Towne and Stalcup, 14 March 1960

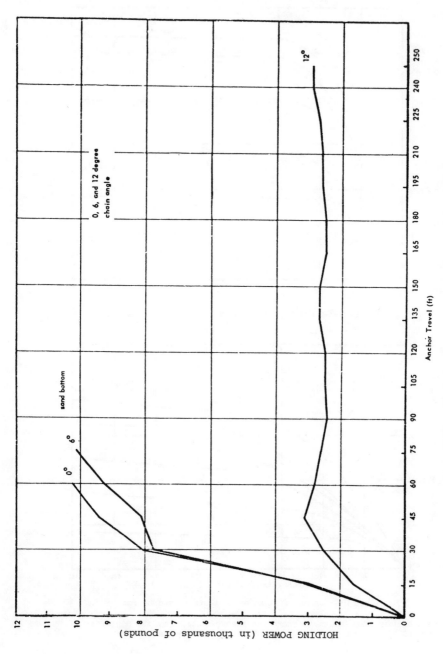

HOLDING POWER (in thousands of pounds)

Anchor Travel (ft)

0, 6, and 12 degree chain angle

sand bottom

0°   6°

12°

Figure 11-5 Graph of average test pulls on 200-lb STATO mooring anchor. with varying chain angles at the anchor shank

Figure 11-2 portrays a series of curves representing the *holding power* of various anchor types in relation to their weights in air. The data comes from several sources, the most authoritative from U. S. Navy technical reports reflecting actual tests on real bottoms.

Notice that all the curves shown are qualified to some extent by their data sources. Also notice that curves reflecting advertising claims are dashed lines. The fact is, much of the data that made up Figure 11-2 is conflicting; differing types of anchors have been tested under differing and mostly unrealistic conditions by various organizations. What is needed is for one nonprofit agency to test a wide weight-range of each anchor type under the same realistic conditions. The organization that has come closest to doing this is the U. S. Navy. But they were conducting their tests for Navy purposes—to anchor and moor big ships. Holding power-to-weight ratios for anchors are not linear and also change with the type of anchor; data cannot simply be scaled down with any degree of accuracy. For the foregoing reasons the reader is cautioned to employ the curves of Figure 11-2 only as a general guide.

The anchors that I would choose for our sample ketch would be these: a 60-pound high tensile *Danforth*. I would expect this anchor to have a holding power of at least 4000 pounds in a *sand* bottom.

For a second anchor I would have a 60-pound *CQR* (plow). Despite the curve shown on Figure 11-2, I believe the CQR will hold as much as the Danforth in sand, perhaps more than the Danforth in mud, and will be better in shingle or weed bottoms.

My third anchor would be an 80- to 100-pound *Herreshoff*, primarily for use in rock and coral. No holding powers are given for these conditions because if a Herreshoff becomes hooked into something solid, the breaking strength of the chain sets the upper limit.

If I were to carry a fourth anchor, it would be a *Northill*. Although Northills are not often seen, they are available on order. And I am of the opinion that an 80-pound Northhill would also be a good substitute for any of the three aforementioned anchors.

I will freely admit that this seems like a lot of iron to put aboard a

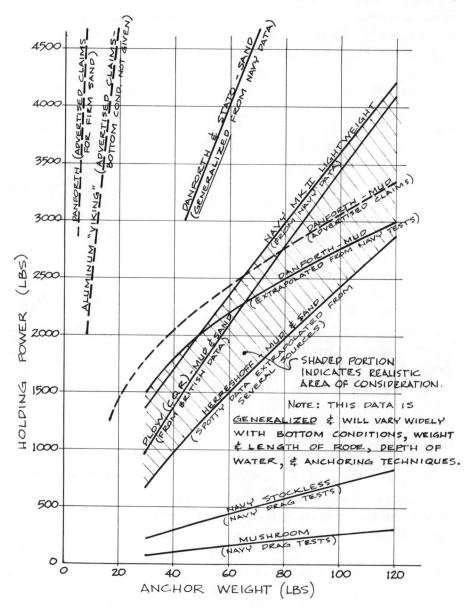

Fig. 11-2 Holding power of anchors.

40-foot ketch; generally we have seen anchors in the weight range of 40 to 45 pounds aboard cruising boats of this size. However, if you want security in 60 knots and more wind, you should carry the bigger sizes. It is true that most cruising boats will put out two anchors in harbors where the stay will be extended, and it is also true that two of the lighter size anchors will probably hold the ship in 60 knots—assuming *good holding ground.* Remember though, most harbor bottoms of the world are mud. Not for nothing do experienced cruising sailors push the size of ground tackle to the largest within their own physical limitations.

Anchoring techniques depend mainly on prevailing conditions, somewhat on the ground tackle, and perhaps to a lesser extent on the handling characteristics of the yacht.

A good anchorage will be protected from wave action, hopefully from high wind and current conditions, will have a good holding bottom, and will not be too deep or too shallow. Such anchorages are popular and are usually crowded, adding another problem— picking a spot that will allow swinging room.

Aboard *Starbound* we follow an anchoring procedure that we can recommend to anyone. It might seem overly cautious to anyone accustomed to anchoring a low-windage fiberglass sloop in local waters, but we have had very few anchoring problems. Bear in mind that *Starbound* is a 35-ton high-windage ketch with a long bowsprit. She measures just under 65 feet from the tip of her bow-sprit to the end of her mizzen boom.

We don't enter a harbor blind. We study the harbor chart carefully, noting our options and getting an idea of depths and bottom conditions. We check the sailing directions (or pilots) and any other publications we might have about the harbor (including books by other yachties). We remember what others have told us, if anything. We rig the anchor well before entering any harbor—there have been a few times when we had to drop it fast.

We do not sail into a harbor unless we know we can do it safely. This supposes preknowledge of the harbor, which a deep-water sailor usually doesn't have. So our diesel is running and the sails come down before we enter.

We have our sounding lead at the ready. (Our depth sounder transducer is 40 feet aft of the point we're interested in.) We use water-pump grease to arm the lead if we want to get a bottom sample. Usually we can get this information from other yachts (if any) in the anchorage. A hail and a polite query can save a lot of time about the best place to anchor too, but in the last analysis, it is your decision where to drop your hook. If the harbor is populated and well protected, odds are the bottom is soft mud.

We pick the spot where the anchor will go down, calculate about a boat length of drag to set it, and make sure we'll have swinging room. If the anchorage is crowded, we'll probably stay to leeward of the yachts already anchored. It is the height of bad manners, as well as being dangerous, to invade the swinging circle of another yacht. If a tidal current is present, the swing on the tide change of all nearby yachts must be considered.

We use the engine to put *Starbound's* bow into the wind at the point we want to drop the anchor. We do this *slowly,* always leaving ourselves an avenue of escape if our first choice looks worse after we get there than it did initially. We reverse the propeller and as headway ceases and the ship starts making slow sternway, we let go the anchor. If there is a wind blowing the bow will fall off one way or the other; we try to have *Starbound's* bow fall off to the starboard since the chain rode fairleads out the port hawse. We always put out a 6 to 1 scope initially before braking the wildcat, which we normally do gently with the propeller stopped.

Now we are anchored, but the hook must be set. We let the ship blow fair to the rode and see if she's holding O.K., then reverse the propeller again and increase power until we're satisfied she's not going anywhere. We are very tender about this last operation to allow the anchor time to settle into the bottom. Also, it gives us time to see just where the ship will sit and if we're going to be happy with it. Now we decide if we want to put out more chain and perhaps a second anchor. If we intend to put the launch over the side, which is usual, we often carry a second anchor out with it. But under some conditions—if it's blowing hard and we know we'll need a second anchor anyway—we'll power forward over our first

Starbound's anchor chain on the dock before stowing.

rode, *always* chain, and drop the second anchor about 20 to 30 degrees off the first and about even with it. This second anchor has 20 feet of chain preceding a nylon rode. As the wind blows us back toward our first position, we let the nylon run out the starboard hawse and as the catenary of our first rode begins to straighten, we'll take a turn of the nylon around the capstan drum and start surging it gently while allowing it to run a bit more. This will set the second anchor and, if done with delicacy, will put us in anchorage with an even strain on both rodes, though the catenary of the nylon will naturally have less curvature than that of the chain.

The evolution takes a little practice but is not really difficult. It is important that the first rode be all chain so that when driving up to the drop point of the second anchor, it will stay relatively vertical and not foul the propeller. Since the placement of the second anchor is 20 to 30 degrees off the first, there usually is not a problem with the chain rode rubbing on the topsides, but one crew member tending a fender can make sure.

We mark our chain rode with paint. Although it wears off and needs to be renewed about once a year while cruising, it seems to be the best method. Since we always put out at least ten fathoms of chain, we commence our marking system from there as follows:

Length (in fathoms)	Link Code
10	1 red, 1 white, 1 blue
11	1 red
12	2 red
13	3 red
14	1 white
15	2 white Repeating Sequence
16	3 white
17	1 blue
18	2 blue
19	3 blue
20	2 red, 2 white, 2 blue
21	1 red
22	2 red
23	3 red

And so on, repeating the sequence of 11–19.

Length (in fathoms)	Link Code
to 30	3 red, 3 white, 3 blue. Repeat sequence again.
and 40	4 red, 4 white, 4 blue. Repeat sequence again.

The nylon rode is marked at 10, 20, and 30 fathoms with 1, 2, and 3 pieces of nylon small stuff passed through the lay with stopper knots on each side.

Stow only *clean* chain and nylon below. A washdown pump with a topside hose is really worth having, not only for the ground tackle but for the decks and the topside baths too. Otherwise you will be relegated to the bucket and brush technique.

The bitter end of the anchor chain should be stoutly attached to the inside of the chain locker by a piece of nylon line of a diameter just small enough to pass through the end link. The line should be long enough so that the bitter end of the chain can come clear through the navel pipe, allowing the nylon line to be cut with a knife if the anchor has to be slipped. If the ground tackle ever does have to be slipped, decide now how you'll buoy it. Use a piece of moderately sized line, say ½-inch diameter, long enough to reach bottom, plus about 10 feet, and bend one end to the chain *outboard of the hawse* and the other end to a buoy—a life jacket will do if nothing else is immediately available. It is unlikely that you'll ever have to slip your ground tackle, but as I've said before, once is enough—and it's too expensive to lose forever.

DINGHIES AND TENDERS

A deep-water cruising yacht must be equipped with a dinghy, or if you prefer, a *tender, launch,* or *gig*. Most yachtsmen prefer the word *dinghy*, which to be desperately accurate comes from a Bengal word meaning a small rowing boat belonging to a larger vessel. The word *tender* usually describes a vessel attendant to lighthouses, buoys, and certain military vessels that use them to ferry stores. *Launch* also describes a small boat, usually with power. A *gig* used to refer to the captain's boat, which in the old days was an ornamented and carefully maintained whaleboat.

Whatever term is used is O.K. nowadays. *Starbound* carries two small boats. An 11-footer we call the launch, which we normally drive with an outboard engine. And a 9-footer on the stern davits, which we call the dinghy and row.

The functions of a dinghy are these: (1) to get crew and supplies to and from shore, (2) to carry a second anchor out whenever necessary, and (3) for recreation such as diving on reefs and exploring places where the yacht cannot go.

Any dinghy intended for deep-water cruising should be rowable. Despite the fact that we carry two outboard engines, there are many times when we have to row—usually when the engine gives out. Then again, rowing is very pleasurable—unless you have a mile to go through choppy water with a heavy load aboard. We usually row the dinghy for fun or if it's just a short haul with not much to carry. But the launch can hold four people and a load of groceries and still make knots against a stiff wind—under power. We find it a valuable asset.

The type and size of dinghy carried aboard a deep-water yacht will depend primarily on the size of the yacht. A 30-foot yacht must necessarily be restricted to the small *pram,* the folding or nested halves breakdown-type, or the small *inflatable.* I would personally prefer the inflatable if my yacht were too small to accommodate a rigid boat, but the preferences of other yachties run the gamut.

Inflatables have their drawbacks. The ones worth having are very expensive. None of them row worth a damn in any but mill-pond conditions, so an engine becomes a necessity rather than a luxury. A plywood sole is required in order to carry an anchor out and is at least recommended for any other use too.

On the plus side inflatables are light and easy to get aboard. They can be stowed topside, upside down under the main boom or forward over the fore hatch—or they can be deflated and stowed below in a very small space, thereby decreasing the ship's windage. Inflating *and* deflating them can be done quickly and easily by a small, noisy, 12-volt electric air pump. They rest quietly at night either alongside or astern. They are very stable initially and make good diving boats. They can carry a surprising amount of weight and are unsinkable as long as the pontoons are intact. (I have included a list of good brands and their manufacturers' addresses at the end of this chapter.)

As yachts get larger, so does the variety of small boats carried, mostly of the rigid type. Before making a choice of what kind of dinghy to carry, the optimum stowage plan for it will have to be worked out. By far, most deep-water cruising yachts carry their dinghies inverted on the deckhouse top and lashed down to the handrails and/or eyebolts secured through the deck beams. Some are carried right side up, cradled in athwartship chocks and have a tight-fitting fabric cover. This is a favorite method of the larger yachts whose dinghies are generally heavier than the average. They are lifted from the water by side davits or a boom that can be rigged for the purpose.

Stern davits also are often seen on large yachts, which are not particularly affected by the weight of a dinghy placed that far aft. The advantages of stern davits are obvious. However, smaller yachts without a great deal of buoyancy aft are advised not to carry them. Their pitching will generally be affected. Also, it is virtually impossible to employ wind vane self-steering when a dinghy is hanging off the stern. The final disadvantage of stern davits is perhaps the most serious: When running before a big sea, a pooping wave can drive the dinghy against or through the davits and destroy the dinghy, or rip the davits loose allowing water below, or smash the helm and possibly the helmsman—or a combination of any or all of these catastrophies.

I will unashamedly admit that *Starbound* has stern davits on which we carry our 9-foot rowing dink, but the bottom of the dinghy is six feet above the water and *Starbound* is fifteen feet wide at the transom. Her aft lines give her tremendous buoyancy, which

has always lifted to any following sea. When we have been washed, the waves have always come over her quarter—never her stern— even with 25-foot greybeards chasing her in 60-knot winds. So if you've got enough yacht—and no wind vane—stern davits are worth having. Otherwise start thinking about topside stowage.

If the deckhouse can accommodate an 11-foot dinghy, then consider that size. If there is only room for a 9-footer, don't get carried away by a larger boat; it'll just get in the way. And consider how you will secure it to the deckhouse. It must be gripped down hard to very solid fixtures.

Be aware that a dinghy carries several appurtenances that must also be stowed: oars, oarlocks, life jackets, an anchor with 6 feet of light chain and perhaps 50 feet of ½-inch diameter nylon rode, bow and stern painters (spliced into place to forestall theft ashore and "borrowing" on board), a bailer (cut plastic jugs still make the best ones), a piece of toweling or sponge to dry the seats, and a waterproof flashlight for night work. If an outboard engine is the normal means of propulsion, there will probably be a gas tank on the sole and running lights will be required. And somewhere aboard there should be a package of plastic containing spare spark plugs, shearpins, cotter pins, and a few simple tools. And if the dinghy is a sailing dinghy, room must be made for sails, mast, rudder, rigging, and boom.

Dinghy construction should be of good quality. I am in favor of fiberglass in lieu of wood because of the reduction in maintenance. There is so much to do on the yacht proper that it seems foolish to have a beautiful, varnished lapstrake dink with polished bronze fittings—as much as I love the type. A dinghy should be unsinkable, with enough built-in buoyancy to support a full load of people even when swamped. It should have lifting eyes, each strong enough to easily support the weight of the boat with its ancillary equipment aboard. A bronze or stainless steel keel strip should run the entire length of the bottom. A wide, tough, but fairly soft, rubbing guard should completely encircle the dinghy at the sheer, about an inch below the edge.

While at anchor, put the dinghy alongside against two fenders,

Gordon in Starbound's *lightweight tender.*

or on a boat boom made from a whisker pole—with an overhauling block. If it is trailed astern, it will sooner or later sneak up on the yacht's transom and thump it. Secondly, do *not* tow the dinghy at sea. It will be swamped or lost and if a deep-water yacht loses her dinghy, the resulting problems at the next port, including costs of replacement in time and dollars, can ruin a cruise.

SURVIVAL AND SECURITY

There is no international law that states a cruising boat must carry a *life raft*. Perhaps there should be. Before our circumnavigation we did some soul searching before laying out $600 dollars for our four-man canopied raft. It has never been out of its plastic container except for a complete test and repack after our return.

A sailor may almost refuse to even consider the possibility of abandoning his sinking ship and taking to a life raft, but a deep-water sailor must consider it. Yachts have been lost at sea many times in the past and with the growing numbers of cruising yachts on the world's oceans, these disastrous incidents will undoubtedly occur more frequently in the future. So let's face it—a deep-water cruising yacht should be equipped with a good life raft.

The only life rafts worth considering are those with a self-erecting canopy for protection against sun, sea, and weather. The canopy should be bright orange or yellow for high visibility and some manufacturers have given them a coating that assures a good radar reflection. The raft should be equipped with at least two separate buoyancy chambers provided with semiautomatic CO_2 inflation.

Rafts are available in four-, six-, or eight-person capacity models and come in a valise-type pack that can be stowed below, or more sensibly, in a fiberglass canister that is chocked and lashed down on deck. Hydrostatic releases are available on the larger rafts but are not recommended for small yachts since a green sea washing across the deckhouse might release the raft prematurely. It is far better to have heavy nylon webbing equipped with a manual quick-release buckle to hold them down or even a piece of nylon line that can be

Gordon stows inflatable liferaft in its chocks aboard Starbound.

quickly severed with a knife. Our raft was delivered with a hold-down strap of flimsy polypropylene webbing with a Velcro closure. It deteriorated within months and was replaced with a piece of ½-inch nylon line.

If the chocks for the raft are through-bolted to the deck, the hold-down strap(s) may be attached to the chocks. But if it is not feasible to through-bolt the chocks, then the hold-down straps must lead to eyebolts or some other permanent fixture outside the chocks.

A *survival kit* is an integral part of a life raft's equipment. But it is impossible to pack all the gear that even a minimum survival kit should contain into the canister with the raft. So a few pieces of the survival kit might go into the canister, but the rest should be packed into a water-resistant valise or in some other handy carrier that is stowed below in a permanent spot adjacent to the companionway.

A list of items we believe should be included in the survival kit are:

*1. Manual inflation pump
*2. Raft repair kit
*3. Collapsible paddles (worthless for making speed but good spear shafts [see item 7] and might be needed to maneuver the raft to a ship's side when rescued)
*4. Sea anchor and rode
 5. Water (At lease four 5-gallon jugs should be carried topside on any cruising yacht (for ferrying water if necessary) and freshened with each fill of the main tanks. Fresh water is lighter than salt water but not by much, so don't fill the jugs completely if you want them to float if dropped overboard. Cut their lashings loose and stow them in the raft or tie them alongside. If time permits, add all the beer on board.)
 6. Food (K-ration type survival food can be obtained at stores that sell backpacking gear. Don't count too much on supplementing these with ship's stores. You may not have time.

*Indicates canister stowage.

Avoid foods with a high salt content. Add matches and can opener. Waterproof packs and cans with melted wax.)

7. Fishing gear (Include trident-type spear heads, plenty of lures, fish hooks, and 50-pound test fishing line. Include a small pair of pliers. This stuff is small and light, so have a lot. Also include two pairs of cheap cotton gloves to handle fishing line.)

8. Shark repellent

9. EPIRB: Emergency Position Indicating Radio Beacon. NASA is currently engaged in a program to put receivers for EPIRBs on board weather satellites. This could effect world-wide coverage and promote timely rescues. (See list of suppliers and manufacturers at end of chapter.)

10. Strobe light

11. Extra batteries for EPIRB and strobe

12. Signals (red parachute flares, handheld red flares, handheld orange smoke flares, signaling mirrors, dye markers)

13. Life jackets (If there's time, throw all you have into the raft and tie them around the perimeter later.)

*14. Inflatable sun stills (at least two)

15. Desalinization kits (several)

16. First-aid kit (burn ointment, PABA paste and pills, seasick pills, nondiuretic laxatives, splint, bandages, antibiotic ointment, adhesive tape, sutures and needles, scissors, tampax for women crew, stainless steel scalpel or very sharp knife, pain killer, aspirin, thermometer, several clear plastic bags to help keep the foregoing dry and to dispose of any bloody waste, any special prescription medications required by you or your crew)

17. Vitamins (primarily vitamin C and a high-potency multivitamin)

*18. Knives (Put one in the canister on a lanyard to the raft and at least two in the survival kit. One should be a folding-type with a can opener. Swiss Army knives are good.)

*Indicates canister stowage.

19. Sunglasses (at least two pair of plastic Polaroid sunglasses and/or clip-ons)
*20. Sea-survival handbook

And if you can grab them in time:

21. Clothes (*Stay clothed* for protection. Grab jackets, shirts, pants, socks, shoes, hats—and wear them. They are protection against heat and cold. Sewing kit.)
22. Navigational gear (Compass; perhaps include a cheap plastic sextant in the kit but grab ocean chart, tables, maybe Bowditch, and make sure your quartz crystal watch is on your wrist.)
23. Ship's papers (Include passports, international vaccine cards, and money, if you have any. These should all be kept with the ship's papers anyway.)

All of the survival-kit equipment should be protected as well as possible against salt water. Cans can be hot-wax dipped as can other metal objects. Film cans can be used for small objects. Keep items such as vitamins and medicines in plastic airtight bottles. Pick everything with an eye toward long shelf life. Put fresh batteries in the EPIRB and strobe light just before departure. If your survival kit is in a valise-type container, treat the seams and zipper (after closing) with Whip-dip. You are not going to open it unless an emergency occurs anyway.

We have included a list of life raft distributors and manufacturers at the close of this chapter. Also listed are some books on survival that we consider to be worth reading and/or keeping on board.

---

*Indicates canister stowage.

SURVIVAL PUBLICATIONS

The following publications have been included for those who may want to delve deeper into the many aspects of survival at sea. We particularly recommend *Survival Afloat* by Don Biggs as an excellent survival handbook. *Staying Alive* by the Baileys, and *Survive the Savage Sea* by Robertson are frightening texts but present accurate and vivid pictures of conditions encountered in actual survival situations.

Angier, Bradford. *Survival with Style*. Harrisburg, Pa.: Stackpole Books, 1972.
Bailey, Maurice and Maralyn. *Staying Alive!* New York: David McKay, 1974.
Baldridge, H. D. *Shark Attack Against Man*. Sarasota, Fla.: Mote Marine Laboratory, 1973.
Biggs, Don. *Survival Afloat*. New York: David McKay, 1976.
Eastman, Peter F., M.D. *Advanced First Aid Afloat*. Cornell Maritime Press, Inc., Cambridge, Maryland, 1972.
Henderson, Richard. *Sea Sense*. Camden, Maine: International Marine, 1972.
Robertson, Dougal. *Survive the Savage Sea*. New York: Praeger, 1973.
————. *Sea Survival*. New York: Praeger, 1975.
Sheldon, Paul B. *First Aid Afloat*. New York: Yachting Publishing Co., 1967.
Wright, C. H. *Survival at Sea: The Lifeboat and Liferaft*. London: James Laver, 1970.

Government Publications

*National Search and Rescue Manual.** (Department of Defense, 1973. SUPDOC, $4.00.)†
Search and Rescue Survival. (Department of the Air Force, 1969. SUPDOC, $2.25.)
Special Study: Survivor Locator Systems for Distressed Vessels. (National Transportation Safety Board, Washington, D.C. 20591, 1972.)

*Extremely interesting and informative guide to the procedures, techniques, and policies followed by Coast Guard and military services in the conduct of search and rescue operations.
†Superintendent of Public Documents, U.S. Government Printing Office, Washington, D.C. 20450.

Survival, Evasion and Escape. (Department of the Army, 1968. SUP-DOC, $3.50.)

Syllabus for Water Survival Training. (U.S. Air Force Training Command, Randolph A.F.B., Tex. 78148, 1973.)

The following publications are final reports of investigations and research projects contracted by the U.S. Coast Guard. A more complete list, which includes the price of each volume, can be obtained by writing to National Technical Information Service, Springfield, Virginia 22151.

Recreational Boaters Requirements and Methods of Distress Notification Using Visual Signals, 1975.
A Reliability Investigation of Personal Flotation Devices, Phase I, 1974.
Inflatable Boat Standard Development, 1973.
Boating Accident Investigations: Fire and Explosion, 1973.
Human Factor Applications in Boating Safety, 1973.
Flotation Standards Analysis Research and Development Report, 1973.
Boating Accident Investigations: Capsizing and Swamping, 1972.
Boating Accident Investigations: Fire and Explosion, 1972.

INFLATABLE DINGHIES

Achilles Inflatable Craft
25 Braca Rd.
E. Rutherford, NJ 07073
(201)438-6400

Annex Int.
1622 SE 10th Terr.
Ft. Lauderdale, FL 33316
(305) 522-0621
"Seaspirit"

Avon Rubber Company
  Imtra Corp.
151 Mystic Ave.
Medford, MA 02155
(617) 391-5660

Inland Marine
79 E. Jackson St.
Wilkes-Barre, PA 18701
(717) 822-7185

Seagull Marine
1851 McGaw Ave.
Irvine, CA 92714
(714) 979-6161

Bonair Boats
15501 W. 109th St.
Lenexa, KS 66219
(913) 888-8484
"Cuda"

Dixie Trading Co.
1526 Forest Ave.
PO Box 90396
East Point, GA 30344
(404) 766-0259

K Enterprises
PO Box 2287
Menlo Park, Ca 94025
(413) 325-9919
"Porta-Bote" Folding Boats

Sevylor USA
6279 East Slauson
Los Angeles, CA 90040
(213) 728-7877
"Caravelle", "Tahiti"

Zodiac of North America
11 Lee St.
Annapolis, MD 21401
(301) 268-2009
Rubber Tenders

LIFE RAFTS

**American Safety
  Equipment Corp.**
7000 NW 46th St.
Miami, FL 33148
(305) 592-3460

Atlantic Pacific Mfg.
124 Atlantic Ave.
Brooklyn, NY 11201
(212) 624-8400
"Apco"

**Avon Inflatables
  Imtra Corp**
151 Mystic Ave.
Medford, MA 02155
(617) 391-5660

Inland Marine
79 E. Jackson St.
Wilkes-Barre, PA 18701
(717) 822-7185

Seagull Marine
1851 McGaw Ave.
Irvine, CA 92714
(714) 979-6161

Datrex
3770 NW South River Dr.
Miami, FL 33142
(305) 638-8220

Dixie Trading Co.
1526 Forrest Ave.
East Point, GA 30344
(404) 766-0259

Eastern Aero Marine
3850 NW 25th St.
Miami, FL 33142
(305) 871-4050

Givens Buoy Rafts
1803 Madrid Ave.
Lake Worth, FL 33461
(305) 582-2477

B.F. Goodrich Co.
500 S. Main St.
Akron, OH 44318
(216) 379-2461
"Crewsaver"

C. J. Hendry Co.
139 Townsend St.
San Francisco, CA 94107
"Sea Jay"

McElfish Assoc.
2615 Love Field Dr.
Dallas, TX 75235
(214) 351-5343

Res-Q-Raft
1402 Norton
Everett, WA 98201

Revere Survival Products
605 W. 29th St.
New York, NY 10001
(212) 565-2660

Survival & Safety
  Designs
1 Fifth Ave.
Oakland, CA 94606
(415) 834-6877
"Sailaway"

Switlik Parachute Co.
PO Box 1328
Trenton, NJ 08607
(609) 587-3300

Winslow Co.
PO Box 578
Osprey, FL 33559
(813) 966-2144

Zodiac of North America
11 Lee St.
Annapolis, MD 21401
(301) 268-2009

OUTSIDE THE U.S.

INFLATABLE BOATS

Dunlop Marine Safety Products
Atherton Road
Hindley Green
Wigan Lancashire WN2 4SH (England)
Tel: Wigan (0942) 57181 Telex 67171

INFLATABLE BOATS AND LIFE RAFTS

Angeviniere
Angeviniere S.A.
63, Av. de Villiers 75017 Paris (France)
Tel.: 227.00.94 / Telex 290995 F

EPIRB (Emergency Position Indicating Radio Beacon)

ACR Electronic
3901 N. 20th Ave.
Hollywood, FL 33020
(305) 921-6262

Narco Marine
Commerce Dr.
Ft. Washington, PA 19034
(215) 643-2900

Seagull Marine
1851 McGaw Ave.
Irvine, CA 92714
(714) 979-6161

Simrad
1 Labriola Ct.
Armonk, NY 10504
(914) 273-9410

12

Tools, Spares, and Bosun's Stores

Literally everything on a yacht must be repaired at one time or another and on a deep-water cruising yacht the repairs must be accomplished *by the crew*. While many repairs can be made in port, many more are made at sea. It makes no difference anyway as far as equipment is concerned, because even in port the ship's crew will still be the ones doing the jobs—and they will be using the ship's tools and spares to accomplish them.

While in Bermuda we had to repair storm damage, which included replacing the mizzen boom track and the outhauls on both staysail and mizzen booms.

In Antigua we pulled the propeller and stuffing box using SCUBA and replaced the cutlass bearing.

Further down the West Indies it was necessary to repair the starting circuit on the Onan generator and replace its fuel pump.

Balboa found us working over the starter motor on the main engine and overhauling the clutch and compass head on the auto pilot.

The Pacific crossing saw us sewing sails, working over rigging, disassembling and cleaning the windlass, and performing various carpentry tasks. And just so we found it with other cruising yachts around the world.

At this point in your preparations, the planning book sections entitled Tools, Spare Parts, and Bosun's Stores should be well crowded with items and the ship's lockers should be filling up. Check your lists against the ones contained in this chapter.

A cruising yacht must carry a large number and variety of tools. They are almost as important as food and water in that basic survival can depend on them. Tools are heavy, often bulky and take up a lot of prime stowage space, space that is dry and handy. Spare parts can be wrapped against dampness and stowed almost anywhere, but not so with tools. Tools must be readily available.

The weight of a full complement of tools such as *Starbound* carries precludes a single stowage area, unless the area is located amidship. The weight of a load of heavy tools carried to one side of the centerline can induce a sizable list, even to a beamy, heavy-displacement yacht.

Aboard *Starbound* we considered every possible stowage area, then shrugged our shoulders and selected the driest, most accessible available—excluding the galley: This was under the forward settee in the main saloon. We compensated for their slightly off-center-line weight by stowing spare parts on the opposite side of the boat under the port quarterberth.

POWER TOOLS

Power tools are nice to have if there is a motor-generator set aboard or some other way to generate a sufficient supply of alternating current. Many areas outside the U.S. use 220-volt, 50-cycle, single-phase current. Some yachts have found it worthwhile to purchase at least a drill motor and matching extension cord for use in these areas. Drill motors powered by 12-volt D.C. are also available. Inverters that can step up 12-volt D.C. to 110-volt A.C. are available, but check its *continuous load capacity* against the drill motor under load. *Starbound* has a 3-kilowatt Onan diesel generator that does a good job: It charges the battery banks, runs the hot water heater for the domestic supply and the heating system when we feel the need for it, and we can use power tools at the same time.

The following inventory of tools lists them in order of importance:

ELECTRIC POWER TOOLS

•Drill motor: ⅜-inch with bits
•Grinder/sander: 3,600 rpm with discs and soft pad
•Saber saw with assorted blades
•Flat bed sander with plenty of sandpaper
•Circular saw with assorted blades, including one carbide-tipped combination blade

HAND TOOLS

The items on this list might seem to be obvious, but only once did *Starbound* have to borrow a tool: a swaging device for Nicopress fittings. On the other hand, we've loaned various tools out several times to yachts that were not so well equipped and /or considered themselves too small to carry a more complete tool inventory.

Machine Tools

•Hammers: ball peen (2)
•Screwdrivers: all types and several sizes
•Pliers: all types and several sizes, including vise grips
•Vises: one large bolt-down type and one small vacuum-base type
•Eggbeater drills: one small and 1 large
•Fixed-size wrenches (spanners: ¼-inch to 1-inch, box and open-end combinations (metric, if required)

•Adjustable wrenches: 6-, 8-, 10-, and 12-inch sizes
•Torque wrench: ½-inch drive, 150 foot-pound capacity
•Socket sets: 2 complete sets with ¼-inch and ½-inch drives
•Allen wrenches: complete set
•Files: several sizes and cuts, triangular, flat, and round
•Punches: one set
•Cold chisels: one set
•Micrometer: 1-inch
•Feeler gauge: two sets (hide one in your personal gear locker as a spare)
•Hacksaws: two holders and various gauge blades
•Tape measures and scales: 12-foot, 50-foot, and 1-foot (straight-edge)
•Taps and dies: complete set
•Easy-outs: complete set

Woodworking Tools

•Hammers: claw (2)
•Mallet
•Hand saws: cross-cut, rip, back (with holder), piping
•Framing square: small and large
•Folding rule: 6-foot
•High-speed wood bits for use with electric drill: ¼- to 1½-inch
•Wood planes: three sizes
•Surform planes: complete set
•Draw knife
•Wood chisels: complete set with sizes from ¼ inch to 2 inches
•Whetstones: large and small
•Circular saw bits for use with electric drill: 1¾- to 2½-inch
•Brace, complete with wood bits, including expansion bit and several sizes of screwdriver bits
•Caulking irons
•C-clamps: various sizes
•Counterbores and countersinks for use with electric drill
•Tapered bits and countersink combinations for use with electric drill

Electrical Tools

- Electrician's pliers
- Soldering gun
- Soldering pencil
- Wire strippers
- Terminal crimpers
- Multitester
- Solder, solid core, resin core, and acid core

Plumbing Tools

- Stillson wrenches: three sizes
- Propane torch with extra tanks of gas, with various tips, bar solder, and soldering paste
- Tubing tools for cutting and flaring

Rigging and Sail Tools

- Nicopress fittings for all wire sizes on board and bolt-up–type swaging tool to accommodate fittings
- Wrenches: large for Norseman, Electroline or similar type terminals on board
- Pipe: galvanized 3-foot section to fit wrench handle for leverage. (This is not a good mechanic's practice but necessary for larger wire sizes, unless special wrenches are on board.)
- Vise (A reiteration: A large vise mounted on a heavy plank to make it portable is necessary to make up mechanical-type wire fittings.)
- Splicing vise, marlinspikes, serving mallet (necessary items if you prefer splicing wire rigging. It is a seamanly art but takes time and practice. We prefer mechanical terminals and Nicopress sleeves for emergencies or very small wire sizes such as used for slings and other devices.)
- Cable cutters for small wire only—say to ¼-inch; cable cutters for large-size wire are almost ineffectual.

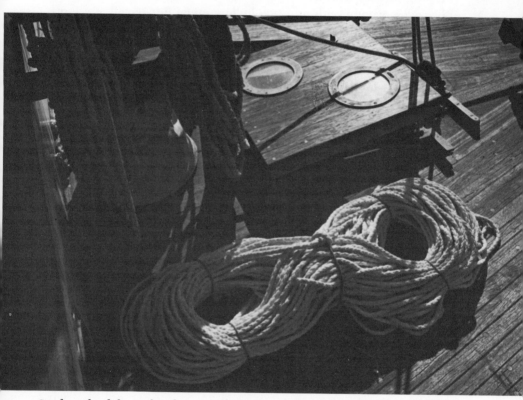

Six hundred feet of eight-stranded plaited Dacron line is flaked for stowing.

•Diamond rods for use in hacksaw holder; they cut through heavy rigging wire and stainless steel plate cleanly and quickly.

•Rigging kit: portable (This can be a box, satchel, canvas bag with pockets, or whatever you prefer as long as you can carry it around. Equip it with roping and sewing palms, whipping twine, roping thread, sail thread, *many* needles of all sizes, a sharp knife, beeswax, wooden fids and two hollow metal fids, small and large. Add a bench hook for sail work and the special tools for splicing braided line if you have any aboard. Put in a roll of chrome leather for chafing gear, sailcloth for patches, and rip-stop tape. Add thimbles and cringles of the size used on your sails and snap fasteners for various covers.)

•Sewing machine with a zigzag stitch. (Sails can be sewn by hand, but a machine is very handy for large boats with large sails. Machines can be purchased which are powered by hand, 12-volt D.C. or 110-A.C. They are fairly expensive but will save money on sails, awnings, flags, and covers.)

•Grommet sets: cutter, punch, and anvil for #1 and #2 spur grommets

Not-so-obvious Tools

•Single-bit ax
•Crowbar
•5-pound sledgehammer
•Short-handled shovel
•Wire swaging tools
•Sheet-metal shears
•Small, flat hydraulic jack
•Ratchet hoist: 3-ton capacity
•Cable cutters
•Propeller puller
•Magnet: 5-pound capacity (stow it far from the compass)
•Magnet: small, on flex cable for tool and part retrieval
•Garden hose: 350 feet, with spare fittings
•Adaptor fittings for propane gas bottle (both male and female)

SPARES

If a yachtie carried every spare item he really wanted to have aboard, he'd sink the yacht. Weight, available space, and money are important limiting factors. But these factors balance as nothing against the overwhelming factor of safety. A deep-water sailor must ask himself, "What items on my yacht will, in failing, prevent or seriously hamper my ship from making it safely to the next or nearest port, which might be 1,500 nautical miles away?" Those items are of first priority.

While planning our voyage, we spent many hours making lists of everything we wanted to carry. Then we categorized and assigned priorities to each item. By the time we balanced what we could spend on spares against the available space to carry them, only the first-priority items were seriously considered—with a few exceptions.

Second-priority items were considered to be those spares which, while not mandatory for safety at sea, were not likely to be found at any except the largest, most modern ports.

Our spares categories are kept broad: Bosun's spares, machinery spares, and electrical/electronics spares.

The following lists are not intended to be agonizingly complete. They include all first-priority spares and some second-priority items. And since the lists are applicable only to our vessel, they are intended simply as a guide for other yachtsmen.

BOSUN'S SPARES

•Sails: main, jib, storm jib, storm trysail
•Line: 300 feet of 1-inch diam., 1200 feet of ⅝-inch diam., 600 feet of ½-inch diam., assorted small stuff. (Note that virtually all running rigging on *Starbound* is restricted to two sizes of line: ⅝-inch and ½-inch.)
•Wire: enough for a spare shroud, a spare headstay, and a made-up spare bobstay)

•Line and wire rope fittings: wire terminals, turnbuckles, toggles, padeyes, shackles, thimbles, etc. (everything needed to make up new standing rigging)

•Blocks

•Paint: enough for three complete paint jobs (with plenty of thinner and good-quality brushes)

•Bedding compound: polysulfide and oil types

•Fiberglass (mat and cloth) and resin

•Underwater epoxy

•Nails, screws, and other fasteners

•Wood: sheets of ½-inch plywood cut to fit under bunk mattresses; 2 x 4s cut to fit in lazaret

•Lead sheeting for gasketing and leak control

•Welding rods: correct type for steel or aluminum hulls

•Cement: approved type for ferro-cement hulls

MACHINERY SPARES

Main Engine and Generator

•Zinc pencils for heat exchangers: 10

•Sea water pump impellers and seals: 4 sets

•V-belts: 2 sets

•Oil and fuel filters: enough to change on schedule; *very important*

•Oil and transmission fluid

•Alternator and voltage regulator: complete spare set

•Starter motor brushes and spare starter motor relay (The motor itself is easy to overhaul, but the relay is difficult.)

•Hoses and stainless steel hose clamps: complete set for all systems (fresh water, salt water, exhaust, oil, fuel, and hydraulics)

•Gaskets for heads, manifolds, pump bodies, etc.: complete set

•Piping/fittings/tubing

•Fuel injectors: a full set is desirable. (I recommend diesel engines for cruising boats, but if you've got gasoline, you'll need sev-

Tool stowage aboard Starbound *is in the area under the settee in the main saloon.*

eral sets of spark plugs and points, and at least two repair kits for the carburator and fuel pump.)

•Water temperature and oil pressure gauges and a spare ignition switch (if in exposed location)

•Steering cables (if used)

•Repair kits for all pumps and heads

•Stopcocks and valves

•Pipe fittings for exhaust system and other systems: various types and sizes

ELECTRICAL/ELECTRONICS SPARES

•Hydrometer: 2 (Put one away.)

•Transistors for auto pilot, chargers, radiotelephone, radio direction finder

•Fuses and circuit breakers for above

•Wire and terminal devices for all uses including batteries

•Diodes for alternator, charger, and radiotelephone

•Light bulbs (for everything) and running-light glasses

•Switches: various types

•Electrical tape

•Sealant

•Silicon spray and sealant

•D-cell batteries (Available almost anywhere, but keep a store of them; buy them by the carton.)

•Refrigerator switch and freon charging kit

•Brushes for all electric motors

•6-volt batteries for spotlights

13

Foul Weather Considerations and Emergency Gear

Foul weather strikes every deep-sea yacht sooner or later but need not necessarily lead to an emergency situation. A cruising yacht has absolutely no good reason to poke her bow into tropical cyclone areas during the season of their occurrence. However, out-of-season storms can strike anytime. The world's weather systems offer no guarantee of tranquil seas to any ship.

The bad weather of midlatitude frontal systems in either hemisphere is a fact of life for a yacht. But the duration of this kind of bad weather is normally 24 to 36 hours at the most—with perhaps only a few hours of gale force winds. If your ship is sound and proper foul weather procedures are begun well in advance, the storm will go eventually grumbling on its way, leaving a sea that is confused for a short while but sparkling under a welcome sun. Then the sea straightens itself out before the prevailing wind and the ship's motion becomes regular once more.

The first emergency most people think about when planning a deep-sea voyage is the "ultimate storm." There is not really very much planning, per se, that a sailor can do to prepare for a tropical storm—one in which the winds are 65 knots and above and the seas get mountainous, measuring 25 feet and more. One really can't train for such circumstances. Of course, if by misfortune you are ever caught by a true tropical storm, the training will be instilled under battlefield conditions. Assuming that your ship is well constructed and meticulously prepared for sea, all that can be done ahead of time will have been done.

While at sea keep a close *weather watch*—even in trade wind areas. Use your radio receivers for forecasts and plot the frontal lows and their troughs on your ocean charts. WWV and WWVH give very general ocean area forecasts every hour—take advantage of them.

If caught by bad weather, the three basic rules are: (1) Stay at sea—don't try to make a port; (2) avoid a lee shore; and (3) stay away from shoal water and areas with currents opposed to the storm wind if possible. I agree that these are good rules, but sometimes they are hard to follow. If you are approaching a coast and a storm comes up behind you, it will be very hard to fight your way back out to sea against wind and wave. Still, that is what you should do on a lee shore unless you are very certain that you can make it to protected waters before the storm hits. Again, this means a tight weather watch. It assumes that you will know that the storm is coming, where it is, and how fast it is moving.

If you've made the ultimate weather error and find yourself at sea with a tropical cyclone threatening your ship, take evasive action as early as possible. Locate the storm and ascertain its direction of movement.

If the information is not available by radio, you should know that swells radiate outward in all directions from a tropical cyclone's center—the longest swells, about four per minute, ahead of the storm's path. Take a bearing on the direction the swells are traveling from. Verify the bearing by adding about 115 degrees to where the winds are coming from. The bearing should be almost the same. Knowing the location, and remembering the projected paths of these gigantic storms, will give you a pretty good idea of your situation and will dictate what your evasive action should be, which is to get out of the storm's influence as fast and safely as possible. Assuming that your ship is in the Northern Hemisphere, if you are in the *navigable semicircle* (the left half of the storm's circulation when looking forward along its path) then the true wind will be backing (shifting counter-clockwise) and you should sail clear (if you can still set sail), with the wind on your starboard quarter. If you are in the *dangerous semicircle,* the *right* half of the storm's circulation, the wind will be veering (shifting clockwise) and you should sail clear with the wind on your starboard bow. Of course, in the Southern Hemisphere, your tactics will become a mirror image of those above. The best tactic of all is not to be caught out by one of these destructive storms.

Avoiding shoal water and adverse currents is usually impossible. One can and must plan the cruise so as not to fight the major currents such as the Gulf Stream and the Agulhas, but ocean voyagers will often find their course laying against one current or another. They are impossible to avoid altogether. And shoal water—well, some delightful cruising areas are all shoal water. All of the continental shelves are relatively shoal and it is true that storm winds blowing across these waters precipitate very steep breaking seas that a yacht cannot oppose—she can only run, which is also hazardous in such conditions.

While deciding whether or not you can beat a storm to protected waters, remember that midlatitude frontal systems travel at a speed of approximately 25 knots in summer to 35 knots in winter. They can move a lot faster than your ship. This means that it is nearly always the correct action to drive for sea room and ride it out. There are a lot of stranded yachts and drowned sailors to prove the opposite is the wrong move. The open sea, even in a big storm, can be a lot safer.

So let's suppose you are out there and you've heard the forecast and "it" is coming. It's a big one with a lot of wind and you know you're going to get hit. What should you do?

First of all, you are permitted to be apprehensive—everyone

At sea, a safety line is of utmost importance.

is—but you are not permitted to panic. A calm skipper, even with subdued apprehension, will have a calming effect on the crew.

Check your sea room. See if you'll have enough to run off before it for as long as you think it will last. If you don't, consider what actions you will have to take to heave to.

If you are already running and the storm is coming up on your stern, a special problem presents itself: You will not be nearly as aware of the actual wind strength. Add your ship's speed to the wind that you feel coming over the stern. The smart thing to do is reduce sail very early. The longer you wait, the tougher it will be! Get the main and mizzen down and then reduce her headsails to a manageable size, perhaps even changing to storm jib. Bag the headsails not in use and *stow them below.*

Start the main engine and keep it ticking over. It'll charge the batteries, which you'll want topped up anyway, and if you have to heave to, it'll help bring her around quickly.

After the batteries are up, secure the engine if you prefer to do without its racket—at least you'll have the knowledge that it is operable, warmed-up, and ready at an instant's notice to give the ship some help.

It is a very valuable feature on a cruising yacht to be able to claw down the sails when off the wind. Sometimes coming into the wind while at sea is just not practicable. We have downhauls on all sails just for this purpose and can douse our gaff main (580 square feet) and our Marconi mizzen (225 square feet) when running before 35 knots. It is a job, but the lazy jacks help and we can manage to secure the sails without damage, even though it takes some time.

Now split up the work, some crew topside and some below. Tie down everything topside, plug all vents, and make sure the plug is in the navel pipe to the chain locker. Put on the hatch and doghouse covers and lash them tightly. Ensure that raft, dinghy, and anchors are secure.

Make a complete check below for loose gear. Nothing should be left adrift. Pump the bilge as dry as possible and keep it that way. *Check it often.* Make sure both manual bilge pumps are clear and working, and also the electric pump. Secure all locker doors and remember which lockers contain heavy articles that might be thrown out if opened in a rough sea.

Put on foul weather gear and safety harnesses when the sea starts getting up. Rig an extra lifeline around the deck edge at chest height. Perhaps one is already rigged; we keep *Starbound's* rigged while at sea, fair weather or foul.

Get any fishing gear in and stowed. If you are trailing a taffrail log, secure it! A familiar scenario is to forget those lines trailing astern, to come up into the wind and end up with the whole mess tangled in the screw. A friend of ours did this and came within a whisker of losing his ship on the reefs of Tonga.

Eat and drink something before it gets too rough. It'll be much harder to prepare food later on—and it's easy to get hungry and thirsty without realizing it when you're scared. Stay warm. A storm will drop the temperature considerably and when you're cold and scared too, it will prey on you mentally and physically.

Try to fix the ship's position as well as possible—take a sight if you can. If you've taken a noon sight, you'll have the last noon position on the chart and can use dead reckoning to closely approximate the ship's position when the storm forces you to take whatever evasive action is appropriate.

There are four prevalent storm management techniques: *heaving to, lying ahull, running off* (either with or without streaming warps), and *lying to a sea anchor* (either off bow or stern). Realistically most deep-water sailors recognize only two of these techniques to be feasible at sea: heaving to and running.

Lying ahull means the ship is stripped of all sail and is presenting her entire length to the storm, alternately wallowing in the trough partly out of the wind, then on top of the wave with her maximum windage getting assaulted. This is a damn uncomfortable technique at best because of the violent motion. It becomes downright dangerous when the seas build up to the breaking point because she can be knocked down flat and overwhelmed. When a ship is knocked down, she'll take the maximum damage to her *lee* side. Water is essentially incompressible and the forces involved are tantamount to dropping the ship onto hard ground. Major damage is very likely to occur and she might even do a full 360-degree roll. A ship might lie ahull safely until the winds get up to about force 8. Then she will have to be run off for safety's sake. While lying ahull, she will drift slowly to leeward and leave somewhat of a slick to windward, which will tend to reduce the seas running down on her—at least until they start to break. But each time she climbs a wave, the wind will push her over; then she'll slide down the back of the wave to the trough, straighten herself up with a snap, and climb the next wave to get hit again by the wind—not comfortable at all, and noisy. I don't recommend it.

Employing a sea anchor off the bow is total nonsense. The ship will lie 90 degrees to the wind just as if she were lying ahull, except that her leeway might be slower. This is because the ship's greater lateral surface aft "holds" in the water while the wind exerts the greater force forward on the windage of masts, rigging, and higher freeboard. *A sea anchor rigged from the stern* has some merit if the desire is to reduce downwind drift, perhaps because of some danger to leeward. But the sea anchor used in this fashion will need to be a very tough item. The forces involved are great. The cute little nylon funnels sold in most marine stores might work for the life raft, but they are worthless for a yacht.

The pyramidal drogues constructed of very heavy canvas and with their mouths held open by two heavy timbers or steel bars fixed at right angles to each other appear as though they'll do the trick. Then there is a sea anchor constructed of two heavy 6-foot long planks (2 x 10s) formed in the shape of a trough, their ends held at the proper angle by welded steel sections to which the planks are bolted. The bridle is all chain, four pieces leading to a gigantic swivel. This arrangement is put out on the heaviest line on board—obviously the anchor rode. It must be very hard to stream or recapture such a monster.

Hal Roth, in his excellent book *After 50,000 miles*, suggests the use of a nylon parachute as a drogue—one 20 to 25 feet in diameter. He has bought one to try out in the next storm that catches him. The idea sounds very feasible. He stresses the importance of

Nasty weather tracks Starbound. *An extra lifeline has been rigged aft.*

a float at the apex of the chute to support the arrangement. And, of course, a swivel must be employed between shrouds and warp.

In the final analysis most deep-water sailors will use the storm tactics of heaving to or running, depending on where their destination lies or how bad the storm gets. *Heaving to* is a nice comfortable way to get through a storm if it doesn't get too bad. The longer-keeled boats heave to better than those cut away aft. With the helm lashed down, a small backed storm jib, and a trysail on the main or mizzen strapped in hard, the yacht should sit easily without a lot of motion. No one has to tend the helm and some rest and food can be gotten. However, if the storm pipes up and the ship starts laboring, it will be time to run off.

Running in a storm is an experience in itself and is my favorite storm tactic with *Starbound* simply because she runs well and has no tendency to surf. A disadvantage is that her helm needs tending. I have run her successfully with the rudder lashed amidships and a storm jib socked down hard absolutely fore and aft. But once in a while, a big wave will cross in from the quarter and slew her stern one direction or the other. For the sake of my nerves, I feel better with someone on the helm to keep her dead before it. Streaming the 300-foot 1-inch diameter nylon anchor warp in a big bight from the quarter hawses slows her down nicely and seems to help quiet the seas aft, as does the slick engendered by her wake. Under those conditions I can also steer her perhaps 10 degrees to the right or left with no penalty. This gives me some leeway to avoid a potential danger to leeward. I've never found it necessary to drag more than the one warp in a big bight, but other deep-water yachts have put out everything but the galley sink.

Our friends on *Triad*, a 40-foot trimaran, were caught in a storm off Rio. The water on the Continental shelf is relatively shoal and the subsequent steep seas and high winds were causing the tri to surf at speeds occasionally approaching 25 knots. They streamed warps, chaining an automobile tire to the end of the heaviest. This stopped *Triad* from surfing for the most part, but Roger Wood told me the chaotic wave action would kick the tire out and she would accelerate for seconds until the tire bit in again. They wanted to put more weight on the tire but couldn't crank it in to do so under the conditions they were experiencing. Even the weight of a heavy chain wrapped around a heavy tire wasn't enough to keep the gear under water.

Other yachts have towed tires with much success, particularly when using them on the bight of a line. A short piece of chain shackled around the tire and made to the line over a saddle of chafing gear seems to do the trick. Of course, there is no way to "trip" a tire because of its shape, so once let out it's out for the duration of the run. The chain needs to be lashed to the chafing gear so as not to work its way off it; therefore the tire and chain cannot be slipped by letting go one end of the warp. If an emergency arose, the whole thing could be cut away, but there would go a nice anchor rode. Perhaps if the chain were secured with a pelican hook, a trip line to the release ring of the hook would jettison the tire and allow the gear to be retrieved. Old tires are plentiful and free; most deep-water yachts carry at least two to use as fenders on the rough bulkheads of foreign port wharves and docks. I heard (second hand) about another yachtie who used a unique drogue when running off before a storm. He simple dropped his 35-pound Danforth over the side on its twenty feet of lead chain and let out all 200 feet of nylon warp. The claim was that it worked very well. I'm not so sure; it seems that the anchor would dive if the flukes were pointed down and then surface if the anchor turned over. I'll have to try it some time under other than storm conditions. I vaguely wonder what would happen if such a rig were being towed in shoal water and the anchor dove to the bottom and grabbed.

What should a deep-water sailor do to prepare his ship? See how the boat heaves to under various conditions. Practice setting storm sails and examine the options for shortening down the rig. If it ever comes to streaming warps, they must be attached to the ship through some very stout fittings; look them over. Plan the method to be used to put out warps and get them back in again. Plan on carrying a few tires on the foredeck—they come in very handy, in any case, for use between the hull and concrete wharves, steel barges, and the like.

Remember that some of the principal dangers of a storm at sea are personal ones. Nervous exhaustion and physical exhaustion should be reduced as much as possible. Cold, wet, hunger, thirst, and lack of sleep all add their toll. And if this toll becomes too great, you will find it increasingly hard to make the proper decisions. Split up the work; don't let any one person take on too much of a load. Stay as warm and as dry as you can. Buy good foul weather gear and safety harnesses—and *use* them. Keep the boat buttoned up tight and the bilges dry. Remember that the main companionway opens aft; when running off, work out a method of signals so that someone below can come on deck without allowing a wave top below.

FIRE AT SEA

There are other emergencies that can occur on a deep-water yacht. A fire at sea can come closer to instigating panic than anything else. An instantly accessible fire extinguisher should be kept in each compartment. If your ship has an enclosed engine space, or small engine room, an *automatic extinguishing system* is mandatory for safety. CO_2 is still the most common system, but the newer, lighter *Freon* systems are gaining in popularity. The new *Halon* systems too are simple, effective, and moderately priced.

Dry powder extinguishers are popular. They are effective and inexpensive, but when used, they make a mess that must be cleaned up—not as important a consideration as the fact that their shelf life can be affected by tropical humidity.

If you are outfitting a new boat for cruising, I recommend 15-pound CO_2 extinguishers—at least three of them—and an automatic Halon system for the engine room that also incorporates a *remote manual actuating device*. If your ship is already equipped with dry powder extinguishers, buy at least one CO_2 extinguisher for use in the galley.

Be aware that the two primary causes of fires on yachts come from fuel systems and electrical systems. Since the number one rule in fire control is to eliminate the fire's fuel source, it is very desirable to have fuel shut-offs and electrical power disconnects outside the engine room.

"*A collision at sea can ruin your entire day.*" I'm sure everyone has seen that tongue-in-cheek chestnut tacked up on a bulkhead. The primary rule to avoid a collision is to assume that every other ship has the right of way. The second rule is to keep a watch, night and day, and to assume that other vessels don't see you or even know you are there; you will most times be correct. The third rule is to try to make your ship visible. Employ a *radar reflector* at all times. Have someone with a radar set check to make sure you show up clearly on the scope.

Running lights must be high enough above the water and bright enough to be seen in a rough sea when the yacht is heeled well down. Running lights recessed into the hull are totally unsatisfactory for deep-water work, and those mounted on the bow pulpit generally are not much better.

The new tricolored masthead lights now permitted under the international regulations are good because they can be seen at a distance and are not subjected to wave splash. Remember, though, that the masthead tricolor is only legal when the ship is under sail. As soon as the engine is started, the ship must have her port and starboard running lights, a stern light, and a steaming bow light mounted higher than the others.

Spreader lights are very valuable if they are bright enough to really light up the decks. Sealed beam types, one tilted to cover the foredeck and the other to cover the housetop without shining in the helmsman's face, can help create order from confusion on a dark night. They can certainly allay any fear that your boat cannot be seen. We found it necessary to light ours on a few occasions in high traffic areas. The fact that two ships changed course to avoid us after we turned on the spreaders reinforced our belief that they hadn't seen us before, despite our very excellent running lights.

Running before big seas.

OTHER EMERGENCIES: FLOODS AND WHALES

Flooding means more than leaking: It means that a hell of a lot of water is coming into the boat. Generally, flooding will occur only if a hull fitting has carried away or if the yacht strikes something at sea. The proper way to combat flooding is to set everyone aboard at pumps and buckets, except one man who determines where the water is coming from. *Any* method to stop the water coming in is excellent. I once used a carrot to stop up a broken pipe. A friend shoved a pillow into a sizeable hole in the bow and yelled for a hammer, nails, and a piece of wood, which he nailed across frames to retain the pillow. A hand over a 2-inch diameter hole where a hull fitting had corroded and dropped entirely away saved a 40-footer from sinking. A jib, worked under the bow from both sides and pulled aft, reduced the water flow through four broken strakes and three broken ribs caused by hitting a floating 55-gallon drum full of "something" at night. This technique of securing a sail across a large area of damaged hull in known as *fothering*.

A question repeated many times, "What did you do about *whales?*" There really isn't anything to do about whales except avoid them. If you sight a whale at sea, stay away from him. If you inadvertently find yourself in a group of them, wend your way cautiously through—even if it means jibing the ship.

Whales are mammals and are believed to be very intelligent. They are not believed to be particularly belligerent, except when they feel threatened. Cows with calves are very protective of them. Bulls can be fractious in the mating season as can all male animals. The problem is that cows may have calves with them any time of the year, and not all that much is known about the breeding season or areas of all species of whales. Calves are generally born in warm water and early in winter. They are not weaned for perhaps six to eighteen months depending on the species. Any female mammal with a baby will tackle anything she thinks is a danger.

One dark night in the Pacific, on the way to the Marquesas from the Galapagos, I was on the afterdeck checking the horizon. I heard a rush of water to windward like a breaking wave and a whoosh, then smelled the same odor an exposed coral reef gives off in the sun—a whale was very close by. A whale's eyesight is poor, but its hearing is acute, so I started the main engine, engaged the propeller, and changed course 30 degrees to starboard, away from the whale's position. I did this to let the whale know that I was not another whale and that I posed no threat. I haven't the faintest idea if this is the correct action to take but it felt right. We heard and saw nothing else that night—and we were very alert.

ON ABANDONING SHIP

If a time ever comes when a sailor thinks he must abandon ship, the first rule is to *think again*. Even if the life raft is inflated, supplied and manned, keep a tether on the ship until she begins to disappear beneath the waves.

It is fairly difficult to actually sink a yacht. They might flood totally or turn over and still remain on the surface. Many yachts have been abandoned to be found drifting days later, still afloat, taking care of themselves. Even if the yacht is awash, she will be easier to spot by rescuers than a raft, so stay with the yacht until she actually sinks.

A lanyard should be attached from the raft to the yacht (inside the raft canister) with a length equal to perhaps the sum of the yacht's beam and overall length. The procedure for abandoning the ship for the raft should be carefully considered. Remove the raft from its canister. Unfold it and lay it out on the water beside the yacht, if you can and as best you can. Then inflate it by pulling the CO_2 mechanism-operating lanyard. Keep the raft as close aboard as possible without damaging it. A strong person should climb aboard first to receive stores, water and equipment, and to help others aboard. Keep the raft tied to the yacht by its lanyard. Add more line if there is a chance of being entangled by the yacht's rig when she sinks, but stay with her until she does. Then and only then should you cut the line.

Take your dinghy if you can. Since a dinghy can be steered it can be used to tow the raft if it becomes apparent that you'll have to make your way either to land or into more heavily traveled waters. A sailing dinghy has a centerboard, so it would even be possible to navigate with some accuracy. If you have a sailing dinghy, keep all its gear stowed with it. And remember to secure it to the raft prior to leaving your boat.

Activate the EPIRB and keep it activated. Stay clothed and as warm as possible, even if wet. A well-equipped raft will keep you in good shape for many days. Erect the canopy for protection against the sun and sea. Keep as sharp a lookout as possible and the flares as dry as possible. The odds are very good for rescue within 48 hours and get increasingly better after that.

Do not fall overboard! Watch your step in rough weather and keep your harness on and snapped into something solid when moving about topside. When moving your safety lanyard from one location to another, keep one hand locked onto the ship. The only harnesses worthwhile are the chest-high harnesses that are easily put on like a sleeveless jacket and fastened with a single, big, positive-release device in the middle of the front. If a harness is easy to get on and off, there will be less tendency to leave it below. Fasten a whistle and a small waterproof flashlight to your safety harness with a lanyard, so that in the event you do fall overboard, you will be more visible at night or can be found by the sound of the whistle.

If you fall overboard, scream bloody murder so that whoever is on board will know it and dump the dan buoy over. The dan buoy pole should project at least eight feet from the water, should float upright even in a wind, and should have a high-visibility orange flag on the top. Attached to its bottom should be a life ring or more commonly now, a horseshoe-shaped personal flotation device (PFD). Attached to the PFD is a strobe light that activates automatically when it hits the water and flips over to its operating position, and a sea anchor to stop the whole works from blowing off faster than you can swim with your foul weather gear on.

The idea is for the man lost overboard to swim to the dan buoy, which he can see from his position in the water, and for the yacht to return to the dan buoy, which the crew on board can also see even though they probably won't see the swimmer until they get to the dan buoy. The yacht should try to get to windward of the dan buoy and create a lee in which to pick up the man in the water.

Unless the person in the water is strong and cooperative, it will be very tough to get him back on board. Grab his safety harness lanyard first and lock it onto something. Tie off the dan buoy, so it will not be lost. Put over a boarding ladder, if you have one, or lash one of your auto tire fenders over so it can be used as a step. As a last resort, use a tackle off the main boom bale or even dump the bight of the sail over the side and get the man into the bight; then roll him aboard.

The smartest thing to do in rough weather is to be very careful.

14

Personal Gear

When choosing clothing for a long cruise, it should be kept in mind that each person does his own laundry and that virtually all laundry on a cruising boat is done by hand in cold water, without bleach. While at sea, clothes are washed and rinsed in sea water. At anchor, clothes are washed in fresh water streams or in buckets and then hung in the rigging to dry. Jeans are, without doubt, the hardest item of clothing to wash by hand but because of their durability should be included in every sailor's seabag. A deck brush and detergent can get even the dirtiest jeans clean.

To prevent colors from fading, clothes should be turned inside out when dried in the sun; but since sun rots fabric they should always be taken in as soon as they are dry. Read the care labels in clothing. If dry cleaning or ironing is recommended, don't take it with you. If you can't wash it by hand in cold water and dry it on the cabin top or in the rigging—forget it!

The one exception would be men's suits. There are some occasions when a suit or a sport coat and slacks would be in order. Some very good, washable, polyester fabrics are available in men's suits, but they usually look better if they are dry-cleaned. Polyester won't mold or mildew as wool and wool mixtures do in the tropics, so it is probably the best choice. Seal them carefully in plastic bags and hang them in a locker. If no hanging locker is available, lay them out flat in the bottom of a drawer.

Underwear for use in the tropics should be all cotton since synthetics do not absorb perspiration well and can cause heat rash. Women's panties are available in cotton, but if lacy panties are a must, they should have cotton inserts.

Clothing for tropical wear is best if it is wrinkle shed and contains as much cotton as possible. Even cotton, when made into a tight weave or too heavy fabric, can be quite uncomfortable when worn ashore in the humidity and heat of the tropics. And one cannot always wear shorts and halters or T-shirts. There are places where halters and shorts or jeans for women and shorts and T-shirts for men are unacceptable to the local people. Two examples which come immediately to mind are South America and Indonesia. In South America for instance, an unaccompanied woman from a yacht may be propositioned, pinched, patted, insulted, and followed by local men if she wears slacks or jeans and a halter or T-shirt (especially sans bra) in public. And in Indonesia, in addition to the proper attire required by the government, one is also required to wear shoes when entering government buildings. A copy of these regulations, given to us in Bali, is provided at the end of this chapter.

Bathing suits are almost universally worn by cruising sailors (those who wear anything at all while at sea). We've seen bathing suits made of almost any fabric one can think of. However, polyester seems to be the most popular—probably because it wears better, fits more comfortably, dries more quickly, and is less prone to fade. Women sailors seem to prefer two-piece suits, and for good reason. They're much cooler than a one-piece and the tops can be dispensed with as the situation warrants. Men most often wear the bikini type, sometimes called the European cut, with side seams only and support sewn in. The laundry situation being what it is at sea, the fewer clothes the better.

Every cruising sailor should have at least one pair of *sunglasses* for use at sea. Glare from the water and from white sails is a real problem. And if you like to read topside, they're a must. Polaroid sunglasses really do a good job, and dark glasses may also help you see obstructions under water that would otherwise not be visible. Photochromatic lenses—the kind that change shade with the brightness of the sun—are really handy if you wear prescription glasses. The pretty, slightly tinted sunglasses that are so much in vogue now are probably worse than useless, since they can make one erroneously think his eyes are being adequately protected. Check with your eye doctor if you have any questions, and if you wear eyeglasses, ask him for a copy of your prescription to take with you.

Since the sun in the tropics can be so brutal, wear a hat. It should be lightweight with plenty of ventilation and should have a wide brim. The wider the brim the more sun protection for your face, neck, and shoulders. Rig a chin strap on your hat for use when sailing so the wind won't blow it over the side. Then wear it even when you are tan enough to tolerate plenty of sun.

White cotton T-shirts are probably the most comfortable item of clothing for sun protection while cruising in the tropics. Try to get them with nylon reinforced necks, since that is usually the first part to wear out. And when they are finally beyond repair, they make great rags for use in the engine room. Light blue, long sleeve, *chambray work shirts* are a close second in comfort and utility. They are usually worn open with the sleeves down for sun protection. However, it has been our experience that the tropic sun can penetrate the shoulder area of these shirts and aggravate an existing sun burn. This is probably due to the dark color as much as the weave of the fabric. Maximum sun protection is always afforded by white cotton. Nylon and other synthetics, even when white, allow much of the sun's rays to penetrate. Even very lightweight synthetics are hotter to wear than a heavier-weight cotton that absorbs perspiration and then cools your skin through evaporation.

Those night watches can get pretty chilly, so a long sleeve pullover cotton *sweat shirt* worn with a bathing suit is nice and comfy. They're also good under foul weather gear when it's not too cold. A lightweight nylon *windbreaker* is good, too. It affords spray protection when riding in a dinghy, but can feel clammy against bare skin.

Another item of clothing is a flat piece of cloth worn tied or wound around the waist and variously called a *sarong, lava-lava,* or *pareu* depending upon the part of the world in which it is worn. And since this garment is worn without anything under it, it is very cool and comfortable for both men and women.

The best shoes for wear on a boat are the Topsider *boat shoes* available at almost any boat supply store. They are expensive, but worth it. They wear well, are easily washed and dried, protect your toes, can keep you from slipping and sliding on wet decks, and may possibly prevent an injury. In short, they are a good investment. They can also be worn ashore, but may require periodic inspections for, and removal of, small pebbles that tend to become imbedded in the soles. If you forget, the skipper will usually remind you when he sees the scratches on his deck. Or you may prefer to keep two pair, reserving one pair for land wear only. Break them in before you start cruising. Blisters on feet in the tropics can become infected. While in Hiva Oa, I managed to contract blood poisoning from a blister caused by a new pair of shoes. Most yachties wear rubber thong sandals ashore in the tropics since closed-in shoes are hot.

Foul weather gear is seldom needed by the cruising sailor while in the tropics. But if it is needed, it should be the best you can afford. Those light plastic-coated nylon suits look great and are really comfortable in a light rain while sailing in the bay or river back home, but at sea they are almost useless. I had one when we first started our circumnavigation in 1973. We were hit by a full storm, between the United States and Bermuda, and the first green water we took on board soaked me to the skin. I guess the hydraulic pressure simply drove the water through the fabric. So for the next three days and nights, I was cold and wet any time I was topside and every piece of clothing I owned was soaked. The first thing I bought when we arrived in Bermuda was a set of good *heavy-duty foul weather gear.* And a proper pair of sea boots—the kind with removable inner soles, small enough to fit with socks only. The suit, then, cost about $90, the boots about $20—more now. And if there'd been a place to buy them while we were at sea, I would have paid anything for them. It was enough to be scared and tired, but to be cold and wet too was almost too much to bear.

Our foul weather gear is Helly Hansen Canor Plarex. The tops pull on over the head and have attached hoods. Some have bib-type pants with suspenders; one set of pants secures with a draw-string. The overall types are comfortable, stay up, and allow free-dom of movement.

Sea boots should be the nonskid boat type with removable inner soles for easy drying and should be small enough to fit over one or two pairs of socks, unless you plan to cruise in cold climates. Then they should be large enough to fit over your boat shoes.

If you want your foul weather gear to last as long as possible and keep its waterproof characteristics, it must be properly cared for. The most important thing is to wash foul weather gear in fresh water as soon as is practicable after hard use at sea and dry it thor-oughly on both sides. It should then be hung (if possible) where it will stay dry. This prevents mold and mildew from forming, and since it is both dry and free of salt, it will not crack or stick to-gether. We usually wash our foul weather gear when we do our first laundry after arriving ashore. And we *always* dry it thoroughly after each use at sea and hang it until it can be properly cleaned. We care for our sea boots the same way.

If there is to be any cold weather sailing, our experience has proven to us that *wool socks* are always the best choice for wear under sea boots since they are warm even when wet. And if you keep your feet warm you've won half the battle. Wear two or more light- or medium-weight socks rather than one heavy pair. The inner pair will become damp from perspiration, but the outer pair will remain dry. And two lightweight pairs of socks dry more quickly than one heavy pair. While off watch, dry the inner pair and wear the outer ones.

Thermal underwear and wool sweaters, pants, hats, and gloves or mittens are mandatory for cold-weather cruising. Then add a water repellent polyester-filled ski-type jacket and pants, or a one-piece suit. Then if conditions warrant, foul weather gear can be worn over this. In extreme cold I use a pair of ski-type fiber-filled water-repellent nylon mittens. If your skin is sensitive to wool, search the better department stores and ski shops in your area for lightweight knitted underwear made with mixtures of wool and silk, cotton, nylon, or polyester. Cotton-flannel work shirts are also good for wearing under scratchy wool sweaters, and they are cheap. Check the Sears or Montgomery Ward catalogs for these items, too. They have some good heavy-duty clothing at reasonable prices. And catalogs can be requested from hunting and sports stores such as L. L. Bean in Maine that offer reasonably priced gear.

If one lives aboard, all of one's personal gear is aboard and should be properly stowed out of the way but available when needed. What should be done, however, is to take a good hard look at what will and will not be needed for extended cruising. Then such changes as will be necessary to provide for the range of humidity, temperature, and weather likely to be encountered can be made. If your cruise plans include cold countries, keep some heavy winter clothes. And if you plan to cruise the tropics, check over your summer clothes. But be sure to keep some warm clothing for night watches or to wear under foul weather gear when necessary. A squall at sea is chilly—even in the tropics!

The *basic seabag* should consist of warm/cold weather clothing and shoes, foul weather gear, passport, personal papers, address book, prescription glasses if needed, sunglasses, prescription medications, toiletries, personal hygiene materials, and a sewing kit. Also camera gear and writing materials. Add one or two paperback books, a diary, playing cards, and pocket-sized versions of games such as chess and you're approaching the luxury class.

For the person who is cruising deep-water for the first time or who is cruising on some one else's boat, a basic seabag list is provided at the end of this chapter. This list includes those items without which you cannot get along comfortably. Since no two people have exactly the same requirements, some may feel that the list is not extensive enough. Add what you want, keeping in mind the type and amount of stowage space available. And never use a suitcase as a seabag. Use only a collapsible seabag—one that can easily be stowed on a boat and that cannot be ruined by sea water.

On most cruising boats the rule for personal gear is to never leave anything lying around the main saloon or other general spaces. Another crew member will usually put it away for you but will probably resent having to do so more than once. Personal articles adrift make a mess, can get lost, and if they're breakable, will usually get broken. If you have something you'd rather not keep in or around your bunk or locker (such as a camera), ask the skipper if there's a better place—but don't count on one being available and don't be disappointed if there isn't.

Take a *plastic bag* along for your dirty laundry, and use it. It is amazing how bad the smell of dirty clothes can be in a small cabin. Don't let dirty laundry pile up. Wash it every day, hang it in the rigging to dry, and put it away as soon as possible.

If you plan to take a camera to sea with you, be advised that salt air (and water) are pure hell on *cameras and associated gear.* Coated lenses are particularly vulnerable and will sometimes be attacked by mold if they're not kept clean and dry. Keep a bag of silica gel in your camera case to absorb moisture. Silica gel resembles coarse white sand in appearance but possesses many fine pores and is extremely absorbent. It is available in small cloth bags and can be purchased in most camera stores. Silica gel absorbs moisture, so it must be dried out periodically. Once a month, after using the galley oven and while the oven is still hot (but turned off), toss in the bag of silica gel for a few minutes to dry it out, then return it to your camera case. This should keep your camera gear reasonably moisture free.

If you already have an expensive camera, consider purchasing an underwater case for it. You'll be able to photograph those storm-tossed waves without ruining the camera and will also be able to get some superb underwater photos when diving.

We have been told by other yachties that a clear plastic bag sealed over a camera works O.K. in the rain, but I'd hesitate to try one on my camera in really bad weather.

If you are considering buying a new camera, have a look at the fine *underwater cameras* available in most camera stores. Dive shops usually have a selection of both underwater cameras and underwater cases available, and there's usually a diver around who can advise you on what's best for you.

If you're a SCUBA diver, bring your own gear along unless the boat has extra for your use. At any rate bring your own regulator and mask. If you have room, bring your snorkel and swim fins too. If you don't dive but like to swim, bring a mask, snorkel, and fins. Tropical waters are so inviting you'll spend lots of time exploring the local reefs or looking for shells. And if you do decide you want to go snorkeling and don't have the gear, your chances of buying what you need are very slim.

Basic Seabag List

Passport (with appropriate visas)
International Certificates of
  Vaccination
Personal papers (including
  driver's license)
Address book
Foul weather suit (with hood)
Sea boots
Safety harness (with whistle and
  light attached)
1 dress outfit
1 pair slacks
1 skirt
1 lightweight shirt or blouse
1 pair jeans
Appropriate underwear (several
  changes)
1 pair gloves
1 hat
1 bathing suit
White cotton T-shirts (several)
1 long-sleeve lightweight shirt
  (light-colored)
1 long-sleeve sweat shirt
1 lightweight windbreaker
2 pair each, lightweight cotton
  and wool socks

1 pair boat shoes (with nonskid
  soles)
1 pair *comfortable* shoes for
  walking
1 pair sandals
1 pair sunglasses
1 pair prescription glasses (with
  copy of prescription) if used
1 each: washcloth, towel,
  blanket and/or sleeping bag
1 knife and fid on lanyard(s)
Toiletries, cosmetics, and
  personal hygiene materials
Your favorite nostrums, pills,
  etc., including sunburn lotion,
  vitamins, and seasick
  medication
1 pocket-sized flashlight (with
  spare battery)
1 pocket-sized sewing kit
Camera gear
SCUBA/snorkel gear
Several medium-sized plastic
  bags for clean/dirty laundry
Pack all in a collapsible
  seabag—no suitcase

15
Habitability

THE GALLEY

The primary work done in a galley is food preparation and the clean-up associated with meals. Secondarily the galley is often used as a handy work shop to fix ship's equipment. It follows then that a galley should be well equipped to handle these jobs and should be arranged so that anyone on board can use it. When a boat is tied up to a dock or anchored in sheltered waters, almost any galley is adequate. But when a boat is at sea, its galley must be functional. Try to imagine preparing even the simplest meal under conditions as rough as some of the rides at an amusement park. Then imagine these conditions lasting for days and you'll have some idea what the cook on a small boat is up against when the weather takes a turn for the worst.

Equip your galley so that everything you use can be secured against falling and/or spilling. The easiest way to start is to install fiddles at least four inches high completely around the edge of the work areas. If you don't want permanent fiddles this high, make them removable. But don't waste your time on fiddles that are only one or two inches high, which cannot possibly keep a hot pan of food where you've put it.

Next, get two or three pieces of ¼-inch shock cord and secure them along the back coamings of the galley work areas so just about anything can be put behind them for safe keeping while you're cooking. With this kind of arrangement, you won't have to hold a container in one hand while you measure out what you need with the other. Without this kind of arrangement, each container must be opened, used, and replaced immediately—a very time-consuming procedure given the awkward stowage that must be utilized on some small boats. Since meal preparation can (and usually does) take twice the time required for the same operation ashore, wasted motion in a galley should be kept to the absolute minimum.

On *Starbound* we have as much galley equipment as possible stowed in racks and hanging on hooks affixed to the bulkheads, secured where necessary with shock cord. Our forward bulkhead holds two dish racks and a cup/glass rack. The cabin side behind the galley sink has a spice rack close to the overhead, fitted with hooks in the bottom on which cooking utensils hang. A piece of shock cord keeps them from banging back and forth. Shock cord is also used to secure the jars in the spice rack and the heavy skillets, which hang on hooks affixed to the cabin side behind the galley stove. We do not store pots or pans in the stove oven. Pans so stored tend to bang around, creating a terrible racket, and must be removed and temporarily stored elsewhere each time the oven is used. It's far better to have permanent pan stowage. If space is limited, try to get pans that nest, such as those used by hikers and sold in camping supply stores.

A good galley sink should be deep enough so water doesn't slop out when the boat rolls and should be large enough to hold more than one dish at a time. *Starbound* has a nice stainless steel sink that is deep and too large. We would prefer a divided sink so that wash and rinse water could be put in both at the same time, the dishes wouldn't slide around so much, and less water would be used. Install a salt-water pump at the sink so you won't have to lug water from topside to wash dishes. Since most dish-washing is done in salt water, this will save time and trouble.

Much has been written about fancy ways to secure the cook while he or she is working in the galley. I personally feel it's much safer to be able to jump out of the way if anything hot spills. But if you do want some means to secure the cook in your galley when the seas are rough, the most simple arrangement is two eyebolts secured to the front edge of the work area, with a rope or strap stretched between and fastened with hooks. This gives the cook something to lean against when needed. The advantage of this arrangement is that the strap or rope can be adjusted to accommodate different size cooks and can be removed and stowed when not in use.

If something more permanent is desired a small wooden swing-out seat could be rigged if a suitably strong, vertical surface is available to attach it to. Alternately, the seat could slide into brackets (somewhat like the pintles on a rudder) fastened to a bulkhead or other vertical surface.

Life in the tropics is much easier for the cook and crew if the galley has either a hatch above the stove or a vent fan so that cooking heat is removed as quickly as possible. This is especially important if the galley is located amidships. Remember, the normal airflow is aft to forward at sea, and forward to aft at anchor. And since the main saloon is always aft if the galley is forward or amidships, the dining area can become so hot as to be unuseable. Not so bad during the day, since people usually prefer to eat topside in the shade of the awning anyway, but at night mosquitoes can keep even the most hardy sailors below. I have seen freshly cooked (rare) steaks attacked by swarms of mosquitoes apparently attracted by the warm juices. So equip your boat with screens before you leave and fit wind scoops and wind sails with them.

There are four basic kinds of fuel used for cooking stoves on cruising boats: *kerosene*, *alcohol*, *diesel*, and *gas* (liquified petroleum gas: LP-gas or LPG). The chart provided at the end of this chapter compares each of these fuels but does not attempt to compare BTUs generated per unit of fuel. Each stove manufacturer has literature available that should contain such information. I have attempted to compare such things as unpleasant fumes and heat released into the cabin by various types of stoves because I feel these are very important factors to consider before the decision is made about what kind of stove is best for your boat. And since stoves for yachts are very costly, a new stove is a major expense. Be absolutely sure of what you want before purchasing a new stove or replacing the one you already have. And remember, a stove that is perfectly adequate for weekend sailing or for use on inland waters may not be even marginally acceptable for deep-water cruising.

Each sailor has his favorite kind of stove and we on *Starbound* are no exceptions. *Starbound* has an LP-gas stove that we have used safely for 13 years. We use LP-gas because (1) it is clean, (2) it cooks quickly, thus saving fuel and releasing less heat to the cabin, (3) it is available almost anyplace in the world, and (4) it is fairly inexpensive.

Our gas tanks are carried on the cabin top in chocks so that if a leak were to develop, the gas would flow harmlessly overboard. The fuel line leads directly to the stove and has a manual shut-off valve in the line. This valve is turned off when the stove is not actually being used, so that gas cannot possibly escape from the stove into the boat. We have found this arrangement to be adequate. And every person who comes aboard is checked-out on the operation and safety requirements of our propane stove.

If I ever had to choose another kind of stove for *Starbound* other than LP-gas, my choice would be kerosene. Several of our cruising friends have kerosene stoves, which they say are good and reliable, and they never have to worry about dangerous gas leaks.

Alcohol is supposed to be a safe cooking fuel because alcohol flames can be put out with water. We know of at least three rather serious accidents involving alcohol fires in which people were burned. An additional problem with alcohol stoves is that many people are sickened by the fumes at sea. And this can be a real problem if the boat has to be secured against the weather. Most cruising sailors we met who were using alcohol stoves said they would replace them with gas or kerosene at their first opportunity because alcohol was incredibly expensive and almost impossible to find outside the U. S.

We met only one yachtie with a diesel stove aboard and he would not use it in the tropics at all because of the excess heat generated. This would, of course, be a definite advantage if one were planning to cruise in colder parts of the world. And as most boats have diesel engines, there is always fuel for the stove.

Every boat should have a backup cooking stove for use if the primary stove malfunctions. Our backup stove is a two-burner portable pressure alcohol stove. We will replace it with a two-burner kerosene stove before we go cruising again. A portable

Cooking Stoves

Stove Type	Fuel			Unpleasant Fumes	Heat released to cabin	Attachments Needed	
	Availability	Cost	Safety″			Vent	Safety
Gas (LPG)	Excellent	Low	Poor*	None	Low	None	Yes†
Kerosene	Good	Medium	Excellent‡	Yes	Medium	None	None
Diesel	Excellent	Low	Excellent	Yes	High	Yes	None
Alcohol	Poor	High	Good§	Yes	Medium	None	None

*The U.S. Coast Guard considers LPG to be a dangerous cargo and prohibits its use on charter boats. LPG is heavier than air so that if there were a leak, it would flow downward to the bilge where it could be ignited by a spark, causing an explosion.

†LPG should be used on a boat *only* if the tanks are stored topside or in a leak-proof compartment vented overboard in such a way that if a leak occurs the gas will flow harmlessly overboard. The lines that carry the gas from the tanks to the stove should always have a shut-off valve between the tanks and the stove, nearest the tanks (and on the inside of the cabin)—even if the stove has automatic shut-off. This valve is kept closed except when the stove is actually being used. With this arrangement there is no possibility of a gas leak occurring in the cabin between the gas tanks and the stove.

‡Except for the initial area of danger when the burners are being primed with alcohol prior to lighting, kerosene is considered to be very safe.

§Since an alcohol fire can be put out with water, it is considered to be a very safe fuel. However, burning alcohol can float on top of water causing it to spread. Probably the most dangerous part of operating an alcohol stove is lighting it, when the burner must be heated before the alcohol is released to the burner. We know one person who was burned when the burning alcohol that had spilled out of the priming cup splashed up into the cook's face when she attempted to put out the fire with water.

″Manufacturers' operating instructions should always be followed *exactly* when operating any marine stove.

stove is particularly handy in the tropics since it can be used top-side when the cabin is too hot to cook in. The little portable one-burner stoves that use solid fuel are used on many yachts for backup or for when it is too rough to use the regular stoves. Since they are small, they stow easily and the fuel can't evaporate be-cause it comes in cans. An additional factor in favor of this kind of stove is that the stove itself is relatively inexpensive. No small con-sideration for something that may never be used.

REFRIGERATION

There are two schools of thought regarding refrigeration on cruis-ing boats. The first (and most often voiced by sailing purists) is that a refrigerator is absolutely useless when cruising, since fresh vege-tables and meats last only a few days and then the refrigerator is empty anyway. The second school of thought is that a refrigerator is an absolute necessity for the health and welfare of deep-water sailors. The truth is probably somewhere between the two.

We have a refrigerator on *Starbound* and believe it is worth the effort required to keep it operable. Refrigeration extends the life of almost all fresh fruits and vegetables, keeps condiments from spoil-ing, and allows one to stock up on meat and fish when it's available. For instance we bought some freshly slaughtered beef the day we left the Galápagos Islands. It was washed and wrapped and kept in our refrigerator at about 36 degrees. We used it over the 26-day crossing to the Marquesas Islands in French Polynesia. The last of it was eaten the day before our arrival and was delicious.

Having refrigeration on board a small sail boat makes life just a bit easier for the sailor who would have to put up with many incon-veniences without it—and it's sure nice to have cold drinks in the tropics.

Having refrigeration saves money since you'll be able to buy larger more economical sized cans or jars of food and will be able to refrigerate what you don't use immediately.

The decision to have refrigeration or not may be difficult to make, but before reaching that decision, be advised that most of the yachties we met on our circumnavigation said they wished they had refrigeration and that they planned to get a good system on board before making any more long voyages.

DINING AREAS (TABLES)

Another important consideration for a happy ship at sea is *good meals*. It's amazing the psychological lift a crew can get from some special goodie (served up by a compassionate cook) after a few hours of hard going. Since food and its preparation are discussed in Chapter 16, let's take a look at the dining facilities.

The table on a boat should, ideally, be out of the way of through traffic. On a small yacht it usually isn't. If the table swivels, tilts up to the bulkhead, moves on runners, or can otherwise be gotten out of the way, the problem of restricted movement and consequent injuries to hips and thighs is somewhat lessened. You may be fortunate to have some such arrangement on your boat, but if not, consider making the necessary changes—especially if your boat is small.

It's nice to sit on a comfortable, dry settee, protected from the occasional dollop of spray that makes its way down the hatch and eat a meal or play a game of chess or cards secure in the knowledge that what you've put on the table will stay there. It's fairly easy to secure objects on a table at sea: rig fiddles. If you don't want permanent fixtures on your beautiful teak table, make them removable. But be sure the fiddles are high enough to do what they're supposed to do: that is, keep things from sliding, or tipping, and falling off when the boat rolls. Arrange the fiddles so that plates, cups, glasses,and condiments will stay put even in rough weather. The alternative is to hold your food in one hand and your cup between your knees while you eat. A small thing—unless you have to do it all the time when sailing in big trade wind swells. Then it can be extremely irritating, especially in rough weather when you need your hands to hang on with.

Some yachts have gimbaled tables, which can be secured when the going isn't too rough. What's too rough? It's hard to say. There have been times at sea when conditions were such that we had no problem keeping everything in place on our un-gimbaled dining table. And there have been times at anchor when we wished fervently for a gimbaled table because the motion created by swells caused us to roll so violently we literally could not keep anything on the table—even with our two-inch fiddles and rubber table pads.

If you intend equipping your boat with a gimbaled table be sure it (1) has enough room to swing, and (2) has enough weight (positioned low enough) to keep it from functioning as a pendulum with the hiccups. The pivot can be constructed like a hanging locker so that a heavy piece of important gear can be stowed in it, thus solving the problem of weighting the table as well as providing a good storage area for a tool box or a sewing machine. It may even be necessary to rig a piece of shock cord to a gimbaled table to keep it in check when the ship's motion becomes too violent. And if your boat is very stiff with a consequent quick motion, you may not be able to use a gimbaled table at all because the motion can cause the table to oscillate, tossing everything off with surprising force.

Remember, the only way to find out how a boat behaves at sea is to actually take her out.

If your boat is a stock design and the builder is a reputable one, it should be equipped with a proper dining table, but don't assume it is. If, for instance, the previous owner of your boat never took her to sea, you would be well advised to check around until you find someone who has been to sea in a boat like yours and elicit as much accommodation information from them as possible. Ask what kind of meals they prepared. If they depended mainly on snack-type foods, find out why. Was it because of an inadequate galley or because the table couldn't be used?

It is perhaps pertinent that very few of the cruising boats we were aboard during our circumnavigation had gimbaled tables, but had instead tables that could be reduced in size as conditions warranted.

HEADS

Heads should be oriented fore and aft, have as near a "normal" sized seat as possible and have enough room at the deck level to brace your feet against the ship's roll.

Prior to departure, check the head carefully for leaks. Foul smells below on a small boat at sea, especially if the boat is secured for bad weather, can literally drive people seasick. Go over the fittings and fastenings with a magnet to make sure they're corrosion-resistant. If any are magnetic replace them with bronze or monel. Check the neoprene line from the head to through-hull fitting. If it is old, consider replacing it before leaving home— where prices are cheaper and everything you'll need is available. If, in spite of your best efforts, your head develops an unpleasant odor while at sea, check its fittings and seals for leaks. Scrub around the base of the bowl with a good detergent cleaner or with a solution of baking soda and water. Once at sea a primary source of odors in the head is poor aim. Sorry, fellas. A good rule is to ask *everyone* to sit when using the head at sea. This shouldn't be a problem since men usually prefer to address themselves to the lee rail anyway.

Make sure head ventilation is adequate. I consider that one should be able to use the head without anyone else below being painfully aware of it. The head should have enough ventilation to remove any odor within a few moments. The boat even when closed against bad weather must still have some air circulation.

Maintaining a head while cruising is almost impossible unless spare parts are available when needed, so an adequate spares inventory should contain those items most likely to fail. We recommend the following replacement parts:

At least one set of all rubber seals and valves
Flapper valves
Gaskets
Seal for pump plunger
Valves for inlet/outlet mechanism

Pump plunger
One set hoses

If space permits, install a shower of some kind in your head with a sea water spray nozzle. It need not be fancy and can be rigged so that it drains either into the bilge (which we don't approve, but have seen), into a sump, or overboard. Topside saltwater baths are O.K. at sea but are not always appreciated by onlookers in port.

Yacht head basins manufactured these days are so small that it is often a problem to use one. If you are stuck with one of these soup bowls, see the stock at your local marine hardware store or look in the marine catalogs. If the prices are too high, check out the local boat yards. They sometimes have a room full of "junk" that has been removed from other boats—and much of this stuff is perfectly serviceable and often of better quality and workmanship than the new hardware currently being manufactured. It is sad but true that much hardware being made and sold for marine use more properly should be used only in recreational vehicles and will not stand up to long-term usage on a deep-water yacht.

BUNKS

Since restful sleep is such an important consideration for the attainment of a happy cruise, it follows that each crew member should have a good place in which to sleep. We will call this place *the optimum bunk*. This optimum bunk must be—above all else—dry! Its ideal orientation is fore and aft. It should be at least 6 feet 6 inches long by 24 to 30 inches wide. It must have a comfortable mattress and a proper bunk board to keep the occupant retained when the going gets rough. An optimum bunk must also be a good place to lie and read. It should have a small directional light that can be used at any time without disturbing others. The overhead of the bunk area should be painted white for maximum light reflection in the daytime. A certain amount of privacy is required even if that privacy is provided only by drawing a curtain. It should have stowage for personal gear—a shelf, a drawer, a clothes hammock—for those things one prefers to have handy. Stowage needn't be fancy but it is necessary. And the optimum bunk must have adequate ventilation.

Enough air is especially important during rough weather, when people tend to feel queasy below and when even the most innocuous odors can tip the scales from mild discomfort to the head-in-the-bucket routine. Sleep in each bunk; try it in the heat of summer. If changes need to be made, make them right away. Don't wait until you're at sea. Check out the ventilation, lighting, stowage, and privacy. Is the bunkboard high enough to do its job well—or is it too high, cutting off light and air? Bunks in the forward and after compartments usually have good ventilation while the boat is sailing. But since the normal air-circulation pattern is aft to forward under way and forward to aft at anchor, it's probably a good idea to check for comfort under both conditions. Remember, most anchorages in the tropics are situated on the leeward side of the land fairly well protected from the prevailing winds, so they can be fairly airless and hot. You may find that a wind-scoop or wind sail installed up forward will be necessary for adequate ventilation.

Pay attention to the bunk's mattress or cushions. They should be soft enough for comfort yet firm enough to provide adequate support. We prefer 4-inch firm foam over a firm base such as plywood. The mattress should be covered in fabric other than a nonbreatheable plastic, which is cold in cold climates, clammy to bare skin at night, and makes you feel very sticky and hot in the tropics. There are so many good washable synthetic fabrics available that I believe plastic cushion covers for cruising boats are a thing of the past.

Compare the following with our optimum bunk.

Pipe berths are, just as the name implies, a frame made of pipe to which a piece of canvas is laced. One sleeps directly on the canvas or on a thin foam mattress placed over it. Pipe berths are hinged to the bulkhead at the outboard side and are supported on the inboard edge by straps secured to the overhead. The hinges allow the berth to be swung up against the bulkhead and out of the way when not in use, and blankets can be stowed behind it. Older boats

View of Starbound's galley. Ernie shows racked stowage.

are often equipped with pipe berths in the forecastle. Folded they take up very little room and allow the space to be used for other purposes. However, if the off-watch are in their pipe berths during the day, the immediate area becomes crowded.

It is our opinion that no more people should cruise on a boat than can be accommodated by standing berths—*except for a very short period of time,* one or two nights at most.

The *Concordian berth* is similar to the pipe berth in that it also folds away when not in use, except that when folded up against the hull, its underside forms a back rest for anyone sitting on the bench or settee in front of it. It is somewhat more satisfactory than sleeping directly on the settee since sleeping gear can be stowed behind it as with a pipe berth.

The *pilot berth* is more like our optimum bunk than any other. It looks like a rectangular box with one side open, but with the bottom edge of the open side raised about eight inches to form a bunk board. There is usually a curtain rigged on the opening to keep out light and to provide privacy and warmth when needed. Lockers or shelves are located at the foot *inside* the berth and a light is situated at the head. In short, a pilot berth is a miniature cabin. The curtain rod should be stout enough to use as a grab-rail and since the placement of the pilot berth is normally above and outboard of the fore and aft settees, the seat of the settee is used for access—a very nice arrangement.

Sleeping directly on the settee seat is a fairly common arrangement on small boats, but the crew of deep-water yachts prefer to sleep anywhere but there—even topside. The biggest drawback to the *settee bunk* arrangement is its temporary nature and lack of privacy. If there are only two people on board, it is not as big a problem—at least at sea. But in port, when visitors are frequent, it becomes an annoyance. The necessity of making up the bunk each time it is used and the stowage requirements for bedding are additional liabilities. So if your boat has bunks in the forecastle, even if they are small, plan to use them when you're on moorings or dockside, and use the settee bunks only at sea.

16
Food, Drink, and Medicine

I once read that to determine the amount of food you will need for a cruise, you simply list the foods you use for one week, multiply by four to get one month's worth, then stock up for however many months you will be unable to buy provisions. In fact you must first take the list, substitute preserved foods for fresh, then make up the food stores list. Simple—until I tried it. My experience has been that finding suitable, appetizing protein, in tins or in the dried state, is difficult. The crew soon becomes tired of beef stew, corned beef hash, spaghetti and meatballs, tuna, and sardines. You will be able to catch fish, but you can't always depend on it. Fish are generally caught near islands, in major oceanic currents, or near the continental shelves. The larger, pelagic fish are sometimes caught in the open oceans but not often from slow-moving yachts. So this leaves you dependent mostly on stores on board.

At the outset of the cruise, you will undoubtedly have many of the luxury items available from the local supermarket as provisions on board. However, these will gradually be used up and you will be faced with the prospect of replacing them with the not-so-luxurious items that are available and that are probably more practical and less expensive anyway. Also, you may find that many items that keep well in the kitchen at home tend to spoil rather quickly when stored aboard a boat. Especially vulnerable are items packaged in cardboard cartons, waxed paper containers, or plastic bags—even when stored in a dry locker.

Sooner or later you have to eliminate many luxury items from the stores simply because replacements are not available or are too expensive. A good example is paper towels. Granted they are great for cleaning up messes, but they can't be washed and used repeatedly, as cloth can, and they take up lots of dry storage space. So take a supply of rags along. Also in this category are paper napkins. One is unlikely to find any to buy, except in large, well-populated cities—and that eliminates most of the places yachtsmen like to visit. We gave up on paper products, except for toilet tissue, after most of ours were ruined when water got into the dry stowage area. It's my opinion that there is no really dry stowage on a boat unless it is in lockers well above the level of the cabin sole, necessarily limited space.

Galley equipment can be a problem if not selected carefully—with a view toward noncorrosive materials. And finding substitutes for fresh foods is always a problem, even if there is a refrigerator aboard.

FOOD

Meat

Real (not chemically) smoked meat will last several months if hung in a cool, dry, well-ventilated place. If kept in a refrigerator, it will last indefinitely. Some Dak brand smoked salami we bought in Curaçao lasted for one year, hanging from the overhead in the galley. We also used smoked hams, bacon, and smoked beef from time to time with excellent results. But be careful to get only real smoked meat. To be sure the meat has been properly cured, read the label. Since properly cured smoked meat does not require refrigeration, if the directions on the label say that it must be refrigerated, it has been chemically "smoked" for flavor only, not to preserve it.

Smithfield hard-cured hams are available in the Eastern United States, but I'm not sure if they're available out west. If the smoked meat in your local butcher shop is hanging from hooks in the ceiling rather than kept in refrigerated cases, you can be certain it has been properly cured and will be suitable to take to sea. But remember, once it has been soaked in water and cooked, it must be eaten or refrigerated. So try to get small pieces or ask your butcher to cut larger ones into halves or quarters for you. If he doesn't recommend this, you can cut chunks off as the meat is needed. If you're interested in smoking your own meat, directions can be found in an excellent book of food preservation called *The Complete Food Preservation Book* (see the list of references at the end of this chapter).

Tinned Meats

Tinned luncheon meats are available and can be cooked with eggs in the morning when the fresh or tinned bacon is all gone, but they will not keep well after being opened, unless refrigerated. Whenever possible, buy tinned meats that contain no vegetables. Fresh potatoes, onions, carrots, and garlic can be added for a stew. The taste is much improved and the dish contains more vitamins.

Many people prefer to can their own meat to take to sea. If you decide to do so, make sure to follow the directions exactly and be sure to use *only* a pressure cooker equipped with a gauge that indicates pounds of pressure being used. Meat must be processed at 240 degrees F or above to protect against botulism. And *botulism will kill you!*

Fresh Meat

We kept freshly killed (not aged) beef for 25 days in our refrigerator (which maintains a temperature of 35–40 degrees F). Freshly killed beef is tough but is good in stews or when pressure-cooked, and after about a week, the meat is tender enough to eat as steaks. Wash fresh meat, pat dry, then wrap in waxed paper and store in the refrigerator.

Cheese

Cheese keeps well if it is a good firm type such as cheddar or gouda. If not refrigerated, it must be kept as dry and cool as possible—not always easy in the tropics, but well worth the effort since cheese is a good source of protein. It is also very compact and thus makes for easy stowage.

Tinned processed cheese is available in countries outside the United States. We prefer regular cheese but have had to use processed cheese occasionally. The standby throughout the Caribbean and South Pacific is New Zealand cheddar. It's sold in most stores throughout the South Pacific but not on the small islands in French Polynesia. Stock up on your favorite cheeses in the United States, where the price and selection is good. Wax-covered cheese and smoked cheese keep well at sea without refrigeration.

It is possible to make cottage and other cheese from reconstituted dry milk. If you plan to try it at sea, take along some Rennet and use the directions enclosed in the package.

If you and your crew like yogurt, take some dry yogurt starter with you and make it using dry milk. Yogurt starter can be purchased from any natural foods store in either individual packets or in small cans. It's possible to make yogurt by using a small amount from a batch you have on hand, but my experience has been that gradually each batch becomes less and less like yogurt and more and more like yeast flavored sour milk.

Eggs

Eggs should be bought fresh, unwashed, and *unrefrigerated*—directly from the farmer. Wipe the eggs carefully, then coat them liberally with petroleum jelly, and store them in egg cartons. It is important to turn the cartons over each week to prevent the yolks from sticking to the side of the egg shells. For safety's sake, after three weeks break each egg into a cup and take a sniff before using it. Most of our eggs lasted for three months when preserved in this manner. If eggs have been refrigerated (chilled), they will last about two weeks, so go to the extra effort to get them fresh and unchilled.

Dried eggs should be considered for use by anyone who intends to do extensive cruising. They come in tins and are available in whole egg mixture, whites only, or yolks only and work well. It is best to buy the yolks and whites in separate containers so that when you need whites or yolks only, they're available. We've used the whole egg mixture with good results in baking and for pancakes. Eggs are virtually impossible to obtain in French Polynesia (except in Tahiti), so stock up well in Curaçao or South America, and take good care of them.

Bread

Bread is always a problem if one doesn't bake. However, salt water bread can be cooked on top of the stove and is satisfying, if not a gastronomic delight. Add a little corn meal to the mixture and it tastes like an English muffin.

Biscuits are easy to make and can be baked in the oven or in a heavy iron skillet on top of the stove. Pancakes can also be utilized as bread, and if your stores contain Masa Harina, you can make your own corn tortillas. Plain tortillas can be made using white flour, lard, and water (see recipes beginning on page 346).

When ordering fresh bread on various islands, we always asked that it be baked twice. After initial baking remove from the oven and cool, then bake again for fifteen to twenty minutes. This makes a rather thick, dark crust, which keeps the bread fresh for as long as a week. If the baker can't or won't do it, do it yourself on board.

Remember, baking uses lots of fuel, so always bake as much as possible each time you use the oven. After the bread is cooled, wrap it in waxed paper or put it in plastic bags, close tightly, and store in as cool a place as possible.

Crackers

Crackers and crispy snacks should be removed from cartons (even if sealed in plastic) and put in cans or jars. However, if purchased in the tropics, they may already be soggy, in which case crisp them in the oven if you have one. If not, use a skillet with low heat. Cool before stowing. This also prevents weevils by destroying any eggs that may be in them. This method also works well for pasta and rice.

Flour

Flour and cereals can be a real problem if not stored properly. The best method we've found is to empty the bags into large cans or jars and put a few bay leaves on top. The bay leaves keep weevils away. I don't know why—they just do. This may also work with pasta and rice, but we didn't try it. If you're really down on weevils, heat the filled tins or jars in the oven (without lids) at 200 degrees F for one hour, let cool, then seal with sterile lids. I treated some rice that way and it kept for two years. It is a lot of trouble, but it works.

Sugar

We purchased raw sugar in large quantities since it keeps well if not wet. I kept a 130-pound plastic bag under the companionway ladder for a year, closing the top with shock cord after each use.

Butter and Oils

Butter can be purchased in tins (outside the United States) but must be kept cool to prevent spoilage. We use fresh butter on *Starbound*, when available, and keep it refrigerated. It stays fresh and is good-tasting for six months or more, and is usually cheaper than tinned butter. Francine Clarkson, on the yacht *Pilecap*, packs her butter in salt with the same result. We also keep a supply of tinned vegetable shortening on hand for use in baking, and use vegetable oil for other cooking. If your boat has no refrigeration, get oil with preservatives if it is available—or buy small jars or tins so they will be used before they can turn rancid. *Rancid oil is very bad for you!*

Vegetables

If vegetables are to be kept without refrigeration, they must not have been refrigerated prior to purchase. Once refrigerated, they spoil very quickly if kept at room temperature. Even if you buy them from a vendor, they may have been shipped in chilled containers, so be sure to ask. Be especially careful on the small dry islands in the Caribbean, where most of the produce is shipped in from elsewhere. Fresh vegetables will keep well when stored in an open basket or hammock in a dry place out of direct sunlight. Potatoes and onions will keep for months in a dry, dark place if one sorts them carefully every week or so and removes any that have become soft or spoiled.

We kept a supply of powdered potatoes to use when our fresh ones were gone but found that they occasionally disagreed with some people—possibly because of the preservatives they contain. Carrots and cabbage should be kept cool and damp, if possible, to prevent shriveling. Peel the outer leaves from cabbage as you use it, leaving the rest of it untrimmed—it will last much longer.

Don't wash vegetables until you're ready to use them. If they're very dirty, wipe them with a dry cloth to remove loose dirt and be sure to check them carefully for bugs before bringing them aboard. Cockroaches are a terrible nuisance and are almost impossible to get rid of once they are established on a boat.

Fruit

Citrus fruit and apples keep well if not refrigerated prior to purchase. Green pineapple will last well, too, but if kept below, the smell of the ripening fruit sometimes causes problems for seasick-prone individuals. Wrap each piece of citrus fruit tightly in aluminum foil and it will last several weeks.

Buy bananas by the stalk and hang from the boom topside, but be careful who you buy them from. We've seen bananas sold by kids in the Caribbean that never did get ripe because they were picked too green. Bananas will all ripen about the same time, so be sure you'll be able to eat them before they spoil.

We bought bananas and limes in Nuku Hiva to take to the Tuamotu Islands (which are dry). The people there were happy to get them, and in return gave us all the coconuts we wanted.

Coconuts

Stock up on coconuts whenever you can. Coconut water is cool and good tasting, the meat good to eat, and the cream made from them is outrageously delicious. Pile them in your dinghy, in the bilge, or anyplace else you have room for them. They keep best if the thick green husk is left on. We've seen shucked coconuts crack open if left in the hot tropic sun.

Breadfruit

Breadfruit is the potato of the South Pacific. It grows on rather large trees, has a bright green bumpy skin and a firm white interior. It is never eaten raw. If cooked the first day it's picked the result is like cooked potato. The second day it's sweeter—more like sweet potato, and the third day it's almost like a sweetened pudding. Polynesians sometimes make poi of breadfruit.

Dehydrated Foods

We use dehydrated vegetables, soups, and fruit on *Starbound* whenever possible. The larger the package, the cheaper they are, so we buy restaurant-size packets and stow the unused portion in jars or cans after they have been opened. The directions for preparation can be put right in the container with the food. If you prefer smaller packets, be sure to put them in heavy plastic bags before storing in the bilge or other food storage areas. The boat's motion will make the packets move, causing holes to be worn in them. This is a fact—it's happened to us. Our dried foods lasted over a year. We used peas, green beans, and sliced apples, reserving them for use when fresh items were not available. Next time around we'll stock up on any dried foods available—especially vegetables. They cost less than like amounts in tins, take up far less stowage space, and you need not worry about tins rusting out and their contents spoiling.

Tinned foods

We always check tins carefully before opening and never taste the contents of questionable ones. If we have any doubts, over the side they go! *Botulism will kill you.* It has no smell or taste, and usually doesn't change the appearance of tinned food. If the lid is puffed up or if there is a loud hiss when you open a tin, throw it away (except for vacuum-packed items, like coffee). We always take plenty of small cans of tomato puree and use it for making tomato juice and for cooking. Concentrated fruit juices in tins are also available (not in the United States) and are inexpensive. They don't taste like the real thing but they're close enough and they don't contain as much sugar as the powdered juice products such as Tang.

Milk

Except in the United States, Martinique, Curaçao, Suva, New Zealand, Australia, and South Africa, we found safe fresh milk impossible to get. We were able to buy fresh milk in the Galápagos but had to pasteurize it ourselves. I've included directions for this process in the "How to . . ." section of this chapter (page 336).

Dry milk keeps best if it is put in airtight containers. We have had boxes of dry milk spoil after only a few weeks at sea. Most countries have whole dry milk available in tins, but we've not been able to find any in the United States. We use it for cooking and for drinking, and never use tinned milk aboard. Dry milk tastes better and takes much less stowage space.

Peanut Butter

Peanut butter is an old standby at sea. It is nutritious and contains protein in rather large amounts, so stock up on it before leaving the United States. But after opening, peanut butter will turn rancid in the tropics if not kept refrigerated, so take small jars if you don't have a refrigerator. Small jars cost more, but it's worth having fresh unspoiled peanut butter for the crew.

Honey, Jam, and Syrup

If you like honey, take a good supply with you. It's hard to find in the Pacific and, when available, is very expensive. We use it on *Starbound* to prevent seasickness or to stop vomiting caused by seasickness.

Jam is also expensive and hard to find in the South Pacific island areas, and some kinds will develop mold growth on top if not refrigerated. Here again, small jars would probably be the solution for those who have no refrigeration on board.

If you like maple syrup, take plenty with you because it is almost impossible to find outside the United States. Genuine maple syrup will spoil if not refrigerated after opening, so if you haven't a refrigerator on board, buy small jars you can use up quickly, or get *maple-flavored* syrup (not genuine), which will keep well at room temperature after being opened. Check the labels and if the directions say to refrigerate after opening—forget it.

Coffee and Tea

Coffee is very expensive and hard to find outside the United States—except in more highly developed countries, or in South America and Indonesia, where it is grown. Take plenty with you. You should be able to buy whole beans in 25-pound bags from a local coffee roasting firm. There are more around than you think, so check the yellow pages in your local telephone book. These firms have a good selection and the price is right. Invest in a hand coffee grinder or use your electric blender to grind the beans as you need them.

As you travel, you'll see green coffee beans for sale. Buy them and roast them yourself. It's easy. The "How to . . ." section (page 334) has directions.

We were able to find tea of one kind or another in almost every country and on almost every island we visited. Tea prices seem to be rather consistent and varieties are pretty good. However, if you have a favorite, stock up on it here in the United States. Do buy it in cans, though. Boxes of tea spoil very quickly.

Condiments

Mustard is available almost everywhere you're apt to sail—and very good Dijon mustard is available in the Caribbean and French Polynesia. If, however, you prefer the plain mild yellow mustard that is available in the United States, you'd better take a few jars with you. Check the label to see if refrigeration is necessary after opening. If so, get small sizes. If not, get a large economy size. Be sure to buy a can of dry mustard to use if you run out. Directions for preparation are printed on the label.

Catsup. I used to think we didn't use much catsup on *Starbound*—until we went to sea. Needless to say we ran out in record time, so I had to make what we needed—and it was very good! Directions are included in the recipe section of this chapter. If you like to preserve your own food, make a large batch and "can" it in jars.

Pickles are fairly hard to find once you've left the Caribbean on your way to the South Pacific, so put plenty on board if your crew likes them. And take the spices and other ingredients needed if you want to make your own pickles en route. I didn't and wished I had. Once again, check the label. Some pickles sold nowadays require refrigeration after opening.

Soy sauce, Worcestershire sauce, and various like products usually don't require refrigeration and since a little goes a long way, they will last quite a while.

Hot Sauce will keep nicely at room temperature, so take along large sizes if your crew likes Mexican foods.

Mayonnaise must be kept refrigerated once the jar is opened.

Failure to do so can result in serious food poisoning. If you don't have refrigeration buy very small jars, or make your own as needed, using my recipe (see page 349). In very hot weather chill the oil and vinegar by placing the containers in cool sea water for an hour or so and put the egg in the water as is.

Yeast and Baking Powder

Buy a large can of dry yeast for baking bread from a restaurant supply store. Since it's dry, it keeps for years if kept tightly closed when not in use.

Baking powder should be purchased in small cans and must be tightly closed after each use. The small cans with the metal top and bottom but with the body made of foil-covered cardboard must be kept in an airtight container, or the contents should be removed and put in a jar or can. Treat baking soda the same way.

DRINK

Liquor

Liquor is very inexpensive (rum $1.50 per bottle) in the Caribbean.

If you plan to cruise through there, take only enough liquor from your home port to last you to the first good supply port (See the "Principal Supply Ports" section of this chapter on page 336). Then buy it tax free by the case and have it put in bond. (But if you're a Bourbon drinker stock up in the United States.) The authorities will ask you not to open the liquor stores until you leave port, so buy a couple of loose bottles (and pay the local taxes on it) to use until you're at sea again.

Wine

If you're a wine drinker, stock up in the United States. French wines are available in Martinique but can be expensive. Our California wines are excellent and reliable wines and the price is right. We've been disappointed quite often in the quality of foreign wines. Even some of the more costly ones vary considerably in quality and taste—even from bottle to bottle.

In French Polynesia decent wine is impossible to find, except in Tahiti and there it is very costly. We found that the trading stores had mostly Algerian red wine. If you're desperate, its O.K. but a far cry from our California product.

It is quite an experience to buy wine at these little trading stores. We'd take our own containers (usually empty bleach jugs since they don't break) to be filled from the huge wicker-covered jugs it's sold from. If the proprietor had more than one jug, we'd sample all and choose the best. The proprietor would drop a wine-stained old rubber hose into the mouth of the jug we'd chosen. Then he'd suck away at the end of the hose until he had a syphon flow started, which he would interrupt by placing a large dirty thumb on the end of the tube. Then he'd fill our containers one after the other, always with the thumb handy to stop the flow.

Beer

The best place to buy beer and soft drinks is everywhere. Some places it's more expensive than others. When we were in Cartagena, Colombia, beer was 9 cents a bottle and Pepsi Cola was 3 cents. Enough said. If you want carbonated water for drinks on board, your best bet is to take a seltzer bottle and a large supply of CO_2 cartridges along in lieu of bulky canned drinks.

Soft Drinks

Coke, Pepsi, and other soft drink syrups can be purchased from local restaurant supply houses. The proprietors won't usually sell retail, so tell them you're stocking your boat for a long cruise and they'll be happy to sell to you.

CLEANING AND LAUNDRY PRODUCTS

Liquid dish washing detergent is a must for deep-water cruising. It is one of the few soap/detergent products that will suds in salt water, so it can be used in place of other detergent and soap products whenever it's necessary to wash clothes, dishes, or anything (including you) with salt water. Take a year's supply if you have room, since quality laundry products can be expensive and hard to find outside the United States.

Laundry bleach is fairly available but costs more on islands supplied by boats. You'll use about the same amount at sea as you use at home. Bleach can be used to purify drinking water, so set some aside for this use.

Take several packages of spring-type clothespins along—refilling the clothespin bag as they're broken or lost overboard. The old-fashioned wooden U-shaped clothespins are not suitable for boat use. They can't be made to fit various sizes of rigging—and that is where your laundry will be hung to dry.

Take several lengths of nylon "small stuff" for clothesline and rig it topside—say between the forward shrouds or between main and mizzen. It's inexpensive and can also be used for securing many things.

HOW TO . . .

Roast coffee: Put several cups of green coffee beans in a heavy skillet on top of the stove. Stir as they brown to prevent scorching. The darker the roast, the richer the taste. Cool, then grind and store.

Bake breadfruit: Put breadfruit directly on stove burner. Turn as the outside becomes charred. When the outside is completely black, it is done. Cut open and use in place of potatoes or rice.

Make coconut cream: Grate coconut meat with a hand grater. Put grated meat in a clean cloth and squeeze to obtain juice. Add about 2 tablespoons water and squeeze a second time. The result is

Nina and Ernie load provisions from a dock in New Zealand.

a thick, lovely coconut cream. Add a little rum, lime juice, and ice for a great drink, or add sugar and thicken with cornstarch for a pudding.

Make poisson cru *(raw fish with lime):* Squeeze juice of several limes into a bowl. Add thinly sliced (strictly fresh) fish and let sit for about 5 minutes. Add coconut cream, a little salt or salt water, and serve. Minced onion can be added.

Pasteurize milk: Heat the milk at 145 degrees F (63 degrees C) for thirty minutes. Cool rapidly, then store below 50 degrees F (10 degree C).

Purify water:

1. Boil water 1 minute (with a pinch of salt added per quart to improve taste, if desired).

2. Add 2 Halazone tablets per quart, then let sit 30 minutes.

3. Add chlorine laundry bleach (4–6 percent solution): 2 drops per quart *if water is clear*, and 4 drops per quart if it is cloudy; let stand for 30 minutes.

4. Add tincture of iodine (2 percent solution): 3 drops per quart if water is clear and 6 drops per quart if cloudy; let stand 30 minutes.

5. If water is otherwise safe, but bilharzia is a problem: let water stand 24 hours before using.

PRINCIPAL SUPPLY PORTS

The most difficult task of the storekeeper on any boat is laying in stores at the outset of a voyage. The second most difficult task is keeping the boat stocked up once underway. Almost all fresh stores are sold by local ladies in the open public markets, so be prepared to bargain in the local language. If you don't speak French, Spanish, and Indonesian (in addition to English), take a small dictionary for each language. Be sure to get the kind that has a section for both languages (that is, English/Spanish and Spanish/English). If you hope to be able to translate local signs, this is what you'll need. The first item is to learn to count money. At the market watch surreptitiously to see what the locals pay for various products.

Keeping in mind that situations tend to change from time to time, but with a view toward making this task as painless as possible, I have compiled a list of *principal supply ports* with my opinions about them. They follow in the order in which we visited them as we sailed around the world—except that I have listed the islands in the Caribbean in alphabetical order.

Castries, Saint Lucia: Moderate prices and good selection. English spoken. Several fairly well-stocked food markets. Good selection of frozen meats and other frozen foods. We bought a frozen turkey and all the trimmings here (for our Christmas dinner). Stock up on New Zealand cheddar cheese and tinned butter. If you have a freezer, get frozen meat here. There is a big department store with excellent selections. Buy fabric, bathing suits, and clothing here. Good water right at the dock in town and the dinghy landing is excellent. Buy fishing gear here.

Fort-de-France, Martinique: Prices about 50 percent higher than in the United States and slightly higher than those in Saint Thomas. Plan to spend about two hours each day marketing, unless you want to take a taxi to one of the supermarkets. Buy fresh fruit, vegetables, fresh spices, live chickens, and eggs at the open market, but be prepared to bargain for each item (in French). Fish is sold in the open fish market near the vegetable market. Don't be put off by the smell. The fish is good. Meat can be bought in the butcher shops in town but is very expensive. This is the place to stock up on all those French goodies. They are available in Tahiti—but expensive! Fresh milk is available. Clothing is expensive. Good French bread and pastries in the bakery shops. Liquor is available at moderate prices. It can be purchased and put in bond—duty free. Good water. LP-gas available. Duty-free shopping. Good docks for landing in a dinghy.

Philipsburg, Saint Maarten: Best food prices in the West Indies. Friendly people. English spoken. Fresh milk, eggs (chilled), cheese, smoked sausage, and variety meats. Frozen meat, good variety of tinned goods. Good selection of liquor at excellent prices—and no hassle with bonding. Fresh vegetables did not seem to be plentiful—probably imported from Florida. There is a supermarket in town. The people were friendly and even changed

U. S. dollars into the local currency. Duty-free shopping. Take a taxi from the market to the waterfront. There is a good dock for landing in a dinghy.

Charlotte Amalie, Saint Thomas: Prices slightly higher than in Saint Maarten but less than the other islands. Several supermarkets, but if you stay at the Caribbean Harbor Club, it is a long walk and you'll need a taxi to bring stores back to the boat—unless you take your dinghy clear across the bay and tie it up beside the rather high cement quay-side walk near town. The other marina along the waterfront is noisy because of low-flying aircraft but is certainly closer to town. Fresh, unrefrigerated vegetables are available from market boats along the waterfront and are about the same price as in the supermarkets. American brands are available, as are many of the luxury items not found on other islands. Meat is frozen. Fresh milk is available. Good dinghy dock. Good water.

Willemstad, Curaçao: Good prices and good selection. All fresh items available. Purchase fresh produce from South American sailing boats along the quay downtown. This is the last chance to stock up on tinned goods and there are several ship's chandlers who can supply stores by the case. We used John Henderson (Curaçao) Co., Ltd. Telephone first. They'll let you go into the warehouse to decide on items you're not sure about, will put your order together, and will deliver to the waterfront. Fresh eggs, milk, and meat are available. Stock up on Curaçao liqueur, good Dutch cheese, and Dak smoked sausage (the hard type). LP-gas available. Good water.

Cartagena, Colombia: Cheap prices. Lots of fresh meat, eggs, and produce are available in the stalls in the open market downtown. You'll have to bargain in Spanish. Buy coffee beans and roast your own. Beer is about 9 cents per bottle; Pepsi and Coke, 3 cents per bottle. Stock up here. When you get to Tahiti, beer and soft drinks cost as much as hard liquor. And hard liquor costs are shocking! Eat in restaurants while here. It is cheaper than using your ship's stores. You *must* tie up at the Club de Pesca or it is probable that your boat will be boarded and robbed, when you are absent, by natives in canoes. Good water at the club. Buy authentic Indian crafts at the government store in town. The selection is good and the prices are even better. There's an old bull ring that has been converted to a movie theater. Take a bottle of wine and buy tickets for seats in one of the old boxes. It's great fun.

Papeete, Tahiti: The most expensive place we visited in the Pacific. Many French goodies are available, but be prepared to pay through the nose. Fresh eggs, milk, fruit, and vegetables are plentiful. Buy them at the open market from the lovely Tahitian women. Get there no later than 0700 for a good selection. Fresh fish is sold in the same place in the afternoon. You can sometimes buy fish right off the fishing boats on the waterfront. Cheese is imported from New Zealand and France. All meat is frozen and very expensive (ground beef from New Zealand cost us U.S.$3 per pound). We found two supermarkets in town: Donald's of Tahiti and Bon Marché, both right on the waterfront. We preferred Bon Marché because it was closer and slightly cheaper but bought our cheese and meat at Donald's. There are many small Chinese-owned grocery stores in town if you care to shop around for the very best prices. They always have at least one person who speaks English and they are polite and helpful—not always the case in French-owned establishments. LP-gas and good water is available. If your boat is tied up near the park, dinghy landing is not easy because you must negotiate the riprap that lines the shore—a slippery operation at low tide.

Pago Pago, American Samoa: Good prices. Many U. S. items available at Burns, Philp & Company supermarket and wholesale store right on the waterfront near town. Toko Groceries Distributors, located outside town, is also a good source. Telephone them first to see if they have what you want, then take a cab and stock up while there. If you have a large order, they may deliver. Fresh eggs (refrigerated) can be bought in the stores, but check at the government office in the public market and order unrefrigerated eggs from them. All fresh produce is sold in the public market. Stock up on liquor and American wines at the government liquor store in town. Liquor prices in New Zealand and Australia are almost as bad as in Tahiti, but their local wines are fair and the beer is great. Stock up on tinned tuna while in Samoa. Buy it by the case from one of the canneries. If you have cockroaches on board, ask the cannery people if they still provide free pest extermination service for yachts. Good water. LP-gas available. Good dinghy landing near the public market.

Suva, Fiji: Good supply port but inconvenient. If you're going straight to New Zealand, stock up only on fresh produce and sugar. Eggs, meat, and vegetables are plentiful, but no fresh milk is available. Duty-free shopping here. Good place to have hand work such as watch repairs done. We had a stopwatch and wristwatch both worked over for about U.S.$6. You will be far from town, so ride the bus for about 10 cents each way. Good dinghy landing at the Suva Yacht Club, if they still allow transient yachts to use the club.

New Zealand: Good prices and everything is available. Dairy products are especially cheap. Good fresh meat of all kinds is available and is also cheap. Stock up on fresh cheese, butter, and meat. Tinned goods cost about the same as in the United States. The tides run about 12 feet, so dinghy landings can be a problem.

Australia: Everything is available and good. Prices are comparable with those in New Zealand, except that meat is a little higher and dairy products are quite a bit higher. If you coast-hop, the farther north you go from Brisbane, the more expensive supplies become. Unless you're tied up in a river, dinghy landing is a real problem.

Denpasar, Bali: Excellent fresh produce is available (except large cooking onions) and is very cheap. Buy green coffee beans for U.S.$1 per kilo and roast them yourself. Eggs cost about 90 cents a dozen. Fresh meat is sold in the open market near the vegetable market, but is never refrigerated. Go early in the morning while it is still fairly cool, check the meat carefully, then if you decide to buy some, get it to your boat as quickly as possible. We ate mostly fresh vegetables while there and depended on our breakfast eggs for protein. Food is so cheap here that many yachties eat ashore instead of using ship's stores. This is not a good place to buy tinned goods of any kind because of the high cost. Take a basket or box when going shopping. One of the little "carry" girls who hang around the market will put it on her head, follow you around while you fill it up, translate for you when necesary, then carry it to the Bemo (bus) station for you. All for 25 rupiahs (about 6 cents).

Christmas Island: Almost everything is available. Liquor is duty free and there is a good selection. Produce and eggs are all chilled, and the meat is frozen. But this is a good place to stock up on tinned goods. Landing a dinghy here can be downright dangerous because of the large swells.

Port Louis, Mauritius: Good prices. Get fresh meat and eggs at the open meat market, and fresh vegetables, spices, and fruit at the vegetable market nearby. Across the street from the vegetable market is an ice cream parlor, and next door is a pharmacy. We stocked up on tinned goods at Lim Fat & Sons Ltd. They are located at 34 Royal Street and will deliver to the quay if you ask them. Dinghy landing is no problem.

Durban, South Africa: This is a big city with lots of supermarkets. Everything is available including some good South African wines. Take on all the stores needed to get to Capetown. Yacht harbors in South Africa are always located on railroad land so are generally a long way from towns, where the stores are. The Point Yacht Club in Durban is an exception. It is only four blocks from town and has a good dinghy dock.

Capetown, South Africa: Same as Durban, but the yacht club is 2 miles from town. This is a good place to stock up on oranges and apples for the long haul to the Caribbean. Try the light white wine called Fleur du Cap, which is inexpensive and good. Smoked meat is readily available and is good but fairly expensive. Your boat will most likely be tied up at a dock here.

GALLEY EQUIPMENT

Yachts making long passages never seem to have enough fresh water on board, so galley equipment and dishes are washed in sea water. Because sea water is so corrosive, each item in our galley was checked with a magnet prior to purchase to ensure that it was stainless steel—except for a cast iron skillet that was used for "baking" biscuits on top of the stove, roasting coffee beans, etc., an aluminum colander (which barely survived our cruise), and a rotary egg beater. The beater was stainless, but one of its fittings was plain steel. It rusted out and broke halfway across the Pacific. It was a year before a replacement could be found. Aluminum doesn't rust but needs to be rinsed in fresh water to prevent deterioration.

A list of the galley equipment on *Starbound* follows. It is all stainless steel except where noted. The only things we wanted that we didn't have were a freezer and a pressure cooker large enough to use for canning.

Propane stove (4 burner w/oven and broiler; porcelain)
Refrigerator (7.5 cu. ft. w/6-tray capacity freezer across top)
Electric blender
Pressure cooker (4-quart capacity)
Skillets (2 porcelain-covered cast iron, 1 cast iron)
Pots and pans (7 assorted sizes w/ lids)
Grater
Knives (4 assorted sizes)
Dish pan and dish rack (plastic)
Cooking spoons (4 assorted sizes; wood)
Can openers (several sizes and types)
Cork screws (2)
Kitchen tools (1 set plus 1 extra spatula)
Hand rotary egg beater (1 with nylon gears)
Whisk (1)
Baking pans (2 cake, 1 muffin, 2 pie, 2 loaf, 1 roaster)
Mixing bowls (2 sets, also used for serving food)
Flatware (service for 8)

Colander (now stainless)
Tongs (2)
Tea kettle (1)
Tea pot (1)
Coffee pot (1)
Flour sifter (1 2-cup capacity)
Measuring spoons (1 set)
Cheese slicer (2)
Measuring cups (1 set)
Ice pick (2)
Salt and pepper shakers (1 set)
Sugar bowl and creamer (1 set)
Dinner plates (8 restaurant-type heavy china)
Mugs (6 heavy plastic and 8 ceramic)
Glasses (12 heavy plastic nesting-type and assorted heavy glass)
Spice rack (1 wood wall-type)
Cooking thermometer (1 stainless steel and glass)
Fishing gear (300 ft. of line, stainless leader wire, assorted hooks and lures, assorted weights)
Clothesline and clothespins
Washboard
String bags for carrying groceries
Nutrition books

Cookbooks

Rolling pin

Vacuum cleaner

Broom

Steam iron (with stainless steel
shoe plate)

FOOD STOWAGE

At this point in cruise planning, the decision has been made as to exactly how much stowage will be allotted to food and related items. So here's what to do:

1. Measure the wet and dry stowage areas and calculate how much food and related items can be put into these areas.

2. Draw up a stowage plan and give each locker a number.

3. Identify each locker by affixing a label to it marked with its assigned number.

4. Make up a card for each locker and list everything you store in it on the card. As items are used, draw a light line through the used item on the card.

5. Check these cards to make up your shopping lists.

6. As the cards are used up replace them, but not before all the ruled-out items have been put on the shopping list.

MEDICINE

When we first started cruising with *Starbound* on the Chesapeake Bay, our medical kit consisted of a tin box of Band-Aids, tweezers, and a tube of antibacterial ointment.

Over the years (and as various accidents occurred), we added niceties such as burn ointment, gauze, bandages, adhesive tape, and various disinfectants—perfectly adequate, since expert medical help was only an hour or two away. But when we contemplated ocean passages of 20 to 30 days, it became evident that we must plan for the possibility of treating serious injuries and illnesses ourselves.

Our research led us to two excellent books that should be in the library of every deep-water sailor: *First Aid Afloat* by Paul B. Shelden, M. D., and *Advanced First Aid Afloat* by Peter F. Eastman, M. D.

Both books contain the information needed to outfit and use a comprehensive medical kit while voyaging anywhere. Prescriptions can be obtained from your family doctor. If you have a cruising friend who is also a doctor, ask him for help.

Obtain a copy of each of the aforementioned books and read them through to become familiar with their contents.

Call your family doctor and make an appointment for the express purpose of going over your proposed kit and obtaining his possible additions and recommendations. Make notes of his comments; then ask him to write the necessary prescriptions.

If you or anyone of your crew has a medical condition that could cause problems, ask your doctor to write a short explanation of the condition and his recommendation for treatment should an emergency arise. Make a few copies and keep them with the ship's papers.

The four most serious medical problems likely to be encountered by a deep-water sailor, particularly when cruising in the tropics, are:

•*staphylococcus infection* (more commonly know as *staph*) that causes boils, septicemia (blood poisoning), and other infections

•*dengue fever* (commonly called break-bone fever), which is an infectious, virulent, tropical, and subtropical epidemic disease transmitted by mosquitoes and characterized by fever, rash, and severe pains in the joints

•*hepatitis,* which is an inflammation of the liver caused by infectious or toxic agents, characterized by jaundice, and usually accompanied by fever. If you swim in a crowded anchorage, you stand the chance of catching hepatitis. If you or your crew show any signs of jaundice, medical attention should be obtained as soon as possible.

•*malaria* is an infectious disease that is transmitted by the bite of an infected mosquito and is characterized by cycles of chills, fever, and sweating. The best treatment is prevention. Have a supply of chloroquin on board, and start the once-weekly doses six weeks prior to entering a malaria-ridden area. Faithfully take the medication each week. On *Starbound* we made the following entry in the ship's log: "Monday is Chloroquin Day." Then whoever wrote the log for that day broke out the medication and we all took it.

VITAMINS

The doctor in the hospital on St. Helena in the South Atlantic, said, "It amazes me to think of the number of cruising yachtsmen I have treated who were in the first stages of vitamin deficiency— slow healing, you know. One wonders why they didn't take vitamins. They're small, easy to carry, keep a long time, and are relatively inexpensive."

We wonder ourselves. We will simply refer you to a book by Adelle Davis, *Let's Eat Right to Keep Fit,* in which she discusses proper nutrition and the use of vitamins to supplement deficient diets.

SOME RECIPES

I have long considered recipes in cruising books to be of little or no value since everyone has his favorite foods and tends to stick with them. However, because it isn't always easy to combine preserved foods into meals that don't taste like day-old dog food, and because it is impossible to find certain standards in other countries, I herewith tender the following recipes that have become good old standards on *Starbound* and on a few other boats as well.

SALT WATER BREAD

1 tbsp. dried yeast
1 tbsp. sugar
1½ cups sea water
4 cups flour

Dissolve yeast and sugar in sea water, then mix in flour. Form mixture into loaf and put into well-greased heavy pan. Let rise 2 hours. Cook covered on very low flame for ½ hour each side.

ENGLISH MUFFINS

Divide salt water bread mixture into 6 parts and roll out on surface heavily dusted with corn meal. Let rise in heavy pan, then cook as above.

CORN TORTILLAS

Mix together: 2 cups Masa Harina (or finely ground corn meal) and 1⅓ cups warm water. Divide into 10 to 12 balls and roll or pat to correct thickness. Cook 1½ to 2 minutes in medium hot pan, turning frequently.

FLOUR TORTILLAS

2 cups flour
1 tsp. salt
½ cup shortening
½ cup lukewarm water

Cut shortening into dry ingredients, add water, and mix with fork. Form into a ball and knead on lightly floured board until smooth and flecked with air bubbles. Grease ball and chill until ready to use. Roll out to 10 to 12 tortillas and cook on very hot (ungreased) griddle—20 seconds on each side.

WATER BISCUITS

1 cup self-rising flour
pinch of salt
2 tbsp. water
1 tbs. butter

Sieve flour and salt. Heat water and butter in pan, then pour into the flour, and mix to a smooth paste. Put dough on floured board, roll out thinly, and stamp into rounds. Bake in moderately hot oven (400–425 degrees) for 10 to 11 minutes until golden brown on both sides. Toss in salt or leave plain. Can be cooked in heavy skillet on top of stove.

UPSIDE-DOWN CAKE

1 16-oz. can fruit (pineapple, apples, cherries, peaches are best)
½ cup white or brown sugar
½ tsp. cinnamon
½ tsp. nutmeg
½ cup butter, margarine, or oil
1 recipe white cake batter

Put everything in a heavy skillet, except the cake batter, and heat to boiling. Turn heat very low (or use heat shield under pan). Pour cake batter on top. Cover and cook about 45 minutes.

CHILI CON CARNE

¼ cup shortening or cooking oil (optional)
1½ lbs. ground beef and 1 cup water (or 2 16-oz. cans beef chunks with liquid)
1 medium onion, chopped (or 1 tbs. dry minced onion)
2 beads garlic (or ¼ tsp. garlic powder)
4 tbsp. chili powder
1 cup solid-pack tomatoes
1 tbsp. paprika
2½ tsp. salt

Combine oil, meat, water, onion, garlic, chili powder, and cook 30 minutes. Add tomatoes and stir until hot. Stir in paprika and salt and simmer about 5 minutes. Serve alone or with kidney beans. Thicken with corn meal and use as filling for tortillas, cover with tomato sauce and grated cheese, and you've got passable enchiladas.

FRYING PAN PIZZA

Make a recipe of salt water bread. Spread part of the uncooked dough on the bottom of a greased iron skillet. Spread this with tinned tomatoes, tomato paste, or catsup. Add sliced or grated cheese, onions, and garlic. Sprinkle with lots of oregano and top with sliced smoked sausage or whatever meat you have. Let rise, then cook on stove top over very low heat as you would salt water bread. It isn't the real thing—but it comes close. If you use enough cheese/meat, it's a fairly good protein meal.

SMOKED MEAT STEW

(This takes about ten minutes if cooked in a pressure cooker.) Cook fresh (peeled or unpeeled) potatoes, onions, sliced smoked meat together in small amount of water until done. Add tinned green beans and serve when hot.

STARBOUND SAUERKRAUT

(Takes about 10 minutes to prepare and 20 minutes to cook.) Put tinned sauerkraut in the bottom of a heavy skillet (not iron). Cover with sliced or grated cheese and top with sliced smoked sausage. Cover and heat on stove top (or uncovered in the oven) until the cheese is melted.

TOASTED CHEESE SANDWICH

Make cheese sandwiches, but add a generous shake of cayenne

to inside. Butter the outside of each sandwich and cook in heavy frying pan on each side until brown and the cheese is melted.

MAYONNAISE

1½ tsp. salt
1 tsp. dry mustard
½ tsp. cayenne
2 egg yolks (or equivalent reconstituted powdered yolk)
¼ cup vinegar
2 cups vegetable oil

Put salt, mustard, paprika, and cayenne into small bowl. Mix thoroughly. Add the egg yolks and beat until mixture is creamy. Add half the vinegar and beat again. Add the oil gradually, ½ tsp. or less at a time, beating continuously until the first ¼ cup has been added. Then add the oil faster, 1 or 2 tbsp. at a time. Continue to beat until the mixture thickens, then add the rest of the vinegar, stirring it well into the mixture. Makes 2½ cups.

TOMATO CATSUP

Puree or tomato sauce to make 5 pints
3 medium onions, chopped (or 3 tbsp. dry minced onions)
3 cups vinegar
3½ tsp. salt
⅞ cup brown sugar
5 tsp. dry mustard
1 tbsp. dry horseradish
1 tsp. black pepper
1 tsp. ground cinnamon
½ tsp. ground cloves
½ tsp. ground nutmeg
1 hot red pepper, chopped (or ⅛ tsp. ground cayenne)

If fresh onion is used, combine tomato sauce, onion, and vinegar and cook until onions are cooked. Put through sieve and return to kettle. Add all other ingredients and simmer 30 minutes. If onion powder is used, combine all ingredients and simmer 1 hour. Pour into sterile jars and refrigerate until use. To preserve (can) refer to food preservation instructions in a reliable book.

YOGURT

Mix proper amount of dry milk and warm (about 90 degrees F) water to make 1 quart liquid. Add ½ cup yogurt (or 1 package of powdered yogurt starter), stir, pour into smaller containers, cover and let sit several hours in a warm place (about 90 degrees F). If richer yogurt is desired, add extra milk powder to the milk mixture.

ITEMS TO STOCK UP ON—IN THE UNITED STATES

Bourbon whiskey
California wines
"American" curry powder
Mexican chili powder
Oregano
Paprika
Pickling spices
Poultry seasoning
Sea food seasonings
Catsup
Cranberry sauce
Mayonnaise
Peanut butter
Canned pumpkin

Pop corn
Canned tortillas
Coffee filters
Toilet paper
Kleenex
Feminine hygiene products
Pins and needles
Rags
Photographic film
Fishing gear
Sea shell, bird, fish, and star books
Cosmetics
Razor blades
Shampoo

ITEMS FOR TRADING AND GIFTS

.22 caliber long-rifle shells (sought after throughout the South Pacific Islands)
lead fishing sinkers, fishing line, and fish hooks
brightly colored cotton cloth
pictures of you and/or your boat
antibiotic ointment
presweetened Kool-aid
Empty plastic containers
Used clothing (in good condition) especially small-sized blue jeans, sweaters, and bras
Paperback books
Magazines (with lots of color pictures)
Playboy magazines (may be illegal in some countries) are much sought after

FOOD AND STORES PUBLICATIONS

Barbour, Beverly. *The Complete Food Preservation Book*. New York: David McKay, 1978
Davis, Adelle. *Let's Cook It Right*. New York: Signet, 1970
Lappé, Frances Moore. *Diet for a Small Planet*. New York: Friends of the Earth/Ballantine, 1971
Wigginton, Eliot, Editor. *The Foxfire Book*. Garden City, New York, 1972
Wigginton, Eliot, Editor. *Foxfire 2*. Garden City, New York, 1973

MEDICAL AND NUTRITION PUBLICATIONS

Davis, Adelle, *Let's Eat Right to Keep Fit*. New York: Signet, 1970
Eastman, Peter F., M.D. *Advanced First Aid Afloat*. Cambridge, Md.: Cornell Maritime Press, Inc., 1972
Leone, Nicholas C., M.D. & Phillips, Elizabeth C., R.N. *The Cruising Sailor's Medical Guide*. New York: David McKay Co., 1979

Sheldon, Paul B., M.D. *First Aid Afloat.* New York: Yachting Publishing Corp., 1964

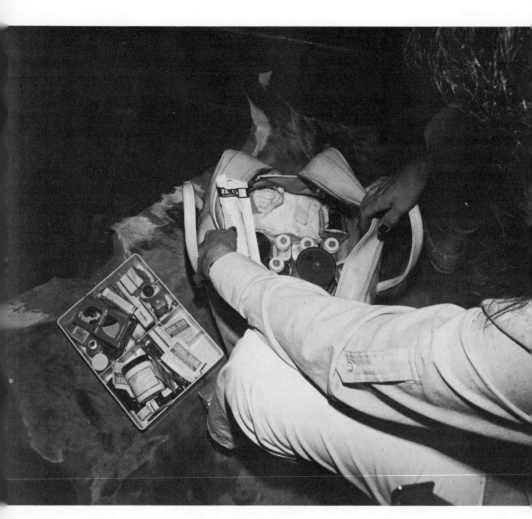

Nina inventories ship's first aid kit.

THREE

PASSAGE

A small vessel is sailing over a blue ocean. The rhythmic swell lifts
her gently, then lowers her into the long glistening trough to rise
again. Her sails are perfect airfoils as she reaches across the trade
winds. Small, flat-bottomed cloud puffs dot the blue sky. The sun,
perhaps an hour high, dries night moisture from the scrubbed
teak and white paint of her topsides, and salt crystals glisten in
thinly crusted, white patches. The morning watch-stander is topside admiring the aerobatics of two sea birds. Small noises ema-
nating from below decks herald the start of another sea day. The
smell of fresh-brewed coffee wafts topside. A radio time signal
beeps incongruously for a few seconds as someone below checks
the chronometer rate for the morning sun line. Breakfast sounds
and aromas from the galley increase. A tropical island lies ahead,
three days to the west.

Supreme content reigns.

17

Getting It All Together: A Check List

Your date for departure is just ahead. Only a few more weeks on the job and you can pack it in. Then perhaps a few weeks of frantic but happy activity and you're away! That is, if you ever work your way through the endless lists of stores and spares, tools and tasks.

It is now time to face up to an incontrovertible fact: If you decide to wait until every job is completed and the ship is just right, you will never leave! There is too much to do; there always is and always will be. So hold to your date of departure and *leave on that date*. Let nothing sway you from that decision. If you are missing stores and tools yet, pick them up at the next port. If there are still a few jobs you want to complete on the boat, do them underway. After all, that's what you'll be doing anyway for the duration of the cruise. There will always be holes in your complements of stores and spares, and there will always be a list of jobs that need doing.

Now that you are within a fortnight of departure, here's a check list of the tasks and chores that ought to have been accomplished by this time as well as the circumstances at sea for which you ought to be prepared.

HEALTH, JOB, KIDS, AND PETS

If you are like us your last physical examination was too long ago. Get a general exam, have any dental work done, and if you wear glasses, have your eyes checked. Be sure to have a spare pair of glasses on board and a copy of your prescription tucked away with the ship's documents.

Put some thought into your career future, if you intend to pursue it. Don't slam any doors behind you as far as your current job is concerned—you may want to return to it.

Get a good correspondence course working for the kids. Put in a few hours a week on their education. You'll probably learn a lot yourself and they will get a better education than is given in most public schools today. The exposure to the world they will get from a deep-water cruise will mature them far in advance of their skateboarding contemporaries.

The decision about pets is a tough one and entirely up to you. Just remember that pets aboard a deep-water cruiser are a disproportionate amount of trouble and will detract from your own pleasure accordingly. Don't forget that in many countries, bonds must be posted for pets and they may not be allowed ashore.

SHIP'S BUSINESS

Have a pot of working cash on board and define the method by which it can be replenished. Have a good idea from which ports you can wire for money. These should also be your principal supply ports. It will take 10 to 14 days to receive money after you've wired for it. Don't let your cash reserve get too low; keep enough to operate with. Have a member of your family, your attorney, or perhaps your bank handle financial matters for you at home. Leave some money in your checking account—an occasional bill will catch up to you.

Obtain your passports and line up your visas as far in advance as possible. Remember that visas are issued for a finite length of time. Some countries will give extensions and some won't. Keep them straight and never allow your visa to expire while you are in that country. Obtain special permits for those countries that require them. Start early on the paperwork—it usually takes some time.

Get all of the required inoculations and make sure they are duly registered on your International Immunization Certificates. Keep the certificates with your passports and ship's papers.

Be prepared to display your ownership documents, your clearance documents from the last port, proof of financial solvency (usually a signed statement will do). Remember that every official will want a crew list—make them up before your arrival.

Obtain a carrying case for all of the ship's papers and working cash. If it's buoyant, waterproof, and fireproof, so much the better.

Arrange your mail drops for those major ports where you will be wiring for money and supplying the ship. Have someone at home, preferably a family member, receive your mail and sort out the junk before forwarding it to you.

PREPARING THE SHIP

Accomplish a complete safety survey of the yacht. Hire professional help if necessary. Start by stripping all the gear out of the boat. This will be a good time to look over your stowage capacity and figure out what should go where. It will also be a good time to scrub down the bilge. And since the boat must be hauled for a hull survey, paint the bottom with antifouling paint before she goes back in the water.

Examine all elements of your ship for signs of electrolysis and corrosion. If you find any, search for the cause, correct it and repair any damage that might compromise safety.

Look at the deck of your ship as the top flange of the hull girder: a prime component of the basic structural system. The joint between deck and hull must cause each to be integral with the other.

Make sure the ship's guardrail is solid enough to transmit impact energy into the basic structure of the ship. Caroming off a piling should not damage the ship.

Ensure that the strength of the deck is adequate, particularly the foredeck in the way of the mast partners and anchor windlass. Make certain all deck fittings intended to take loads are through-bolted and bedded down well. If the decks are metal, all fittings of dissimilar metals should be insulated from the deck.

Plug the cockpit drains and fill the cockpit with water. Then remove the plugs and see how fast it will drain out. Three minutes should be the *maximum*; my personal maximum is one minute.

Ensure that all deck stowage for bulky items such as rafts and dinghies have heavy chocks and lashings.

Ports and lights larger than two square feet should have storm covers of ½-inch tempered plexiglass. All ventilation penetrations should have deck plates provided. All hatches must be very sturdy and gasketed against leakage. Securing methods must be positive and strong.

Dodgers, awnings, and covers are extremely useful both at sea and in port. Shade and rain protection are important in the Tropics.

Good sized toe-rails, coamings, and bulwarks keep crew and gear inboard and also make good foundations for stanchions, tracks, and padeyes.

Double lifelines, as high as possible, are mandatory around the deck's perimeter.

Check for deck leaks: Every penetration should be bedded, gasketed, booted, baffled, caulked, seamed—and maintained.

Make certain your rig is strong. Wire of ⅜-inch diameter is a common size for a 30-foot cruiser. Three shrouds for each side of each mast is a minimum. Wire end fittings should be a mechanical (swageless) type so they can be made up with a vise and hand tools. If your ship has the streamlined swaged terminals, either replace them before leaving or take along plenty of swageless fittings for spares. Include toggles, to make up the difference in wire length when you have to cut off a cracked swaged fitting.

Carefully examine each piece of rigging for strength, material compatibility, fit, and alignment. Look for corrosion and other indicators of incipient failure such as hairline cracks. Lubricate all threads and bearing surfaces. Take close-up photos of masthead gear for ready reference. Measure each piece of wire and line and enter the dimensions in the planning book.

Try to consolidate all line on board into one size—two at the most. Buy rope by the 600-foot reel—it'll save money. Strip the reel, flaking the line as you go. Whip a few turns of small stuff around the flaking bights and the line will stow into a small volume in the lazaret.

Carry enough rope in the bosun's locker to replace all running rigging at least twice.

Use line with a large enough diameter to take a full strain on it with your hands. ½-inch diameter should be the minimum size used, but ⅝-inch diameter is much easier to handle.

Eight-strand plaited rope is nonrotating, easy to splice, allows a good grip, does not hockle or tend to tangle, and can be coiled. We recommend it.

Sails should be polyester (Dacron) of a heavier weight than weekenders employ: Perhaps 8-ounce, American weight, should be the *lightest* material used. All seams should be triple stitched with extra-heavy reinforcing at the corners. Use plenty of chafing material and the toughest hanks and slides available. Have at least two extra jibs/genoas and, if possible, an extra mainsail. Storm sails should include, as a minimum, a storm jib and trysail, built very strongly and roped all around. Learn how to use them *before* you need them!

MAKE SURE ABOUT MAIN EQUIPMENT

Every deep-water yacht needs a windlass to handle both chain and nylon rodes and the relatively heavy anchors required to keep the ship safe in the varying conditions that will be encountered. The windlass should operate manually, even if its normal mode is electric or hydraulic. It must be bolted strongly to the foredeck structure, which must be sturdy enough to handle the strain that will be imposed.

A deep-water yacht must have a form of self-steering. Either auto pilot or wind vane are the co-favorites: the wind vane for boats of approximately 45 feet and smaller, the auto pilot embraced by larger boats with motor generators. The trick to ensure dependable operation of either system is to buy a good unit. They are expensive but well worth the price.

A deep-water yacht should have a diesel-fueled main engine. Gasoline is not as economical as diesel and gasoline engines have trouble-prone ignition systems, but the primary prejudice against gasoline is the very real danger of fire and explosion. It has been calculated that the fumes from one cup of gasoline have the *explosive power of seven sticks of TNT.*

Look carefully at all maintenance aspects of the main engine—*you* will be doing all of it.

Two battery banks are necessary, one for engine starting and one for ship's service. Batteries must be kept clean and dry, and solidly fixed in their operating position.

The alternator should be a heavy-duty marine type with a big capacity.

The wiring system should be a two-wire system, not the old, common-ground, one-wire type. Installation of all electrical components must be meticulous—a most common cause of fires aboard is faulty electrics.

Fuel tanks should be of monel or steel. Steel tanks should not be galvanized inside. Stay away from integral fiberglass fuel tanks— minute quantities of fuel can leak right through the fiberglass. Stainless steel is not suitable for fuel, either. Pit corrosion can occur quickly.

Tanks must be held in place by solid structure—when they are full, they are heavy. Tanks must be vented and baffled and isolated against vibration and electrolysis. They should be fitted with clean-outs, have good ventilation around them, and should be accessible.

Ground tackle is one of the more important systems on a deep-water yacht—don't skimp on it. Wind drag will account for most of the force the ground tackle will resist. Calculate the drag force for your ship and use the tables included in Chapter 11 to pick the right size of chain and nylon rodes.

Carry at least three anchors and enough tackle to use all three concurrently.

One rode should be all chain: Buy High Test chain to take advantage of a large factor of safety.

Nylon rodes should have a working load limit in exces of the maximum calculated holding power you will need. The working load limit should never be in excess of 40 percent of the tensile strength. On *Starbound* we use 30 percent. The Cordage Institute uses a very conservative 10 to 11 percent to protect themselves from product liability suits (see Table 11-2, Chapter 11).

Every cruising sailor has his favorite anchor. The CQR, Danforth, and Herreshoff lead the parade. We recommend one of each, but caution that you remain aware of the limitations of each anchor's design.

Remember that good heavy anchors hold better than good light anchors. It is best to choose anchors as heavy as are within your physical limitations to handle, keeping in mind that it is possible to use a tackle to swing them inboard.

DINGHIES AND LIFE RAFTS

Every cruising sailor develops his own anchoring procedure, based on his ship's handling characteristics, bow configuration, type and weight of ground tackle, and its handling gear, all tempered by his own personal preferences developed through experience. Experience is the key word, and it takes time to get that experience.

A deep-water cruising yacht must carry an adequate dinghy. *Adequate* means that it must be able to perform safely the toughest job it will be called upon to do: to carry out and drop a second anchor—at night, in a short steep chop, with the wind blowing like hell. A dinghy's most common function is to get crew and supplies to and from the shore. The second most common use is for recreation: diving, swimming, and exploring. There are many small boats on the market that will perform the common functions satisfactorily. It is important to choose a tender that will perform the one tough job that must be done. If it can do that, it can do the others.

Inflatables, the good ones, are very serviceable tenders, but remember that they are very difficult to row against wind. If you choose an inflatable, pick a good outboard for it, but *do not overpower*. Choose an engine with the maximum rated horsepower recommended by the boat's manufacturer and it will perform every job you might realistically expect of it. The outboard should also have a worldwide service organization; OMC (Johnson, Evinrude), Mercury, and Seagull parts and service are found almost everywhere. Carry a large selection of spares though. An outboard always seems to act up in the most remote areas.

Recommended dinghy stowage is topside, upside down, in chocks and lashed firmly in place. Unless you have a large yacht, 50 feet and above, stern davits are not advisable, although side davits might be well employed.

Carry a life raft. Buy a good one with a canopy. Stow it topside and develop a plan for its use. Put together a survival kit and stow it near the companionway. Probably you will never use it, but it would be foolish to bet your life on that probability.

REPAIRS: DOING THEM YOURSELF

When a repair of any kind must be made to the yacht, the crew must provide the know-how, the labor, the tools, and the spare parts—even in port. In a foreign port the odds against obtaining the needed parts or materials are high and we find it difficult to remember many instances when a skipper found it necessary to hire outside labor. Generally it costs too much and the quality of workmanship is less than your own. I'm referring to *general* repairs; there may be times when a specialist is needed—electronics, inert-gas welding, major sail repairs. To sum it up, the deep-water yacht must carry tools and spares for every conceivable job. (If I owned a steel boat, I'd have a small welding/burning outfit on board.)

LEARN HOW TO DEAL WITH STORMS

The best preparation for foul weather is to avoid the really bad storms by good planning, to learn enough about weather to know what to expect from the normal systems, and to keep a tight weather watch.

Keep all the sea room you can manage if you're caught. Do not run for a harbor—head, instead, for deep water if you possibly can.

Avoid a lee shore, shoal water, and adverse currents. (Though we've never learned how to do that when approaching a continent.)

Learn how to use your radio to get weather forecasts and learn how to plot the lows and troughs.

Shorten down your rig very early, especially when running—the wind will be blowing harder than you will first realize.

Use your engine to help your control—don't be too much of a purist.

Secure everything topside and below and keep the bilge dry. Split up the work and stay calm. Stow the fishing gear and logline. Get something to eat and drink (nonalcoholic). Put on something warm under your foul weather gear and your safety harness over it.

Stay on course, if you can, until the ship tells you she doesn't like it anymore—then heave to or run, depending on your destination. If the ship is hove to and it gets too rough, then run her off. If she starts running too fast, drag warps.

Be conscious that there is always a fire hazard aboard. Don't get careless. It's easy to do so. Check your extinguishers and the automatic one in your engine room. Poor fuel systems and electric circuits cause nearly all boat fires.

Keep a watch night and day. If you are single-handing or sailing short-handed—perhaps just man and wife—sleep during the day.

Make the ship visible. Install your running lights well above the water and use good quality gear that really shows up. Assume that other ships do not see you; they probably don't.

Check your bilge often. Know how to shut off all through-hull fittings very quickly without fumbling. Practice damage control techniques, if only in your mind.

Stay the hell away from whales! I heard one innocent soul say, "We saw this whale blow so we ran down on him to get a picture . . ."

If you must abandon ship and take to the raft, stay tethered until the yacht actually starts to sink—*it may not.*

Do not fall overboard. If you manage it with no one else topside, chances are you'll never be found. A person alone topside should have his safety harness on and secured. Check out your man-overboard gear and procedures.

PERSONAL GEAR

Personal gear can be added to from port to port, so for the most part it is wise to start out with a fairly loose seabag. Basically clothing comes down to staying warm when it's cold, comfortable when it's warm, dry when it's wet, and presentable when ashore.

Protection from the sun is important for the sake of your skin and eyes. A cool breeze at sea can be deceptive: The sun will still be working.

Buy good-quality foul weather gear and boat shoes. They are worth the price.

If you are a serious photographer, keep your gear in a foam-lined impact case with a few bags of silica gel tucked around.

Buy a leather bag with a stout shoulder strap so you will be able to lug your gear around when exploring ashore. We realize most American males think carrying a bag is slightly effeminate—that is, until they go ashore in a foreign port and realize that it is both essential and common practice. Also, the bag is used on board to keep your very personal stuff stowed: passport, personal papers, address book, glasses, medication.

LIVING ABOARD

Put some heavy thinking into the habitability of your ship. It is your home for the duration of the cruise and seemingly small annoyances on weekend cruises can become horrendous on an ocean passage.

All lockers must have stout securing devices. Work areas and tables must have high fiddles. Use shock cord wherever necessary to secure galley and other gear. Put in a good stove with an oven. Use LP-gas or kerosene—alcohol is not very efficient and is expensive and hard to find.

Refrigeration is very worth having if you can fit in a unit, and nowadays there are so many small, good refrigeration set-ups for yachts, there's no reason to be without one.

A good table is an important item. It's a social center for any yacht and serves for every function that demands a flat surface: eating, drinking, writing, charting, repairing, or just plain leaning and talking. A table needs fiddles, removable if you desire. Gimballed tables are not generally seen much anymore—most yachties feel that they are not useful enough to bother with and I tend to agree.

Heads should be husky, comfortable, and oriented fore and aft. The water level in the head should match the water line of the ship to help preclude flooding. The valves and intake/discharge lines should be of good quality and maintained faithfully. Stories of yachts being flooded through the head are common and usually the result of cheap gear in the first place or poor maintenance. It is a fact that no sailor has ever wanted to get down on his knees and work on the head. It is also a fact that most sailors put it off until the head breaks. If it breaks at sea, it can flood the boat. Keep it maintained and keep spare parts aboard.

What it's all about. At sea en route to Tahiti. Under squaresail, Starbound runs free.

Each crew member on a deep-water yacht should have his own berth: a nest of his own. He should have light to read by, ventilation, and places to stow his gear. A curtain for privacy is a nicety too often overlooked. A bunkboard, preferably made from easily stowed canvas, will stabilize him against a heavy roll. Climb into each bunk aboard your ship and contemplate what it needs to become a decent nest.

FIRST LAP: A SHAKEDOWN CRUISE

It is now time to consider a shakedown cruise. Perhaps you've already made one, or even several short weekend cruises to break up the continuous workload of preparing for the big one. All to the good, particularly if your ultimate crew has been with you on the short hops.

Now, if you have time before your long dreamed-of departure date, and with your ship loaded with gear, a final shakedown hop would be very advisable.

In our sailing area sailors perform this most valuable enterprise as the first leg of their voyage. They say their goodbyes to family and friends and sail the 130 miles down the Chesapeake Bay to Norfolk. By the time they arrive there, a few problems have already cropped up. So they pause for a few days, square away the jobs, pick up the inevitable missing bits and pieces and drop further south through the inland waterway to Morehead City, North Carolina. By then both sails and auxiliary have had a workout and a semblance of order should become evident. At this point, if their confidence permits, they can set sail for Bermuda or Antigua, or perhaps cruise the coast to Florida staying inside the Gulf Stream. Or they can remain in the Inland Waterway to the next city where perhaps additional tasks must be performed. The options are myriad.

But they are on their way and so should you be.

18

On Being at Sea

It is a memorable experience to stand at the helm of your small ship and for the first time watch her bow drive outward for deep water. The land fades into the sea off the stern and becomes a thin, blue line, and then disappears. Dusk announces itself as the sun drops below the horizon and a tangible night approaches like a dark blanket being pulled across the sky, increasing the initial *we're-at-sea* apprehension of the crew.

A radio program of music provides a mental stabilizer of familiarity, as does an evening meal: something simple and nonspicy on the first night out. Stomachs feel a bit uneasy—perhaps not so much from the ship's motion as from that natural apprehension engendered by a totally new experience.

The skipper tries to assume a casual attitude as he listens to a fair weather forecast for the fourteenth time—and goes over in his mind again all of the completed items on the check-off list prepared against departure. As the ship sails on into the night, the crew slowly relaxes and the off-watch members try to sleep, very aware of the hiss and burble of the ocean sliding past the hull just inches from their reclining heads.

In the old days, when a yacht wished to set sail from its own country, it would simply leave—assuming that the weather was fair. Things have changed. There now seems to be a semilegal requirement, at least in the United States, to file a Float Plan with the port captain's office or with the Coast Guard. I'm not sure of the reason—perhaps it is a direct result of the incredibly high number of incidents in recent years in which private boats have called for rescue or assistance.

Eric Hiscock, in his latest wonderfully readable and informative book, *Come Aboard* (Oxford, 1978) states: ". . . and again and again there are government threats that because of this we shall all have to pass tests and our vessels be inspected; not only would that restrict our freedom but it would cost money to pay the bureaucrats who are so keen to protect us from ourselves. Such ideas need to be strongly opposed, for we must be allowed to go unrestricted on our suicidal way, otherwise our precious freedom, which already is being eroded by immigration laws, will be lost. In most walks of life there are little men who delight in controlling their fellows, and we must do all we can to keep their poking noses and prying fingers out of yacht cruising and voyaging, which at present are occupations open to any man or woman with a free spirit and an ability to rely on his or her own guts."

Every deep-water sailor I know agrees as I do with Eric Hiscock's sentiments. But if you are required to file a Float Plan it will probably save a hassle to go ahead and do so. American ports are particularly peculiar about it, just because of the aforementioned high incidence of screams for help, none of which come from deep-water sailors on well-prepared yachts manned by well-prepared crews.

Contact the proper authorities ahead of departure, pick up a Float Plan form, fill in all the standard data pertaining to ship's description, safety gear, radio calling frequencies, and names of crew members—all of the information that won't change—make several copies of the form and file them with the ship's papers.

Then, when you are called upon to come up with one of these documents, fill in the name of your last port and your next port and turn in the form.

There exists one type of bureaucratic organization of which I am inordinately fond: the meteorological offices. Whenever departing from a port that has any kind of forecasting facilities, I pay them a visit. I have always been treated courteously and have been given all the information at hand, including complete up-to-date copies of synoptic charts showing just what we might expect to encounter in the way of weather along our route. It is common to have one, two, or more meteorologists leaning over a chart table, intensely interested in the voyage and the route, doing their best to keep us out of trouble. Several times, when locked into a port by bad weather, I have been on the phone to these kind people twice a day. I can still hear them: "Ah, the American captain! I think you may be in for a bit of luck tomorrow. We have a large high pressure system coming in from the southwest that should give you fair weather for the next three to four days. . . ."

Big ships are another good forecast source. Most of them carry equipment that will receive and print the latest synoptic diagrams and they are not stingy with them. We've found that the master or first officer of a big ship is usually willing to give a yacht a hand— even as busy as these people always are.

A deep-water sailor should never push his departure if the weather is not cooperating. It is so much more pleasant to just relax in port until the wind is fair. While sailing around the south coast of South Africa, we were hung up in Port Elizabeth for seven days while a boisterous southwesterly howled. Each morning I would telephone the "met" office and listen to the negative report, then would go sightseeing. We watched dolphin being trained at the sea aquarium. We visited the snake park and the museum, and strolled the countryside. Mostly we worked on *Starbound*, read books, and wrote.

When setting out to sea, be it the first or fiftieth time, the skipper has a responsibility to lay out the departure plans for the crew. He should fill them in on the weather, spell out the safety rules,

Gordon on watch in the trade wind belt.

and assign the tasks to prepare the ship for sea. Everyone's questions should be answered to at least a degree of satisfaction.

The "Bligh syndrome" does not belong aboard a cruising yacht. While the captain is still "the captain," a large helping of democracy should exist. We have met a very few yachts on which the skipper walked roughshod over the desires of everyone else on board, naturally resulting in an unhappy ship. The skippers usually wised up and mended their relationships, but I can think of two cases where the cruise was terminated in misery.

My own *modus operandi,* involving what Nina is fond of calling my "departure address" to the crew, calls for a final get-together a few hours before departure. If we plan to leave very early in the morning, I try to have it the afternoon before.

The first order of business is the weather. The second is the status of fuel, fresh water, stores, and spares; these items usually require last minute topping-off. It is a familiar sight to have the dock lines singled-up, or the anchor hove short on a single rode, and to see Nina coming alongside in the launch with her net shopping bags full of fresh bread and fresh vegetables.

Perhaps one of the crew has forgotten an important errand, or to mail a letter. Maybe the skipper has been so busy he's forgotten to cash in his remaining local currency, or to pick up a case of beer. One thing is certain: It is a happier ship if no one has forgotten anything. One of the jobs a skipper must do is to stir memories and give the crew time to make those last-minute runs ashore.

Safety rules should be spelled out (again): Cautions about the care to be taken when alone on deck, man-overboard procedures, locations of life jackets, and when safety harnesses are to be worn are all items of importance. "One hand for the ship and one for yourself" is always a basic rule at sea. It is so easy to become careless because of familiarity with a job. I always tell the crew that jumping or running is not allowed on *Starbound*—step and walk to whatever job is at hand. Broken bones or sprains on board are usually a result of being in too big a hurry. *Look* and *think* before tackling a job. The strains involved in the lines, wire, and chain on

a cruising yacht are enough to do severe damage to any part of the human anatomy that comes into contact with them.

Make certain that everyone's health is good: Toothaches, earaches, diarrhea, infections should all be taken care of before departure. A sick crew member can be a big liability once you're at sea.

Check immunization certificates again before clearing to make sure that all shots required by the health authorities of the next port are going to be valid.

Assign the tasks to prepare for sea. Everything topside and below must be in its place and secure. Rig lifelines and make sure that all running rigging is free and that standing rigging is secure.

Get the dinghy on board and completely secured before weighing anchor: It's too much of a distraction to mess with while working your way out of harbor.

Give a seasick remedy to those who may need it at least one hour before departure and again at departure. Certain ones such as Triptone will not induce sleepiness but are not effective once the seasickness begins.

After the anchor is weighed, try to keep the ship in quiet water or perhaps drifting bow downwind until the anchor is on deck (or housed) with a temporary lashing on it. It is wise to keep it ready for use until well clear of the harbor. This technique kept *Starbound* out of serious trouble on two occasions: once when the engine died at a most inopportune time and again when a steering cable parted.

Once the harbor is cleared the anchor should be housed in its seagoing position and lashed hard into place with no opportunity for the slightest movement under *any* conditions. The chain should be unshackled from its shank and stowed in the locker, and the navel pipe plugged. A cover should be lashed over the windlass.

Set up the *watch bill* and deck log. The deck log and the ship's log are two different things. (We've reproduced a typical page from *Starbound's* deck log at the end of this chapter.) It is a simple and valuable record of distances run and sea and weather conditions encountered. Using the weather reports from our radio receiver and correlating them with our continual deck log recordings gives us a good general idea of what is happening with the weather in our area of the ocean.

Entries in the deck log are made at the end of each watch, or more often if necessary to record something of an unusual nature such as lightning on the horizon, a wind shift or changing sea condition, or perhaps a ship sighting. Course changes are always recorded and we also use it as a sort of rough engine log, entering instances when the engine was needed or how long the generator was running.

There are many different watch methods used on deep-water cruising yachts. All yachts tailor their watch bills to fit the crew makeup and number on any particular leg of their passage, taking into account primarily experience—age and sex having relatively little impact on the issue. A young girl with plenty of sea time will stand a more efficient watch than a grown man with no experience.

Aboard *Starbound* we stand no formal watches during daylight hours since our auto pilot does the steering. Someone is always awake to keep an eye on the ship, the sea, and the sky—usually two or three are on deck.

When only three are aboard, we usually stand 4-hour night watches: 1900 to 2300, 2300 to 0300, and 0300 to 0700. With four aboard—our favorite crew size—we stand 3-hour watches: 1900 to 2200, 2200 to 0100, 0100 to 0400, and 0400 to 0700.

"Peggy-for-a-day" is a good technique for a cruising yacht to employ. We take turns being Peggy, our *nom de guerre* for the person who does all the cooking and associated clean-up work for the day. With four aboard the person who stands the morning watch becomes Peggy. This works well because the morning watch-stander is already awake and by 0700 has not only decided what to fix for breakfast but is ready for a cup of coffee. When the off-watch begins to stir—usually between 0800 and 0900—Peggy informs them what is planned for breakfast (a subject sometimes open to negotiation), then prepares it, and serves it. If the person who stood the 0100 to 0400 watch is still in the sack, Peggy feeds him when he wakes. It is important to get enough sleep and a crew member is *never* rolled out just to eat with the others in order to make it easier on Peggy.

When the breakfast mess is squared away, it is time to think about lunch. Remember that meals are mostly prepared from scratch—a time-consuming process and one that takes some thought and imagination to make the chow palatable.

Peggy gets a short afternoon break until time to start dinner. And when the dinner dishes are finished, it is pushing 1900 hours, at which time Peggy finishes the long day by taking the first watch.

The advantage of having the first watch is that at 2200 the watch is turned over and Peggy goes to bed—no longer Peggy—and sleeps all night, awakening to a hot cup of coffee and a breakfast served by the next day's Peggy. This democratic system works very well and evenly divides the cooking chores.

It is not a good procedure to have one person doing all the cooking simply because it is nearly a full-time job—and not very much fun at that. Various cruising acquaintances have tried it—usually assigning "Mama" to the job—with near mutiny resulting within a short period of time. The only way it will ever work is if a cook is hired, as some of the larger boats do, and paid well.

We find it fun to take turns cooking. A lot of imagination is turned loose in the galley and the meals seem much more varied than if one person were doing it all. Nina retains her title of chief storekeeper and acts in an advisory capacity to keep meals and stores balanced. She is also occasionally called on to act as cooking instructor, which she is willing to do as long as verbal advice will suffice. Requests for a demonstrative lesson are greeted with a laugh (she knows better than to get involved on some other Peggy's day). Only if the captain is head down in the bilge on his cook day will Nina take over the galley for him.

We've tried several watch systems. If the weather is bad, we'll keep two on watch at a time, especially if it's so rough the helm must be tended—a rare occurrence. Sometimes with just three on board we'll stand 3-hour watches, the evening and morning watches belonging to one person who gets six hours sleep between them. The natural rotation allows, as it should, a different watch

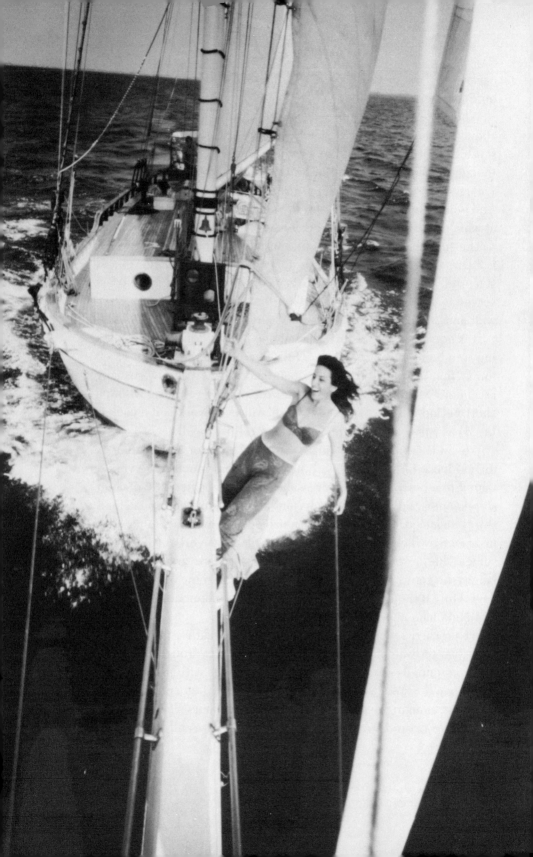

each night. The morning watch-stander is still Peggy for the day but doesn't end up the day with the evening watch, taking the 0100 to 0400 instead.

Sailing couples will usually stand alternate watches during the night and then catch up sleep in the daytime, the reasoning being that a ship is more likely to sight a yacht during the day than at night. Singlehanders will do much the same, often staying up all night and sleeping much of the day, with time up for a noon latitude sight.

We have known couples, and singlehanders too, who simply sack-in during the night and put their trust in God. Admittedly they don't do this in shipping lanes. Frankly I don't think this is a wise practice. I have faith in God, too—but I've seen too many ships go by *Starbound* at night when we were far out of the shipping lanes.

An inexperienced crew member should never stand a watch alone—not until the skipper feels that the crew member can handle it and the crew member feels so, too.

Children, as watch-standers, present an interesting problem. Mental maturity and experience, far more than physical size, will dictate their capabilities. We met a twelve-year-old girl on one yacht who was a better watch-stander than many older boys we became acquainted with. But even young children, say 8 to 10 years old, should have the experience of standing a watch with an adult. There are many things for them to do and see, and consequently learn. A ten-year-old, though a child at the beginning of a long cruising experience, becomes an experienced seaman by the end of it. No adult learns as fast.

In the long run, each cruising yacht will develop its own watch bill based on the number and experience of those aboard. The techniques developed will change as the crew matures. The captain should keep a sharp eye out for personal idiosyncracies and switch his bill around accordingly. Proper sequencing should be given some thought. Aboard *Starbound* it is always Gordon—Nina—Ernie—Gordon—etc. This is because Nina likes me to wake her, which I do gently. And Ernie likes Nina to wake him

Enjoying the sweep of the seas. Nina on the bowsprit of Starbound.

because she brings him a cup of coffee and gives him enough time to become fully alert. But I usually wake up instantly and totally aware with one shake of the shoulder—Ernie's technique. It is wise to keep such small things in mind when making up the watch bill. It is one more small way to keep the ship running smoothly.

The standing watch orders for *Starbound*, posted on the cover of the deck log, are these:

1. Call the captain if *any* problem arises, including weather changes, or if you see any lights you do not understand.

2. Check horizon for ships *every ten minutes*; then ensure that compass course and set of sails is correct.

3. During rough weather wear safety harness and stay locked on.

4. Stay off bowsprit and rigging unless someone else is on deck.

5. Check bilge after calling/waking your relief, *every* watch— keep it dry!

6. If rain threatens, secure ports, hatches, and doghouses. Check topside and strike down binoculars, pillows, etc.

7. Wake your relief ten minutes before the hour.

8. 1900–2200 watch-stander turns on running lights.

9. 0400–0700 watch-stander turns off running lights.

10. Be careful. Watch your footing; Do not run or jump. Do not attempt difficult jobs alone. *Do not take chances*—it's a long swim to shore.

The Ship's Log, unlike the deck log, is a formal and legal document. It is the official record of your boat's cruise. In the case of large vessels, the log entries can be referred to as evidence in legal actions. Such is also the case for yachts. Therefore, all entries should be accurate and conclusive.

A loose-leaf binder should not be used for the Ship's Log. It should be a bound book so that pages cannot be removed. All entries should be made in ink.

Some yachtsmen use a proper log-book with part of each page printed in columns, such that much of the information shown on our sample deck log sheet can be entered. We feel that this is a waste of time and prefer lined paper. However, we do make certain that each course change is entered, together with the log reading and the Greenwich Mean Time (Consolidated Universal Time), as well as the ship's time. We write up the log each evening, sometimes oftener when at sea, and mention everything of interest. Reference back to the deck log is often made for information entered by watch-standers.

"A place for everything and everything in its place": Nowhere does this familiar homily have more meaning than aboard a deep-water cruising yacht on passage. Peggy will take care of the galley and is also tasked to give the head its daily scrub and the cabin sole its brush-up. But that's all Peggy should have to do. There should *never* be a need for anyone on board to put away anyone else's personal gear or clean up anyone else's mess. The quarters aboard a yacht are too close for that. Each individual should keep his gear stowed in the space assigned to him. Soiled clothes should be kept in plastic bags and washed as soon as possible—each person doing his own laundry. Jobs requiring tools should be completed with dispatch and all equipment restowed immediately. If a particular tool is left out and lost, there is no way to buy another—not at sea and, often, not in a foreign port.

It is quite important to maintain a regular schedule for meals— for health as well as economy. If the crew is constantly snacking on the ship's provisions, it is wasteful and cannot be afforded when operating on a finite quantity of stores. Also, the nutritional value of snacks cannot approach that of balanced meals. It works the other way around though: Regular balanced meals will naturally reduce the crew's desire to snack.

We keep a "goody locker" on *Starbound*. It is labeled as such and the crew is free to take anything from it any time of the day or night. All items put in the goody locker have been removed from the food stores list so that no accountability is necessary. Our goody locker usually contains crackers, bread, peanut butter, hard candies, cookies (if we have any), small cans of sardines, instant soups, and just about anything people like to snack on. Gingersnaps seem to be a favorite—and any freshly baked items made specifically for that purpose: A pan of cookies or cinnamon rolls, or an unfrosted cake are always welcome. If any goody locker items require refrigeration, they are labeled as such and put in the refrigerator. Especially tasty leftovers will usually be eaten if made part of the goody locker stores. It is wise, however, with items such as candy bars to replace them as needed instead of putting out the entire supply at once. The crew always appreciates it when the storekeeper "finds a few more" when the stock becomes low. Regular meals help to stay really abusive raids on the locker so the night watch can almost always find a goody to go with a cup of coffee.

Privacy aboard a cruising yacht is difficult to attain and very necessary for every member of the crew. A certain amount of individual privacy is attained by simply standing a night watch, which is one of the reasons why cruising sailors tend to remember those lone instances on deck with a large degree of pleasure.

Make sure the forecastle and head doors can be closed. Curtains across bunk openings are better than nothing—even though they cut down air circulation, at least they allow the option of drawing them. Mutual consideration for others, *including children,* is mandatory for maintaining a happy ship.

Getting enough sleep on a passage is not difficult after the first few days. Once again, the attainment of privacy is a big help, but as the sea days pass by, most of the crew will find themselves able to snuggle into their bunks for a few hours at almost any time. Once again, mutual consideration is beneficial. A sleeper should be allowed as much quiet and privacy as is possible for as long as possible. Who knows? If the weather takes a bad turn, the whole crew might be on call for 24 to 36 hours.

We have known people to take sleeping pills of one kind or another to help them sleep on passages. We consider it a bad practice. The sleep is not as restful as natural sleep and the pill-taker wakes up dopey and irritable. It is far more healthy to get plenty of exercise during the day. Of course, the larger the boat the easier it is to exercise. We can, and do, walk laps around *Starbound.* But we have seen problems on some cruising yachts that have been

Even at sea maintenance is part of the daily routine. A windlass is overhauled.

brought about by laziness or ignorance. Since I have seldom seen any true laziness among cruising people, I must conclude that the problem is ignorance—at least of certain facts. The human body needs exercise—lots of it—to maintain its normal functions. Getting enough vitamins and minerals is also very important. If the shipboard diet is not balanced well enough to provide these essentials—and this is very likely—then supplementary vitamins and minerals should be carried and taken faithfully. We highly recommend a high-dosage multiple-B capsule every day, along with a minimum of 500 milligrams of vitamin C. A very important mineral supplement to carry aboard is a calcium-magnesium mix in tablet form, which is commonly sold under the name Dolomite. Milk is our richest source of calcium, but very few cruising sailors drink enough milk. It is easy enough to carry in whole powdered form, but we are continually surprised that many cruising families carried it only "for the children." The best sources of magnesium are nuts, soybeans, and green leafy vegetables such as spinach, chard, kale, and beet tops. These foods are eaten infrequently even on shore. It is indeed rare to see them included in the supplies for a cruising boat. The thing about calcium and magnesium is this: They are both natural tranquilizers and are extremely effective against insomnia, irritability, and nervousness. They are even more important in their activity with relation to other vitamins and minerals.

During our circumnavigation no one aboard *Starbound* ever fell heir to the physical problems displayed by many other ships' crews. Eat wisely, exercise, and take vitamins and minerals. Exercise can be of the "free-ex" type: Bends, stretches, situps, push-ups, and running in place are all good. If the main shrouds have ratlines, it is fun to run up one side, cross over on the spreader, and come down the other side. Try it three times the first day and build up to ten times or so. Constipation problems at sea, as well as many other problems, are caused primarily by a poor diet and lack of exercise. Children are generally quite active on board and their diets are better tended than are the diets of those doing the tend-

ing ("Drink your milk—it's good for you!"). But we can't help remembering a woman on one yacht being taken to the hospital after
a long ocean cruise, in great pain and unable to walk. The diagnosis
came out to be severe constipation and leg cramps caused by a poor
diet and extreme inactivity. So, stay busy, play games, exercise,
drink lots of water—and eat right.

Fishing at sea is not only fun, it is a great way to supplement the
ship's stores with fresh protein. Since a fish caught at sea and
cooked immediately bears little resemblance in taste or smell to
the ancient chunk of whatever is being sold in your local grocery, it
behooves the man who "doesn't really care for fish" to try it. In fact
the fishing we have done at sea has rather spoiled us for any fish
from a market—it is just not the same product.

Aboard *Starbound* we put out 100 meters of 100-pound test
monofilament with about 10 feet of wire leader attached to it with a
good-sized swivel. For lures we've tried everything, including
making our own, but we've had the best luck with a little red rubber squid about 6 inches long, whose waving tentacles conceal a
barbed double hook of about 4–0 size (about ¾ inch between barb
and shank). With this rig we generally caught fish of about 15
pounds: mostly tuna, but often a mahi-mahi (dorado or dolphin
fish), and sometimes a wahoo, my favorite. A 15-pound fish provides a lot of meat, and a bigger fish would be wasted unless you
can freeze some of it. Frankly we'd rather eat fish freshly caught, so
we stay with the same size gear. A salmon trolling reel is handy to
have. These are big, simple, ungeared reels made of plastic with a
crank fixed to one side. They can be easily clamped to a shroud, a
davit, or a stanchion. They have a simple friction brake that can be
partially set so the line won't part if a fish strikes the lure. A small
plastic tool box can be loaded with several spools of line, a coil of
leader wire, and a variety of lures, sinkers, swivels, and hooks. A
heavy gaff with a 6-foot handle is a necessity and should be stowed
topside in a handy location. The handle should be fitted with a
wrist strap to avoid its loss—a big ocean fish is very active.

The faster the yacht's speed the more likely it is to pick up a fish:

6 to 7 knots seemed to always attract a tuna or mahi-mahi to the lure. But I guess there is no set rule, because we caught a big wahoo when puttering along at 3 knots.

Trolling at night is not a good idea. All we ever caught at night were snake mackerel, and two of those times other fish ate the mackerel before we knew they were on the line. Quite a few times we pulled in a bare leader wire from which the lure had been neatly snipped. We guessed that a shark had taken fish and lure, and it amazed us that a fish could bite through that tough stainless leader without breaking the nylon monofilament.

Keep a watch for flocks of sea birds diving and feeding on the ocean. The old fishermen's stories about always catching fish if you sail through such an area is true. We have always caught fish when we've done it. But watch out for whale sharks when doing so. They are not considered to be dangerous since they feed on plankton, very tiny fish, or on scraps left in the water by feeding fish; however, they are so big that if hit by a small boat, the impact could do considerable damage to hull or rudder.

On every passage it is important to maintain a continual weather watch. Despite the wealth of weather data available by radio, the cruising yacht's first line of defense is still a sharp eye on sea and sky, and a lot of common sense. If a lot of cirrus starts coming in and the clouds start to form a thickening cover, you can usually count on some rain and perhaps a shifting wind, along with some nasty gusts—even in trade wind areas. If a cross-swell starts to form and causes the ship's motion to become irregular, it is wise to ask yourself why—and to keep the weather watch even more actively. We often saw signs of lightning at night that came to nothing, and in the morning were still under a beautiful blue sky with our puffy little trade wind cumulus keeping us company. But a few times the signs of lightning increased until a sharp little squall drove right over the top of us. When it becomes apparent that the ship is going to catch some weather, even though it might be short lived, then it's hit the deck and shorten sail. Even the small, localized squalls can have some heavy wind in them.

It is also common sense for the captain to listen to what the crew has to say. Some people have a better "feel" for the weather than others. Perhaps the combination of subtle changes in barometric pressure, humidity, and temperature stirs their atavistic senses and cause them to feel uncomfortable. When our son Ernie says, "I don't like this—let's dump the main," then we dump the main. More often than not it turns out he was right. Besides, there is no penalty when erring on the side of safety except a bit of exercise.

On celestial navigation, no matter if your instruments, calculations, and plots show you that everything is O.K., if your common sense starts arguing with them and you don't feel quite right about it, if you begin trying to reach a bit for arguments to explain away an apparent inconsistency, then it is time for a serious reappraisal. Trust your senses, at least until you can prove that the funny feeling was just something you ate. When crossing the equator for the first time, I committed the classic error of not remembering the change in rules for calculating the azimuth of the stars we were shooting. And our friend Ray Kukulski was making the same error, each of us working separately. So our calculations agreed, except that we were *both* wrong and our actual position was about 40 miles south of our plot on the chart—not too serious an error far at sea, but we were coming down on the Galápagos Islands and couldn't afford an error. Our sights for the previous two days were scanty because of poor visibility, so we were prepared to accept our plot as accurate—except that we were both bothered about it for no explainable reason. So we went topside and looked at the stars and their reflection in a glass-smooth sea and talked about it—and simultaneously looked at one star we had both shot and realized we were looking northwest and our azimuth had come out southwest. So we raced below and reworked the final parts of our calculations and replotted the position to find we were 20 miles south of the equator instead of 20 miles north. And our "funny feeling" was dispelled.

The above incident was just one of several during our circumnavigation when we paid attention to our senses telling us that all was not as it should be. One bright morning in the Pacific, at least 1200 miles from the nearest land, we were having breakfast. I sud-

Landfall, Starbound heads for the harbor of Durban, South Africa.

denly felt as if I should go topside and look around—a huge Japanese trawler was coming right down our throats less than 500 yards off the bow! We sheared off to port and the trawler was abeam before its startled helmsman appeared in the pilot house and "discovered" us. The lonesome sea, indeed! What was it that told me I should take a look around? Perhaps I subconsciously heard, or felt the vibrations of, the trawler's engines.

Use your eyes while at sea. Look for sea birds and learn to identify them. Some of them spend their entire lives at sea. Then when you see a land bird, one that flies to sea for dinner and returns to land each night, notice the time of day and which way he is flying. You can then calculate the approximate distance from shore. Look for jet planes, too. The big commercial jets usually stay right on track.

Floating sea weed and other flotsam may indicate land, up-current from your boat. When you approach land with a shelf far to sea, the wave patterns will change noticeably. Also, large rivers can change the color of the water for a hundred miles out to sea. The Amazon is a particular case in point. When there is a noticeable change in ocean water coloration, keep a very sharp lookout for floating trees or other large debris that might cause damage to the hull of your ship.

Try out various navigational techniques. Get your longitude at sunset without a sextant. Simply use the exact time the upper rim of the sun disappears at the close of a very clear day. You might even see the flash of green. Then work the shot just as if you used a sextant set at 0 degrees. Since it is an upper-limb shot, you will be working with negative angles, which are covered in H.O. 229. Your resulting line of position will be almost north and south and will give you an accurate longitude.

Some day, just for fun, assume that your radio has fallen overboard and the chronometer packed it in and you must in some fashion reestablish the correct GMT for navigational purposes. Watch the sun as it approaches its zenith. Take a series of shots and plot their altitudes on a vertical scale against an assumed time (from any clock) on a horizontal scale. Carefully draw the curve and it will be a perfect parabola with the apex up. Then bisect the parabola with a vertical line that strikes the time scale and you will have the assumed time of local apparent noon. Compare this against the almanac data, estimating as closely as possible your assumed longitude, and you will know how slow or fast your assumed time is from GMT—and you will be accurate within a few seconds.

Bowditch is full of methods that are interesting to play with and will provide you with a greater understanding of the celestial ins and outs of navigation.

I find it amusing to remember when all those glittering stars in the night sky meant nothing except beauty to me. After a few weeks of night watches, the constellations became old familiar friends as they wheeled from east to west and dove into the sea.

There is a lot of maintenance to be done on a ship while she's in port—and that maintenance doesn't stop when she goes to sea. As a matter of fact, sea time, especially in good weather, is a fine time to do all the jobs you didn't feel were crucial enough to do before leaving port. There are always quite a number of them because there are always more jobs than can ever be completed—a ship is never totally up to scratch. The best maintained yachts only approach it.

A fair weather passage presents a fine time for ship maintenance with perhaps the exclusion of painting the masts and the hull. Even in a flat calm the underlying swells will induce a roll that makes it uncomfortable to be aloft in a bosun's chair or alongside in the tender. We know of yacht crews that have tackled both jobs at sea with some measure of success but admitted that next time, they'd save it for a quiet harbor.

Painting and varnishing is usually restricted to cabin sides, hatches, bulwarks, and the portions of masts that can be reached from the deck. Below-decks painting can be done if the crew have good sea stomachs. Paint fumes tend to upset some people who would otherwise be O.K.

Maintenance while under way is most advantageously performed on the ship's mechanical equipment: The anchor windlass and sheet winches are always prime candidates for cleaning and greasing. The main engine and motor generator can have their lube oil

and fuel oil systems worked over, filters and all, with the expenditure of only a few quarts of perspiration. A five-gallon container can be used to hold old oil until it can be disposed of at the next port. We never dump oil overboard.

Just consider the broken galley locker hinge . . . and that damn split in the teak louver . . . the toilet needs a new seal in the pump shaft . . . and the propeller shaft needs a few turns on its stuffing box . . . whoops, the fire extinguishers haven't been weighed for a year . . . check the tension on the alternator belts . . . I'll bet the pencil zincs in all three heat exchangers: main, transmission, and MG are nearly gone . . . and when was it that we last lubed the taffrail log . . . speaking of which, it's time to overhaul the log line and scrape off the goose barnacles 'cause it has only been a week but they're a half-inch long already . . . better think about recoding the anchor chain pretty quick—the color is nearly off the links . . . and it's such a *helluva* pretty afternoon. . . . Let's crack a cold beer and get into a hot game of Hearts or 500!

Timing the port arrival is always exciting. It's a real adventure, in the best sense of the word, because your guts are on the line. I never feel casual when entering a foreign port. It's a big new kick every time.

Try to enter a foreign harbor in the daytime. Planning for 0900 hours during a working day is always best because you will probably get through the entrance formalities much faster. And if it takes longer to work your ship into an anchorage than you'd planned, there is the whole day before you.

One cruising couple we know likes to come to port on Sunday or another religious holiday. They like a day's rest after a long passage to sleep and clean up the ship, and if there is still fresh water aboard, a shower without salt in it. When the officials drop in next morning, our friends appear like the couples seen in the advertising pages of the yachting magazines. Remember though, entering some ports on holidays or "outside office hours" may result in overtime charges.

Whichever way is preferred, it is wise to study every piece of information you have gathered on that port and country. First of all, it is necessary to know on what days religious and other holidays fall. The officials generally speak English, *but not everywhere*, so at least learn some key words and phrases of the prevalent language. The monetary system must be committed to memory, as well as the rates of exchange, which can vary in some ports between bank and money-changer. Know something of the local customs so you can avoid embarrassing yourself or others. Study the geography, at least in general—and the history, at least in brief. And read accounts of other yachties who have visited the same ports.

Many ports ask, or even require, that visiting yachts observe large ship methods and radio in ahead of time to request entry into the port, giving their identity and ETA (Estimated Time of Arrival). We always try to reach the port by radio the evening before our morning ETA. Sometimes we raise them—if not, we try them again in the morning when we are close in.

Study the sailing directions or pilots in conjunction with the harbor charts before entering, but don't put total faith in them. If there is a seeming conflict between them, ask the port for clarifying information when you make contact. Then enter with all eyes aboard on watch.

And now is the time to remember: *You* are the foreigner in a foreign land.

DECK LOG

YACHT "STARBOUND"

Day | Date | Month | Year

| TIME | COMPASS | LOG | WIND | | BAR | SEA | | SKY | REMARKS | INITIAL |
			KTS.	DIR.		HEIGHT	DIR.			

19
Ports of Call

Before entering any foreign port, make sure the correct flags are properly flown. Your country's ensign should be flown from a staff right aft if the ship is under power, which she most likely will be. And the ensign should be of a decent size: One inch on the fly (the long direction) for each foot of overall boat length is a good working rule. The courtesy ensign of the country being visited can be about half that size, but really should not be any smaller than that. The courtesy ensign should be hoisted *close up* under the starboard main cross-tree. Port officials in foreign ports expect transient yachts to display the flag of that country. In some places they may impose a fine on a yacht not flying a courtesy ensign and/or ask that you buy one from them at an exorbitant price. We have heard from other yachtsmen that South American countries are particularly ready to do this. Remember that the courtesy ensign should be the *merchant* ensign of the country, not the national ensign, when there is a difference between them.

When entering a country for the first time, hoist the yellow "Q" *flag,* which should be flown directly under the courtesy ensign if the ship only has one mast. Aboard *Starbound* we fly "Q" just under the starboard mizzen spreader—and it is a good sized flag, 18 X 24 inches, so as to be more readily visible from shore. The "Q" flag means: My vessel is healthy and I request free pratique—freedom of the port. Once the vessel is inspected, the officials will generally request that you take in the "Q" flag. If they don't, take it in as soon as they leave.

We Americans are rather lax about flags and flag courtesy while cruising our own waters. But for an overseas yacht, correct flag etiquette is important if not mandatory. One of the problems on an extended cruise is simply how to find and purchase all the different courtesy ensigns that may be required. We managed this problem by *making* them all.

Before setting out on our cruise, we scrounged around two or three sailmakers' lofts and obtained a lot of scraps of discarded spinnaker cloth in nearly all the colors of the rainbow, although we tried to get most of it in red, white, blue, black, green, and yellow. The flags of simple detail are easy to make, but some of them have complicated patterns, the most difficult having shields or other emblems almost impossible to reproduce exactly. Nina overcame this obstacle by cutting the shield out of white ripstop nylon, putting the detail on it with waterproof, colorfast paints (once she used wax crayon) and then basting the shield onto the flag. We saved a lot of dollars by making our own flags. Nina also put together a complete set of signal flags for *Starbound* out of ripstop nylon. Several days of hard work were involved but resulted in a handsome set of flags of much higher quality than can be purchased.

If you choose to fly a burgee, it should be flown from the main truck on a swivel-equipped pigstick. We fly ours if we plan to use the yacht club facilities of any port we enter. But much more often, and always at sea, we carry a small white nylon windsock on the stick, which gives us a better indication of wind direction than the burgee and also saves it from wear.

When entering a port, follow entrance directions the port captain's office might have transmitted by radio, but proceed with much caution. Many foreign harbors have extremely tight quarters. Don't poke your ship's bow into a tight spot unless you can see a way out of it.

Information about the port that may have been gleaned from sources at the last anchorage should not be followed blindly. Harbors are always modified in one way or another; Navigational aids can change too, as can official procedures. We cannot think of a single foreign port that we found to be just as described. When entering Suva, Fiji, we originally intended to lay *Starbound* up to the large ship's wharf right in front of the custom's office, a small building on the waterfront. A cruising skipper we'd met in Tahiti had told us that was what he'd done a few years before. But farther down *Isles Sous le Vent*, we heard more recent information: We were supposed to go to the quarantine anchorage and drop the hook there, with "Q" flying, until visited by the health authorities. This advice matched the *Sailing Directions*. Discretion being the better way to sail, we made the harbor in daylight and dropped anchor in the area designated by a purple-inked circle on the harbor chart marked "Quarantine." After an hour's binocular search of the busy shore, we began wondering if we'd done the right thing. But then a launch separated from one of the larger yachts at anchor off the Royal Suva Yacht Club and ran up to us. We'd last seen the skipper in Samoa. He wouldn't come aboard: "Not until you've been given pratique. They're strict here!" He let his launch rest just off our quarter and told us the story of a yacht skipper who, the week before, had anchored off the club and gone ashore in search of the officials. When he found them, they ordered him to take his yacht to the quarantine anchorage until visited by the health authorities. Then they let him sit there for three days. However, during our stay in Suva, we found the officials to be somewhat officious but quite efficient—and the city was entirely delightful.

The Royal Suva Yacht Club played host to all transient yachts at that time. There was a nominal weekly fee, which we considered fair. We've lately heard though, that transient yachts may no longer use the club's facilities. This is a trend that is spreading because of the increasing large numbers of cruising yachts passing through the ocean's major crossroads. The various yacht clubs that used to pay considerable deference to cruising yachts when they only had three or four each year, have found that twenty to thirty and more, all at once, play hell with the proper conduct of the club's primary business, which is to cater to their membership. Most of today's yachties should try to understand this new attitude—getting hot about it does nothing to enhance the reputation of overseas yachts.

At any rate, the port officials will generally advise you, at least in a busy port, where the transient yachts are anchored and that is the best place to go. It is a lot of fun to have company nearby, and cooperation between yachts is the keynote—mutual protection when yachts are left untended not being the least of advantages.

A deep-water yacht entering a foreign port will always have to deal with customs, immigration, and health officials. Depending on the country, there may be separate *agricultural regulations* for which one must satisfy a separate official. Sometimes the Navy gets into the act, as they do in Indonesia. In French Polynesia we found that the French Navy was fully aware of all yachts' movements throughout that very large area. Of course, much of the very close surveillance was due to the nuclear testing France was conducting at that time.

In some small ports perhaps only one official will take care of all functions. He may choose to come aboard or you may have to go ashore and find him. The procedure is a bit different in every port. If other yachts are present it is a good idea to give them a hail and ask about the entering procedures—it can save a lot of time and occasional grief. If you find yourself on your own, then anchor and if no one comes in response to your "Q" flag after perhaps two to three hours, row ashore and find the port captain's office—that is, if you have arrived during working hours. Keep in mind that night and Sunday arrivals can lead to one of two things: Either no one shows up because offices are closed or someone shows up and hits you with expensive overtime charges.

When I was a small boy, my mother told me that first impressions are very important to most people. She made sure I remembered it. The appearance, attitude, and personal conduct of a tran-

Starbound *at rest in Robinson's Cove, Moorea.*

sient yacht's crew can easily affect the yacht's reception in various ports around the world. Before entering a new harbor aboard *Starbound*, we would take last minute baths, in fresh water if we had it to spare. The men would shave, Nina would do her hair and put on something feminine—never lost on port officials. I'd have Nina give me a trim if I looked too shaggy, and Ernie, whose hair was quite long then, would tie it back neatly. We would put on shirts and shorts (sometimes even slacks in the larger ports) and at least Nina and I would wear sandals or boat shoes. *Looking* like ladies and gentlemen, we were received as ladies and gentlemen. I am hard put to think of a single port where we were harassed.

The ship is always clean and neat at sea, but we'd give her a last minute brush up. We'd always have coffee or tea to offer officials and on a rare occasion we might offer an alcoholic drink, depending on the port, the officials, and the time of day. It is something that needs to be played by instinct.

Port officials should always be taken very seriously, and entrance (and departure) procedures should be handled in an efficient, businesslike manner. This does not preclude a friendly attitude, something that should be prevalent at all times whether or not you really feel that way. A professional, businesslike mien should forestall anyone trying to take advantage of you—baksheesh is sometimes asked for —a fairly rare occurrence that can happen in the smaller ports of underdeveloped countries.

All of the documents for ship and crew should be ready—the faster the entry formalities can be dealt with, the better. Make notes of any rules offered relative to country, harbor, or customs and ask polite questions if necessary. *Read documents before you sign them.* Do not display any cash. If proof of solvency is required (rarely), a signed statement will usually do, otherwise your last bank statement should suffice. We have never had to produce more than a statement.

If asked if there are drugs aboard, they are not talking about the medical kit, so don't volunteer its contents. If asked about guns, declare them. If an official boat search is required, stay friendly and give them your complete cooperation.

Firearms have definite assets and liabilities on a cruising yacht. Everyone must decide for themselves as to whether or not they're worth carrying. Their assets are obvious: for protection and to hunt with. Their liabilities are that they are a real pain in the neck to get in and out of some countries, and they call for a good deal of maintenance and careful storage to prevent their deterioration.

Handguns are the big problem. They are made primarily for personal protection and many countries with internal problems will not let you keep them aboard for fear they will be stolen (or sold). Rifles and shotguns are looked upon more as hunting weapons and do not bear the stigma attached to handguns. So if you intend to hunt in some countries—and it can be well worth the time—carry a rifle, shotgun, or both. They can still be used for protection if necessary. But we would advise that handguns not be carried— they are more trouble than they are worth.

If firearms are carried, they should be kept in a full sheath, lano-lined lambskin on the inside and zippered shut, with a large packet of silica gel crystals added to absorb moisture. The silica gel can be baked out in the oven once in a while to refresh it. Keep weapons in a locked cabinet or at least stow them where they cannot be readily found if the boat is broken into. Ammunition should be packaged in waterproof wrappers and stowed in a cool, dry place. If you intend to hunt, ask the port officials how to obtain permission to do so.

If the visited country's policy is to put your firearms in bond, or otherwise retain them until your departure, you may have to carry them to the custom's office, the police station, or the armory, along with all ammunition. A receipt will be given to you, which should contain complete descriptions of the weapons, including serial numbers and an ammo count. Leave the weapons in their sheathes and give them a last protective coat of oil before turning them over—some storage areas might be damp, particularly in tropical ports.

All papers given to you by port officials should be kept in order in the ship's documents file, which should be restowed in its proper place after all entrance formalities are complete. These various pieces of paper, none of which seem to be the same size, are important from a bureaucratic standpoint and if misplaced or lost may cause an inordinate amount of trouble when it is time to leave—or even at the next port.

Entry completed, it is time to make contact with other yachts, assuming there are any. A first query might have already been made, on the fly, to get information about anchoring and entry, but now a friendly visit in the launch is in order, to say hello and to find out about money exchange, mail, laundry, stores, fuel, water, and the availability of repair facilities. Learn the best place to land the dinghy and how secure it will be. Determine if language difficulties might be encountered.

Take it easy for the first few days ashore. Unlike tourists we sailors don't have to try to do everything at once. First of all, go to the bank or money-changer and convert some dollars, not too many to begin with. Then head for the post office if mail is expected. Perhaps arrange for the laundry to be done if there are any public facilities. Check out the markets to see what food stuffs are available and buy some fresh vegetables, meat, milk, and bread for dinner. Make sure the water supply is pure before drinking it and get a line on the facilities for putting water and fuel on board. Think about topping your tanks early in your stay.

If a haulout is planned, try to schedule it early at an available facility. If your stay is going to be an extended one, you might not want to paint the ship's bottom until just before departure, but all shipyards in the world seem to be always busy, so at least get on the schedule as soon as possible. At the same time scout the marine facilities to find out the extent of available parts and spares.

The status of the crew's health should be carefully considered. A review of immunization certificates is in order. A requirement for a doctor and dentist presents the problem of how to find a competent one. First, query the other yachts. Someone aboard might even be a doctor—we've met several—or they may have already investigated the medical picture ashore and can make a recommendation. If you find yourself in a major port with an American Embassy within reach, even by telephone, they will be able to make a recommendation. In fact any country's embassy may be contacted for information. English will always be spoken by someone and generally embassy personnel try to be of help. Religious organizations are another possible source of information. The church always knows where the best doctors are to be found.

There are other sources. While in Martinique I broke a corner from a molar and needed a dentist to repair it. I met an American girl working in a bank who had been living in Martinique for some time. She steered me to an excellent French dentist who fixed the tooth very nicely and charged me only twelve dollars. Bargains can still be found.

On some small islands there may be only one place to go if more medical attention is needed than can be given on the boat: the *infirmary*, which may not have a doctor, per se, in attendance. There might be just a nurse or student doctor available. Usually, though, they are able to set a simple bone fracture, perhaps take some stitches. We even heard that an appendectomy had been performed in one of these small, almost open-air "hospitals." But if something really complicated turns up, they will either try to stabilize it until you can sail to a large port with modern medical facilities or, as a last resort, fly in a doctor—if there is an airstrip on the island. The medical people in the small, isolated places do fairly well though. They are like the old-time small-town practitioners, almost as extinct as the buffalo in the United States, and who, not being specialists, know a hell of a lot about plain doctoring.

We did not sail *Starbound* 'round the world just to sail 'round the world. All the years of our lives, we've dreamed of visiting far places, exotic lands, strange peoples with different customs, chaotic streets in foreign cities with a polyglot of languages being spoken: "Lotus lands" we call them, for only semantic reasons. And of course being romantics, probably to an extreme, Nina and I believe that the only suitable, sensible, realistic way to experience our Lotus lands is to sail to them in our ship—a true romantic can do no less, and how we love the sailing!

Upon arriving at our various ports of call, the urge to explore is strongly with us. The harbor area gets the first close examination because as sailors there is always a strong, traditional link with the waterfront. Then we wander through the port town, traveling in

Shoreside. Common transport in Tahiti is "le truck."

ever widening circles as we go upon our various errands for the ship. We return each night and share our experiences, learning from each other. But then, as the ship's requirements become satisfied, we begin to ponder the surrounding countryside, and further.

What fascinating experiences we have had! We climbed a mountain to find a Polynesian *marae,* an ancient and sacred temple located high in the hills above Melville's famed Taipi Vai. We paddled across incredibly beautiful Lake Bratan, which fills the caldera of a semiextinct volcano in Bali, and tried to gaze upon the Temple of Ulu Danu, seeming to float upon the lake waters, misty in the early morning, without weeping because of its beauty. We wandered the narrow, walled walkways of Kuta Beach under a full moon and listened to the chant of the *kerchak* ceremony. We saw the Emerald pool of Dominica and climbed the riverbed at the head of Nara inlet on the Barrier Reef. We swam with seals in the Galápagos and experienced the roar and mist of mighty Victoria Falls in Rhodesia. And we met many fascinating, wonderful people.

We don't usually make any explicit advance plans for exploring. Once anchored in a new port, the plans just happen along. Another yacht's crew might tell us of a beautiful place or one of the local people may mention something of a fascinating nature, far inland. Some days one or two of the world-wandering young backpackers would come visiting and talk about where they'd been, and we'd start to figure a way to see . . . whatever.

For those who like to explore—especially the faraway places that tourists have never been able to spoil—keep some good hiking shoes and backpacks aboard. It's the only way to get to many of the real beauty spots of the world: the places not sullied by man—at least, not yet. And remember the words that should be law: Take nothing but pictures! Leave nothing but footprints!

Nina and I saw a lot of Bali by *bemo,* the small Japanese-truck buses. Then we'd walk for miles. Another way to see a lot of country when roads are present is to rent a motorbike. The small 120 to 200 cc. machines seem to be available for rent in many ports. But the best way to really *see,* is on foot: One has time to feel the earth and smell the scents.

We have thought hard about buying a motorbike for the ship, but machinery like that is such a big maintenance problem. Our friends who sailed *Topaz,* a big, green Baltic Trader, around the world, had two motorbikes on board. They would condition them for a sea trip with consummate care, spraying them and wrapping them in plastic and tarpaulins. At the next port the motorbikes would be infected with corrosion problems despite the care. We decided to think about a motorbike acquisition a while longer. Perhaps it will depend on where our next venture will take us, and certainly on whether the handiness is worth the maintenance and stowage problems.

When the exploring is complete and the seasonal changes begin reminding one that it is time to head toward the next port, when your ship is ready and her lockers are full, when the meteorology people have stated that the winds are fair and storms are rare— begin your clearance procedures!

Start by contacting the port captain's office and *verify* the procedures for departure. Let the port captain know when it is you wish to leave. A favorite technique is to clear the day before, because clearing can be an all day run-around or a ten-minute office visit, depending on the port. Having been cleared, the crew is obliged to return to the ship and leave at first light next morning. A few ports won't allow this—a ship must leave immediately on receiving her clearance. Sometimes the officials will bend the rules if the skipper uses some diplomacy and promises to keep the crew aboard until departure.

Keep all clearance documents in order in the ship's file. They will be requested at the next port where they'll want to see where you've been and to make sure you've brought no communicable diseases into their fair land. I don't blame them—and I have been told by yachties from other countries that U.S. port officials are among the world's toughest.

The ship's departure time, assuming the weather is fair, should

Shoreside. A train ride to the "tablelands" of the northeast coast of Australia.

depend, if it is going to be a short hop, on your estimated passage time to your destination. If you are heading for a port only a few days distant, it is advisable to turn it up in the morning so that you've got all day to get in. If there are reefs to run and the pass through them is on the east side of an island (a rare occurrence in the Pacific), you will want to get through the pass sometime in the morning with the sun behind your shoulder, giving maximum visibility through the water. If the pass lies on the west or northwest side of an island, the most usual place for a pass to be for an island in the trade wind area, the pass should be entered in the afternoon, again, with the sun behind the shoulder, eliminating glare from the water's surface. (The only time I ever ignored this rule, I hit the coral heads of the south reef of Night Island on the Great Barrier Reef. By pure luck we did not have any hull damage, striking the *bommies* directly with the heavy bronze shoe plate.) So if your way is west, as is the way of most sailing ships in tropical waters, you'll still want to turn up a port in the morning so as to have the time to do whatever you'll need to do to get the yacht safely into port.

If there is a long sea passage to make, clear the port whenever it is most convenient. We've even made night departures when it was easy to get clear of the harbor. Usually, though, we leave the night departures for those times when we have just a short hop and want to arrive in daylight.

Taking our ship to sea is as exciting an experience as we've ever had, and as pleasurable. The curious thing is that after doing it so many times, it is just as exciting—perhaps more so, because we now know better what the sea can hand out if our planning is bad or if capricious Mother Nature decides to give us a small whack on the sprit. But it is vastly satisfying being aboard our ship at sea in good weather—which, with good planning, is most of the time.

Nina and I were musing pleasurably about how soon we could leave our jobs and cross another ocean. We recalled some memorable days and nights we have spent at sea. Nina in particular remembers the nights:

"Passage nights are all memorable, but two night watches in particular stand out vividly in my mind because they were so pleasant.

The first was during the passage from Curaçao to Cartagena. "Grumpy" (our auto pilot) was turned off. Seated on the transom seat cushions aft, with my safety harness secured, I watched the large following seas lift the stern, then the bow, as their tops foamed by down *Starbound's* sides. I sang amateur opera aloud to the accompaniment of our transoceanic radio and the swash of the seas, and admired the night. There wasn't much moon—just a sliver—but the stars shown brightly above the myriad tiny stars in the water. Highlighting the scene, occasional huge round things deep down in the water glowed bright blue, like a flashbulb exploding, then faded away and back into the wake as *Starbound* flew on her way.

"A second memorable night watch was on the passage to Dili in Portuguese Timor (now Indonesian following a *coup d'état*). We were in the passage between Timor and Wetar Islands. "Grumpy" was steering his almost perfect course and I stargazed as most night watches are prone to do. Gordon's watch jacket kept out the chill and I sat on the inboard edge of the main hatch with my legs dangling down into the main saloon, my back against the mizzenmast. The Pleiades were playing ring-around-the-rosy with the truck of the topmast. A meteor shower was in full swing and it streaked the sky singly and in groups, hour after hour. And I thought: Tomorrow, Indonesia! That was a night."

Nights at sea are grand, and so are the days: The sunrises turning the trade wind clouds pink, then gold . . . the flying fish for breakfast, fried golden brown . . . fresh water showers on deck, the soap sudsing under a tropical downpour . . . the squaresail and raffee bellying out before the trades, curvaceously fair . . . blue-green and gold mahi-mahi on the fishing line, destined for the pan . . . the satisfaction of placing a noon fix on the chart, verifying a fine day's run . . . the delight of a good lunch served by "Peggy," along with a cold beer and maybe a hotly contested card game in the afternoon . . . the preparation for evening star shots and an accurate fix, because the next port of call lies not too far over the blue of Capricorn horizon.